W9-CPD-909

FAMILY, GENDER AND KINSHIP IN AUSTRALIA

Anthropology and Cultural History in Asia and the Indo-Pacific

Series Editors:
Pamela J. Stewart and Andrew Strathern
University of Pittsburgh, USA

This series offers a fresh perspective on Asian and Indo-Pacific Anthropology. Acknowledging the increasing impact of transnational flows of ideas and practices across borders, the series widens the established geographical remit of Asian studies to consider the entire Indo-Pacific region. In addition to focussed ethnographic studies, the series incorporates thematic work on issues of cross-regional impact, including globalization, the spread of terrorism, and alternative medical practices.

The series further aims to be innovative in its disciplinary breadth, linking anthropological theory with studies in cultural history and religious studies, thus reflecting the current creative interactions between anthropology and historical scholarship that are enriching the study of Asia and the Indo-Pacific region. While the series covers classic themes within the anthropology of the region such as ritual, political and economic issues will also be tackled. Studies of adaptation, change and conflict in small-scale situations enmeshed in wider currents of change will have a significant place in this range of foci.

We publish scholarly texts, both single-authored and collaborative as well as collections of thematically organized essays. The series aims to reach a core audience of anthropologists and Asian Studies specialists, but also to be accessible to a broader multidisciplinary readership.

Titles in the series

Domestic Mandala:
Architecture of Lifeworlds in Nepal
John Gray
ISBN 0 7546 4538 X

Aboriginal Art, Identity and Appropriation
Elizabeth Burns Coleman
ISBN 0 7546 4403 0

The Making of Global and Local Modernities in Melanesia:
Humiliation, Transformation and the Nature of Cultural Change
Edited by Joel Robbins and Holly Wardlow
ISBN 0 7546 4312 3

Family, Gender and Kinship in Australia

The Social and Cultural Logic of Practice and Subjectivity

ALLON J. UHLMANN
University of Missouri, St. Louis, USA

ASHGATE

© Allon J. Uhlmann 2006

All rights reserved. No part of this publication may be reproduced, stored in a retrieval system, or transmitted in any form or by any means, electronic, mechanical, photocopying, recording or otherwise without the prior permission of the publisher.

Allon J. Uhlmann has asserted his right under the Copyright, Designs and Patents Act, 1988, to be identified as the author of this work.

Published by
Ashgate Publishing Limited
Gower House
Croft Road
Aldershot
Hants GU11 3HR
England

Ashgate Publishing Company
Suite 420
101 Cherry Street
Burlington, VT 05401-4405
USA

Ashgate website: http://www.ashgate.com

British Library Cataloguing in Publication Data
Uhlmann, Allon J.
   Family, gender and kinship in Australia : the social and
   cultural logic of practice and subjectivity. -
   (Anthropology and cultural history in Asia and the
   Indo-Pacific)
   1. Family - Australia 2. Kinship - Australia
   I. Title
   306.8'5'0994

Library of Congress Cataloging-in-Publication Data
Uhlmann, Allon J.
   Family, gender and kinship in Australia : the social and cultural logic of practice and
   subjectivity / by Allon J. Uhlmann.
      p. cm. -- (Anthropology and cultural history in Asia and the Indo-Pacific)
   Includes bibliographical references and index.
   ISBN 0-7546-4645-9
   1. Family--Australia. 2. Family--Australia--New Castle (N.S.W.) I. Title. II. Series.

HQ706.U55 2006
306.850994--dc22

                                                                              2006008606

ISBN-10: 0-7546-4645-9
ISBN-13: 978-0-7546-4645-7

Printed and bound in Great Britain by Antony Rowe Ltd, Chippenham, Wiltshire.

Contents

Contents

Series Editors' Preface

Andrew Strathern and Pamela J. Stewart

We are very pleased to be able to include Allon Uhlmann's study of kinship relations in the town of Newcastle in New South Wales in our Series on Anthropology and Cultural History in Asia and the Indo-Pacific. This is a closely observed and tightly constructed study which contributes to the work of theorizing and describing gender and kinship in contemporary contexts within industrialized urban societies. This it does in at least two interconnected ways. First, it challenges the idea that the nuclear domestic family is in crisis in Australia – an idea that circulates in political and popular discourse within Australia and also elsewhere. And second, it does so by extending a concept that has proven very useful in understanding diachronic processes of familial relationships generally, the developmental 'cycle' of the domestic group. In 1958 Jack Goody edited a volume of studies on this topic, with an Introduction by Meyer Fortes, and it set the scene for a succession of studies following its basic rationale (Goody 1958). As less sociological and more deconstructive-interpretive ways of looking at kinship emerged in the 1980s, the approach was dropped in favor of particularistic disquisitions on the special character of Euro-American notions of 'kinship' and the recent effects on these of new forms of reproductive technology. Uhlmann's analysis returns us to the seminal work of Fortes and Goody as well as to the quotidian contexts of kinship as it is practiced in urban environments. In brief, his argument is that many, though perhaps not all, of the variations of patterns in domestic residence can be seen, not simply as deviations from a nuclear family normative structure, but as stages in the formation, consolidation, attrition, splitting, and dissolution of the nuclear family. Underpinning this approach is the point that the nuclear family remains an ideal focus of reference for kin relations and residence forms generally. The nuclear family is thus the ideal family; or, as Uhlmann puts it, using the terminology of Pierre Bourdieu, the doxic family. In this regard, he appeals also to schema and embodiment theory as propounded by George Lakoff and Mark Johnson: the body boundary as a container enclosing an essence. The family is seen as like a boundary device also, excluding outsiders. Throughout his study Uhlmann combines insights of this cognitive kind with sociological analysis, thereby enriching both. He also does not neglect the historical dimension, giving us an extended sketch of the transformations of family patterns from early times of colonization onward.

A further interesting feature that emerges from the container schema and its normative accompaniments is the downplaying of material interests within the boundary of 'the family': the family as the center of sharing and thus 'love'. But 'family' can also be a locus of conflict and competition. Externally manifested solidarity of siblings may be matched internally by their intense competition, for example. Spousal conflict may lead to divorce. Struggles with parents may lead children to split off. Uhlmann refers to the glossing over of such conflicts in terms of Bourdieu's idea of 'misrecognition', although in practice people may be aware of the contradictions that are involved in familial relations.

In terms of technical discussions on kinship Uhlmann's carefully documented study also bears on another issue: that of filiation versus descent. There are no strongly defined descent categories as such in Newcastle, and effective recruitment to social positions is via filiation. Yet, in a broader sense, notions of ancestrality are present, since relations among cousins depend on an idea that goes beyond immediate filiation. We could perhaps speak of steps of filiation rather than descent here; but the idioms people use clearly indicate there is an idea of descending ancestral connections linking people together; so that descent in a general sense is recognized, even though it does not produce descent groups. This is not surprising, for even if such groups can be defined primarily in terms of descent, they do not emerge as effective groups unless they are centered on definite shared activities or interests in property or ritual values, as Jack Goody also pointed out long ago.

Finally, Uhlmann raises the interesting question of why people have children. He answers this question in part by way of recourse to Pierre Bourdieu's concept of habitus. The question is real, because bringing up children is hard work and is often seen as a sacrifice. Uhlmann briefly invokes cognitive dissonance theory here, noting that reasons given for having children might be seen as post hoc rationalizations and a defense against any notion that the sacrifice might not actually be 'worth it'. However, he rejects this explanation in favour of a processual approach. Parents invest themselves in their children, and the more they do so the more important it is for them to see this activity as worth while; especially, we might add, since in a sense it may continue for their lifetimes. At a more general level we might suggest here that the ultimate clue lies in the concept of sacrifice. A sacrifice is a gift made to some cause or project which is considered to have considerable value, and in order to obtain a return. In cultural terms, the return may be computed, and the answer to the initial question sought, in the ideal definition of the family itself, i.e., that it must include children. If 'family' is bound up with the definition of 'achieving personhood' and family means having children, it follows that people who are motivated to seeking personhood through the idea of the family would be motivated to have children. As Uhlmann himself points out, 'family' is also expanded into further discursive realms, including ethnicity and the nation. It becomes a connecting or bridging metaphor linking different domains of social experience together, and gaining further power as a result of this process.

These remarks cover only a few of the many themes that emerge from this finely described, carefully analysed, and interestingly theorized ethnography, which adds significantly both to ethnographic knowledge and to wider debates on kinship, ideology, social class, gender, and social practice generally.

Reference

Goody, Jack (ed.) (1958), *The Developmental Cycle in Domestic Groups*. Cambridge: Cambridge University Press.

To the Novocastrians, whose generosity and hospitality made this book a possibility; and to JR, whose insistence and toil made this book a reality.

Acknowledgments

This book was made possible by the generosity and patience of a large number of informants, respondents, and participants in the ethnographic component of this project. To protect their identity, these people will remain anonymous.

I would like to thank the following organisations and people for their help in the conduct of the fieldwork: Family with Adolescents Support Centre; Relationships Australia; Leone Forsythe of the National Association for Prevention of Child Abuse and Neglect; Newcastle City Mission; Working Women's Centre (especially Doone Turnbull); Salvation Army Welfare Service; Fay Exton from Adolescent and Family Counsellors, at Redhead; the Westlake Adolescent and Family Counsellors; Graeme Stuart of the Community Youth Development Project, Barney Langford of the 2–5 Youth Theatre; WEA Hunter – Helping Early Leavers (especially Tony Johnson); the Islington Branch of the ALP; the Jewish Community of Newcastle, Talk of the Town Toastmasters (formerly the BHP Toastmasters); Sally Jamieson of the Hamilton Chamber of Commerce, the Newcastle Workers Club; Greg Heys, Lord Mayor of Newcastle; Mr Allan Morris, MP (Federal Member for Newcastle); Serge Zorino of the TLC; Mick Savin of AWU-FIME; Bob Ritten of CEPU; Denis Nichols of AMEU; Nicola Hirschhorn and Chris Morley; Glenn Beatty; Michael Robson and Theresea Hughes.

The following have given of their time and energy, and contributed (knowingly or otherwise) to the intellectual development of the research, and to its culmination in book form: Ahmed Abou Zeid (Alexandria); Lois Bryson (Newcastle); James Carrier (*JRAI*); Carolyn Court (Ashgate); Ann Curthoys (ANU); Rebecca Emigh (UCLA); Jim Fox (ANU); Deane Fergie (Adelaide); Kingsley Garbett (Adelaide, *Social Analysis*); Don Gardner (ANU); Ghassan Hage (Sydney) Alexandra Jaffe (CSULB); Don Handelman (Hebrew Univ); Christine Helliwell (ANU); Ian Keen (ANU); Al Klovdahl (ANU); Peter McDonald (ANU); Deirdre McKay (ANU); Shelley Mallett (La Trobe); Andrew Metcalfe (UNSW); Francesca Merlan (ANU); Ruth Milkman (UCLA); Nancy Munn (Chicago); Mary Patterson (Melbourne); Nicolas Peterson (ANU); Jane Read (Jane Read Editorial Services); Kathy Robinson (ANU); Larry Saha (ANU); Mary Savigar (Ashgate); Michael Shalev (Hebrew Univ); Pamela J. Stewart (Pittsburgh); Maila Stivens (Melbourne); Andrew Strathern (Pittsburgh); Jennifer Uhlmann (UCLA); Andrea Whittacker (ANU); Hillary Winchester (Newcastle); Caroline Wintersgill (Ashgate); Sylvia Yanagisako (Stanford).

I am grateful to Berghahn Books for permission to integrate material from my article 'Incorporating Masculine Domination: Theoretical and Ethnographic

Elaborations', *Social Analysis*, April 2000, **44**(1): 142–161; to Blackwell Publishing for permission to integrate material from my article 'Intertwined Refractions: The Mutual Constitution of Gender Style and Class Fraction in a Deindustrialising Australian Town', *Journal of the Royal Anthropological Institute (Incorporating Man)*, September 2001, **7**(3): 449–466; to Elsevier and to co-author JR Uhlmann for permission to integrate material from 'Embodiment below Discourse: The Internalized Domination of the Masculine Perspective', *Women's Studies International Forum*, 2005, **28**(1): 93–103; and to the *Australian Journal of Anthropology* for allowing me to integrate material from my paper 'The Dynamics of Stasis: Historical Inertia in the Evolution of the Australian Family', *The Australian Journal of Anthropology*, April 2005, **16**(1): 18–30.

Chapter 1

Introduction: The Project and the Field

This book is intended as an ethnographic report into kinship, family and gender practices; as a critical exposition of the current social scientific understanding of such practices; and as a theoretical and methodological treatise on practice.

The project originated in ethnographic fieldwork among workers and their families in the Australian town of Newcastle, New South Wales, from late 1994 until early 1996. The fieldwork unfolded in various phases, each lasting a few months. In the first stage I conducted interviews with union organizers and local politicians, and also started approaching potential informants. In the next phase I conducted formal interviews with community organizers, with professionals and activists in areas of family, youth and gender, and with family and relationship counsellors. At the same time I was keeping close contact with several families – learning about and sharing in their daily lives – while conducting a series of formal and informal interviews with other informants. In the following stage I continued my work with ethnographic informants, while starting to formulate preliminary observations. In the final phase of my fieldwork I focused with my informants on exploring and elaborating my preliminary observations, rather than on trying to generate new observations. In this phase I also conducted focus groups.

In total I maintained rather close and continuous contact with around fifteen informants. I also administered four focus groups (two with men, two with women) whose participants numbered between five and six each, and conducted interviews (both formal and informal) with many more. Some of my informants came through contacts I established in the union movement, others through personal contacts, a few through community organizations (such as the local branch of the Australian Labor Party, a Toastmasters club, religious community organizations, and adult technical and continuing education institutions). A few neighbours in the 'rough' inner-city suburb of Islington where I lived also became informants. Some of the youth I interviewed were contacted through a few community organizations that deal with young people, such as a youth theatre group. The participants in the focus groups were recruited through the distribution of fliers at shopping centres, followed by phone interviews.

This description might convey the impression of a well-organized ethnographic fieldwork, carried out in a premeditated and systematic manner. In reality, however, much of the fieldwork unfolded haphazardly rather than by intentional pre-planning. For example, I had originally intended to focus my study on workers in a particular industrial site, using that site as a bounded community of sorts. I chose one steel-making plant of BHP – the largest Australian-based multinational at the time – and proceeded to get the approval of the manager of the site. This approval was subsequently revoked by BHP's head office in Melbourne. The reason for denying me access was most likely a reluctance of top BHP management to have outsiders in the plant just as they were about to launch a massive downsizing drive. The extent of the planned closures and the intentional escalation of industrial conflict were not known to either workers or local management at the time I began my fieldwork. Once the negative response arrived from BHP's corporate headquarters, workers, especially staff members, were warned by management in no uncertain terms not to cooperate with me in the study. I decided not to try to recruit any more informants from among employees at that workplace, and did not put any pressure on those who bowed to company pressure and decided not to continue. While I continued working with a few of the workers, I gave up on my original attempt to delineate a clearly bounded population. I subsequently relied on the snowball method to recruit further informants. Another dead end in my research was my attempt to use social network analysis, which I had originally hoped to integrate into the study. As it turned out, I had underestimated the amount of data which such an analysis would both generate and require. I concluded that, given the great restrictions on my resources, I could not pursue this avenue of research.

As a result of the collapse of my strategy to bracket off a bounded community, my increasing realization of the limits on my resources, and the abundance of well-resourced statistical data on Australian families, I decided not to attempt survey work or other quantitative data collections, and rather to focus on in-depth, qualitative studies. As I proceeded to concentrate on qualitative work, I continued to experiment with different research methods. Towards the end of my fieldwork I conducted four focus groups. These proved surprisingly useful in the data they provided. I conducted two focus groups with men, and two with women.

While all informants contributed to the research voluntarily, those who participated in the focus groups were paid A$40 for their participation. Professional childcare was also provided to participants, free of charge, during the sessions. Initially I tried to recruit participants on a voluntary basis, but met with very little success. One common practice among some researchers with low budgets is to get a pre-existing group of people, such as a club committee, to participate as a group in a focus group. I decided not to follow this route, as it is an essential aspect of the focus group methodology that participants should be strangers to one another. Furthermore, Newcastle is saturated with commercial research companies who run focus groups, and who pay their participants. This had created an expectation, which was not unreasonable, among potential participants that they should be remunerated for turning up at an allotted place at an allotted time for the interview.

This shift in methodology towards an exclusive focus on qualitative research was only possible because of the abundance of solid quantitative data on family practices published by such sources as the Australian Bureau of Statistics (ABS) and the Australian Institute of Family Studies (AIFS). It coincided with a general shift in my interests from providing a description of the patterns of practice, to trying to understand the logic of practice. This shift was influenced by the fact that the practice of my informants was rather disappointingly common. An original hypothesis I had entertained before heading off to the field – namely that terminal monogamy was being replaced with serial monogamy – fell flat. My informants did not take lightly to divorce and separation, nor did they experience it as an integral part of the normal life experience. Divorce and separation were still very much marital breakdowns rather than integral stages of a novel life trajectory.

Further, confronted with the realities of my field I found it necessary to raise fundamental questions that ideally should have been answered by works in other disciplines. For example, while much statistical data exists on family-related regularities of practice, the current historical and sociological literature does not provide a useful analysis of what is changing and what is not in the practice of kinship and family. Moreover, the analysis of the logic of these patterns of practice is not very useful by anthropological standards. For instance, it is not clear from the literature if changes in aggregate patterns of practice reflect what, following David Schneider (e.g. Schneider 1980, 1–8), one might call normative changes, or perhaps changes at the cultural level.

In confronting the cultural level of practice I also came up against one of the most frustrating and fruitful limitations of ethnographic data – the silences and lacunae in the data that result from the fact that what is taken for granted escapes explication. These silences are all the more interesting as they were echoed in much social research, and resonate with much of the experience of both producers and consumers of anthropological research alike.

My shift in focus towards the logic of kinship practice led me to an in-depth engagement with the work of Pierre Bourdieu. This engagement began while in the field, but grew in intensity in the period following my return. In the process I had to re-evaluate the very questions, concepts and theories that had guided my research. Bourdieu's theory of practice came to form the analytical backbone for the discussion below. However, in the course of bringing it to bear on my ethnographic data, I found it necessary to modify several aspects of his theory, and to integrate elements of cognitive sciences and phenomenology into the broad scheme of things. Specifically, work on metaphor and categorization in social sciences opened the way for me to explore the way the lived world is organized in practice even when this contradicted formal logic; and the phenomenology of embodiment allowed me to reintroduce the body – as physical reality – into the analysis. Thus this study became an opportunity for me to develop an eclectic methodology to analyse practice.

In sum, then, this work is ethnographically driven, but is not an ethnography in the narrowest sense of the word. Rather, it is a broader exploration of various theoretical issues relating to the kinship practices which were observed in the field. The ethnographic component of the research joins in with other historical, sociological and demographic data to provide an object for analysis. The analysis that follows serves two functions. One is to provide new information about and greater insight into a critical field of practice. The other is to showcase an analytical approach to practice.

Before delving into the analysis in the chapters that follow, I should better situate my fieldwork, and my informants.

The Context of the Fieldwork

Newcastle at the time of my fieldwork was in the throes of a major political-economic structural shift. From the early years of the twentieth century Newcastle's economy had been based on heavy industry. However, major structural reforms that flowed from the increased globalization of the economy resulted in the progressive exodus of heavy industries from Newcastle, beginning in the early 1980s and culminating in the mid-1990s. For example, in the early 1980s BHP was the town's main employer. In 1982–83 BHP shed well over 10,000 employees, reducing its workforce to around 3,000. Beginning in 1995, BHP began progressively restructuring, eventually winding down virtually all operations in the city. More generally, by the time of my fieldwork heavy industry's share of employment in Newcastle had dropped substantially. The largest employer in Newcastle in 1995 was the University of Newcastle (Boreham and Hall 1993; Metcalfe and Bern 1994; Metcalfe and Bern n.d.; Docherty 1983; Mills 1997; Sexton 1997; Hextall et al. 1997; Greg Heys (Lecturer in Social Work at the University of Newcastle and Lord Mayor 1995–9), personal communication; Serge Zorino (Trades and Labour Council), personal communication; Mick Savin (AWU-FIME Amalgamated Union), personal communication; Bob Ritten (Communications, Electrical and Plumbing Union), personal communication; Denis Nichols (Automotive, Metals and Engineering Union), personal communication).

This was part of a national trend that saw manufacturing's share of the formal economy drop, while tertiary service industries increased their proportion. Over that period capital grew stronger in relation to both organized labour and the state apparatus. This was reflected economically in the drop in the ratio of wages to profit, in the wages' share of production costs, and in the wages' share of the national income. The structural shift was accompanied by the rolling back of social spending by state and federal governments, the pacification of labour, and a progressive deterioration of the labour experience. Unionization rates dropped, unemployment increased, as did casual and part-time work. Full-time work entailed progressively longer hours of work and greater effort, in conjunction with a decline in job security. Good jobs became rarer, and degraded jobs proliferated. Apprenticeships which had previously been important in securing young people's economic independence became very rare indeed. All these transformations affected the labour market unevenly. Consequently, the economic and social inequalities within the working class increased, so that the best-off of the working class – invariably core employees in well-unionized industries – shrank in ratio, but were doing comparatively better than before. At the same time the people at the bottom of the heap increased in numbers, and were worse off. Newcastle itself failed to develop any alternative economic bases to the rapidly fleeing heavy industries, and was exhibiting, in a magnified form, all the ailments of the national structural transformation (Gittins 1997; McGregor 1997; Connell and Irving 1992; Boreham and Hall 1993; Greg Heys ((Lecturer in Social Work at the University of Newcastle and Lord Mayor 1995–9)), personal communication).

My Informants and their Class Position

My ethnographic informants came mostly from the shrinking traditional industrial working class. The vast majority could be classed as members of what Bourdieu (1984) has dubbed the dominated class which can be glossed as working class. When analysing the dominant class – that is the various social, cultural and economic elites – Bourdieu distinguished between dominated and dominant fractions. This distinction can also be applied to the working class.

Among my informants there was a higher representation of members of the dominant fraction of the working class, than of the dominated fraction of the working class. They included tradesmen, semi-professionals, foremen, mid-level clerical workers, trade unionists and their families. They were mostly from Northern and Western European extraction, or at least identified with the 'non-ethnic'/'true-blue' mainstream society. While my informants' age range varied, my main focus was on men and women in their twenties, thirties and forties.

In adapting Bourdieu's relational scheme to my working-class informants, I distinguish between two class fractions – the dominated and the dominant – according to the segment of the labour market to which they are attached.[1]

The Australian labour market, like all modern capitalist labour markets, is segmented (Boreham and Hall 1993; cf. Sawyer 1989, chapter 3; Edwards 1979; Norris 1993). The distinction I am drawing between the dominant and dominated fractions of the working class relates to the distinction often drawn between the primary and the secondary labour markets in various studies, for example the distinction between the 'secondary' labour market, and 'subordinate primary' labour market in Richard Edwards's formulation (Edwards 1979). The secondary labour market offers casual employment and dead-end jobs, is characterized by great worker mobility, low skill level, low investment by employers in employee training, poor working conditions, job insecurity and ultimately, low wages. The labour-market participation patterns of those who sell their labour power on this market can be typified by great horizontal job mobility (normally between employers) and a lack of promotion, and is typically accompanied by high levels of

---

[1] The dominant fraction is referred to as the aristocracy of labour in some formulations, is included in the middle class in other formulations, or is counted as working class in yet other formulations. So long as the class structure is taken as a heuristic device, the consequences of these different formulations are not great. They all tend to point to a structural divide between the groups I distinguish as dominant and dominated fractions, and which others might distinguish as middle and working class.

unemployment. By contrast, the primary labour market, which is largely organized around large corporate employers' internal labour markets, provides workers with better working conditions and greater job security. Positions that are filled with labour power bought on the primary labour market normally require greater skill levels than those that are filled on the secondary labour market. Employers invest more in training and maintaining such employees. The primary labour market, which normally takes the form of a manorial internal labour market (see Norris 1993, 98–113), contains the jobs of the old industrial working class, and the lower-level clerical, service and supervisory positions. Workers who sell their labour power on this labour market normally enjoy higher levels of unionization, exercise greater control over their labour process and, ultimately, earn much higher wages. Compared with those from the secondary market, they are more likely to stay with their current employer, more likely to win promotions and more likely to advance up the skill and remuneration levels. Further, in transition between industries, workers tend to remain within their segment of the labour market. This was particularly visible during my fieldwork, which occurred at the peak of deindustrialization in Newcastle. All those whom I encountered who had made the transition from blue-collar work to white-collar jobs of the primary labour market had been employed in the primary segment in their original industry.

I class those who live in households whose income derives primarily from the secondary labour market as the dominated fraction of the working class, and those whose households rely primarily on the primary labour market as the dominant fraction of the working class.

Members of the dominant fractions of the working class directly dominate members of the dominated fractions of their own class in various contexts. The following instances reflect the specificities of my fieldwork site. At the workplace, the secondary labour market jobs in large firms would usually come under the supervision of the firm's core workforce, which was composed of those who were attached to the primary labour market. In other words, the members of the dominated fraction of the working class came under the supervision of the dominant-fraction members of the working class. Similarly, in formal grassroots organizations such as lay church groups, unions, ALP branches, single-issue organizations or parental mobilization around schools – those in leadership positions were much more likely to be members of the dominant fractions of the working class, rather than their counterparts in the dominated fractions. Another form of domination occurred in the home-rental markets. Many members of the dominant fraction invested in real estate, usually in the cheap, impoverished, inner-city suburbs. These investments required a relatively modest initial capital investment, which was one reason they were popular. Also, being members of the working class, my informants were 'good with their hands', and often used their embodied cultural capital (that is, their manual skills) to improve the real estate and increase its value. The loans taken to finance the acquisitions were paid off from the rent collected from tenants. The tenants on such properties were very likely to be members of the dominated fractions of the working class, who could not afford even the initial investment to gain a mortgage to buy a family home. Through this relationship between landlord and tenant too, then, members of the dominant fraction came to dominate members of the dominated fractions of the working class. Even in State agencies that manage and control the working class (e.g. police, Department of Social Security), those employees who directly interacted with the public normally belonged to the dominant fraction, while clients or those subjected to the work of these agencies were usually members of the dominated fraction. Finally, occasionally a member of the dominant fraction of the working class might try to set up an independent small business. When such businesses became successful enough to require the recruitment of employees, the latter were most often members of the dominated fractions of the working class. All these instances of daily domination of the one fraction by the other represent a major structural fault line which cuts across the working class (cf. McGregor 1997, 55–56, 89–93, 199).

Further, the daily conflicts within the working class – either through direct domination as I described above, or merely through exclusory practices like the closed shop at unionized workplaces – continuously put the dominant fraction and its style in opposition with that of the dominated fraction and its style. (I will return to the intertwining of class structure and gender style in chapter 8.) Nevertheless, both fractions shared their basic position in the social structure – namely opposition to the social, economic and cultural elites – and were furthermore not separated in a clear-cut fashion. Mobility between the two fractions occurred frequently. During my fieldwork, at a time when heavy industries were fleeing from Newcastle, mostly offshore, the most common mobility was downwards through redundancy and unemployment, from the dominant fraction to the dominated fraction. More importantly, most of my dominant-fraction informants had little which had distinguished them as adolescents from fellow White working-class Australians who ended up in the dominated fraction. To my informants, adolescence seems to be a limbo of sorts from which some emerge in the course of their early adulthood to the dominant fraction, and others into the dominated fraction. This is exemplified, among other things, in the fact that siblings may quite commonly find themselves in different class fractions. For example, in one set of siblings among my informants the two elder brothers were in secondary manual labour positions, the third brother was in a salaried middle-level supervisory position (in charge of training in a heavy-industry plant), and the youngest sister was an academic, specializing in education, and very much in the cultural elite.

In fact, reproduction of class-fraction location down the generations was fraught with uncertainty. Youths were not usually guaranteed a place in the dominant fraction. Their acquisition and internalization of the discipline of work and on-the-job training which are part of the disciplining process that makes the respectable working-class male was by no means certain. If they should fail to market their labour power on the primary labour market, working-class youths were likely to miss out on training opportunities, and consequently fail to develop the cultural capital which is necessary for access to the primary labour market. Such a situation would almost certainly assure them a permanent place in the secondary labour market. This, and the fact that spatially and socially the two fractions were not separated very clearly, limited the divergence of styles in that class, including patterns of kinship and family.

I have noted above that my informants largely belonged to the dominant ethnic group. Ethnicity and Aboriginality are strongly connected with the division into classes and fractions. Marginal groups are more likely to be represented in the secondary labour market, and thereby in the dominated fraction of the working class. This may be attributed in part to poverty in cultural capital (e.g. formal qualifications, English literacy), poverty in social capital (social contacts are critical in recruitment to primary labour market jobs and assist in membership in trade unions), as well as economic capital (which can be converted into marketable cultural capital through further education and training) (cf. Boreham and Hall 1993; McGregor 1997, 265–266). These issues are easily forgotten when dealing with the dominant ethnic group, and the temptation is to focus on largely economic aspects of class as if ethnicity and Aboriginality are only meaningful categories in the analysis of the practices of non-mainstream people. In fact, non-ethnic, mainstream and true-blue are as ethnic as any category.

The Chapters that Follow

The remainder of this book relies on my original research and on published material to explore Anglo-Celtic Australian kinship practice. By Anglo-Celtic I wish to designate the dominant cultural tradition in Australia that has its roots in the British Isles.[2]

Chapter 2 sets the stage for the analysis that follows by briefly sketching the historical evolution of contemporary Australian kinship, family and gender practices.

Chapter 3 draws on contemporary scholarship to describe the current reality of kinship and family practices. The pervasive sense of recent cataclysmic crises and shifts in the family is shown to be unjustified. Aggregate changes in practice result, in part, from demographic shifts and are therefore an exaggerated indicator of actual changes in practice. Some changes are afoot, though, such as the lengthening liminal phase between social and economic independence of youths, and the emergence of a clearer distinction between a childbearing and a child-rearing phase. But it is rather the historical continuity and resilience of kinship and family practices that is remarkable, as expressed, for instance, in the gendered division of

---

[2] I should hasten to add that the adjective 'Anglo-Celtic' itself was not spontaneously invoked by my informants. The adjective is commonly used among the intelligentsia, and although my informants had heard and understood the term, it was generally redundant to them, as Anglo-Celtic is none other than unhyphenated Australian, often referred to as 'true blue' or 'Aussie' (see below, pp. 85–87).

labour. This resilience is particularly stark at the cultural and normative levels of practice, to which the discussion then turns.

Chapter 4 addresses the nuclear family – the prototypical family – which is at the core of my informants' kinship practice. The prototypical family acts as a realized category: it is both a model *of* reality in the sense that it reflects the general practice; as well as a model *for* reality, in a sense that it becomes a prescription or a set of blueprints that members of society – conceived of in this study as social agents – follow. The prototypical family is modelled after an idealized prototypical person. Both prototypes are strongly inflected by the container metaphor that cognitively and experientially structures them. The prototypical family is the cognitively basic family: all other forms of family are defined as such by reference to this prototype. The analysis belies the putative significance of Australian peculiarities, such as the centrality of the mate in the family structure.

Chapter 5 further develops these notions by considering alternative family practices, ranging from the homosexual family to some totally idiosyncratic arrangements. Family practices form a graded and radial category. To qualify as an alternative, a type must be defined as family by reference to the prototypical family. Moreover, at the very same time that alternative family practices challenge specific aspects of the prototypical family, they reinforce others. This is part of the explanation of the family's remarkable historical resilience.

Moreover, the family is embedded within broad webs of meaning which chapter 6 begins to analyse with a discussion of the broader kinship system and its underlying logic. The analysis focuses on kinship terminology and associated etiquette. The significant principle that structures relatedness is filiation. The extended kin are organized and mobilized as social categories of ego-centred kindreds. The kinship system is predicated on, and reinforces divisions into individual persons, divisions by age, and by gender.

Chapter 7 then explores how gender and gender relations are internalized into the very embodied subjectivities of social agents. This includes orientation to the body, modalities of motility, techniques of the body and non-deliberative linguistic practices. An idealized notion of reproduction serves as the cognitive and cultural basis that motivates the construction of gender in abstract contexts. Genderedness clearly inflects social practices, with family and domesticity being feminized, as opposed to other contexts which are masculinized.

Following chapters 4 and 5 that explore the family, and chapters 6 and 7 that delve further into the experiences of kinship and gender beyond the confines of the family, chapter 8 broadens the purview of the discussion even further to the political economy in general. Contrary to much economistic commonsense, the Australian experience clearly demonstrates how kinship, family and gender practices have conditioned the very structure of modernity and capitalism. For example, the study demonstrates how class location and gender styles are mutually constitutive, without either being an epiphenomenon of the other. Moreover, the structure of the market economy, including the social relations of industrial production, the labour market and the patterns of economic expansion and growth in Australia have been critically affected by the structure and function of the field of kinship, family and gender.

   Chapter 9 briefly recapitulates the theory of practice that underlies the discussion, and further develops the heuristic economics of practice – in contrast with the common substantivist approaches – that inform the analysis. I raise such seemingly trivial yet theoretically intractable questions like why people have children, to show that interests do not precede practice but are constructed in the very process of practice. I engage with other family practices to demonstrate that much of practice is coordinated implicitly through the commonality of dispositions that results from the similarity in formative social experiences; and to show how the logic of practice, which is much fuzzier than formal logic, can endure many contradictions and lends itself to such symbolic politicking as manipulating the interpretation of given social interactions. The discussion throughout the book was based on an understanding of kinship and gender as a social field. Chapter 9 concludes by emphasizing the interpretative arbitrariness of such fields by showing how the logic of practice transcends such artificial fields, for instance through the application of homologous mental structures to analogous situations.

Chapter 2

The Historical Evolution of the Australian Family

This chapter briefly sketches the historical evolution of the Australian family to set the stage for the analysis that follows. The embeddedness of the family within broad social, political and cultural processes is emphasized, as is the inseparability of the historical threads of kinship, family and gender.

The nuclear family has been the structurally prevalent family form in Northern and Western Europe for many centuries (Goody 2000; Goody 1983; Mcfarlane 1987). Yet the internal workings of the family and its function within the social order have shifted considerably, along with the evolution of the European political economy. Historians recount that up to the emergence of capitalism, the nuclear family was firmly embedded within broader social networks. With the advent of capitalism, families were increasingly dislodged from earlier bonds of authority, kinship and estate which engulfed the feudal family. With early capitalism households became privileged sites of small-scale commodity production for the quickly expanding impersonal markets. In this early capitalist household there was a division of labour between the genders and between the generations, but all householders' activities were explicitly geared towards production (Goody 2000, chapter 9; Zaretsky 1986, chapters 1–2).

Household size did not change dramatically with early capitalism. In England for the most part of the past millennium the typical household numbered five residents. While the underlying dispositions and normative conventions did not change much when Britons emigrated or were transported to the Antipodes, the special conditions of early settlement (like the inclusion of indentured workers in households) skewed the demographic picture. Before the 1860s, European households in Australia averaged over ten residents. Conditions changed gradually through the middle of the nineteenth century. The demographic and social structure of the colonies began normalizing by the early 1860s, following the gold rush. Households were organized around nuclear families, but were commonly not exclusively nuclear-family households. Affluent homes normally included servants and governesses. Bourgeois households might also include apprentices and journeymen. Established working-class households often supplemented their incomes by taking in lodgers – normally working-class men. In 1901 11.3 per cent of Sydney households included at least one lodger. In addition, both bourgeois and working-class households might have included, usually on a temporary basis, relatives in need, such as women, children and the elderly. On the other hand, among the working class in the cities, by the end of the nineteenth century, many men did not live with their families, but rather moved in pursuit of employment (Snooks 1994, 63–69; McDonald 1995, 10; Gilding 1991, 32–35; Zaretsky 1986, chapters 1, 2).

In Australia, as in comparable societies, the disconnection of the immigrating nuclear family from its original community was definite and absolute. Those who emigrated from the British Isles left mostly as individuals or in nuclear-family groups, not as communities. Upon arrival in the colonies, early settlers did not recreate strong community networks in Australia. The agricultural technology and the political economy of farming made it impossible for most early settlers to support large family groups on the land. Furthermore, in the bush,[1] families were isolated because of the great distances and the poorly developed transportation system (Aspin 1994, 31–34; Grimshaw 1983, 31–39).

Compared with England, patriarchy – that is, the authority exercised by the male head of the family over his dependants – was attenuated in Australia for various reasons. The demands of frontier society meant women were involved in production and the material support of the family long after Victorian bourgeois women were confined to hysterically wallow in unproductive domesticity. This need for women's labour combined with the over-supply of men to put women in a good bargaining position in the marital markets. In addition, rich families with substantial patrimony who exercised control over their children by virtue of the estates they owned were proportionally far fewer in Australia than in England, making young adults, *ipso facto*, much more economically independent. Finally, the fragmentation of the household in pursuit of distant employment left many women in full control of, and responsible for, the household (Grimshaw 1983, 38).

In pre-industrial colonial Australia the essence of family life was the material maintenance of the household. In the cities, an increasing share of families came to rely primarily on wages for income. In such proletarian families, children would join the workforce and support the family, while mothers would typically support the family income through productive activities such as taking in lodgers, laundry work or the performance of piecework for factories. But the father of the family remained the main breadwinner. Often family members might reside elsewhere in pursuit of work. The father and the sons might follow seasonal or distant work, and girls might move to affluent households to work as live-in servants. In such fragmented households it was the mother of the household – the practical hub of the family – who would permanently reside at home. The paucity of broader support networks and the weakness of civil society meant that in the early stages of colonization the fate of patriarch-less families was grim. Then, as now, abandoned, orphaned, or otherwise homeless children were most vulnerable. This economic dependency on men also spelt disaster to those women and children who were unfortunate enough to depend on a violent or economically dysfunctional male.

---

[1] In Australian English 'the bush' denotes the countryside and the rural sector, as opposed to cities and the urban sector.

Pre-industrial bourgeois families were already moving away from production and focusing on consumption. Young bourgeois children, especially boys, were put through lengthening and deepening educational processes to secure their entry into the burgeoning professional ranks. Bourgeois women became domesticated and circumscribed in their maternal role (Grimshaw 1983, 31–39; Burns and Goodnow 1985, chapter 1; Gilding 1991, chapters 2, 3, 4, 6).

***

The rise of industrial capitalism – which arrived in Australia only in the early twentieth century (Connell and Irving 1992, chapters 4, 5) – meant that production was increasingly removed from households and socialized in factories. Throughout the European cultural sphere work became increasingly commodified as labour markets developed. For the working class at least, the kind of work one did constituted progressively less of one's identity. Rather, being a worker was what constituted one as working class. One's identity and self were increasingly disconnected from one's trade, and invested in the home and family. This is how the domestic sphere became the sphere of privacy, as against the public sphere. Home was the site of one's individuality, where one could be oneself, and not just a cog in the large industrial machine. Increasingly, the essence of the family shifted from production to the pursuit of happiness and satisfaction, meaningful personal relationships, and the exclusive site of love and eroticism. But while generally the home became the site of the personal, of individuality, of lifestyle and hobbies, the public domain became the idealized site of calculated utility maximization, that is, the rationalist selfishness of *homo oeconomicus* (Goody 2000, chapters 9, 11; Zaretsky 1986, chapters 1, 2).

The division of labour between the genders came to take the form of the division between production, which was masculine and socialized, and the domestic domain, which was feminized and privatized. The industrial relations regime came to be premised on the specialization of men in breadwinning and women in homemaking. Such informal activities as hospitality and backyard dairy farming, which women had normally controlled, were displaced by the economy of scale of commercial production. Even in market niches where women had carved out an independent existence, they found themselves squeezed out by the new breed of entrepreneurs and the State. Thus, throughout the nineteenth century prostitution and midwifery were largely controlled by women. In fact, sex work was the highest paying employment for independently employed Australian women. This changed around the late nineteenth and early twentieth centuries when politicians and police, through legislation and regulations, enabled pimps and physicians to seize control over these two industries, with the consequent deterioration in women's working conditions and income in both industries (Gilding 1991, 55, 58, 83). The marginalization of women's economic activity continued well into the inter-war period.

The on-going process of separating the household from production is by no means complete, though. For example, some women mind children for pay while carrying out their own child-minding and household tasks. This phenomenon is distinct from the arrangement whereby centrally organized production is carried out in the home, textile piecework being a case in point. In the latter instance work is clearly separate from household chores. With child-minding, on the other hand, household chores are used to generate income. In addition, those businesses which are owned, run, and operated by families still retain much of the character of the families of early, pre-industrial capitalism. Moreover, while some production such as the manufacture of clothing is still being socialized, other tasks, like laundering, are being retaken by households, mostly as a result of technological developments that enable these tasks to be done more easily in-house (Game and Pringle 1983, 92; Bittman et al. 1999).

Early conflicts between and within labour and industrial capital eventually led to the evolution of the family wage as the governing principle of industrial relations (Connell and Irving 1992, chapter 4; cf. Zaretsky 1986, 47 ff.). The family-wage system in Australia was crystallized in 1907 in a ruling handed down by Justice Higgins in the Harvester judgment. His ruling required that every working man should earn wages sufficient to maintain a wife and three children in frugal comfort (Game and Pringle 1983, 86). The principle of the family wage formed the foundation of welfare capitalism in Australia throughout the century. It was a male wage-earner's welfare system. It operated through the labour market, to which members of the working class gained access either directly, as workers, or indirectly, as dependants of workers. Direct welfare payments and other welfare programmes that operate outside the labour market have never been given much prominence compared with other OECD countries. Furthermore, the regimentation of the labour process made it harder to balance caring obligations with full participation in the labour market, thereby accentuating the feminization of caring and the labour-market marginalization of women (Boreham and Hall 1993; Bryson 1995; Weeks 1995; Grimshaw et al. 1994, 199 ff.).

Industrial capitalism saw the emergence of childhood as a qualitatively distinct life stage. These changes reflected the increased mechanization of production in the nineteenth century, and the declining demand for child labour. Childhood was born of industrial capitalism's need to develop a progressively skilled workforce, and out of the bourgeoisie's earlier increased reliance on education for social reproduction. Educational institutions proliferated and school attendance increased, initially in bourgeois circles, and then progressively in the proletariat. The expansion of education throughout society was accompanied by the exclusion of children from production. Laws were introduced to eliminate child labour and enforce compulsory full-time education. Children were removed from the formal labour market, and were less available to carry out housekeeping activities. They became increasingly dependants, and an economic burden. These transformations profoundly affected familial authority and the channels of social reproduction throughout the White anglophone world. Specifically, the elite, through the State, sought to exert more influence on the social reproduction of the working class, and to bring working-class children more effectively under the influence of the prevailing power structures. Children, for their part, were exposed to greater influences outside the family household, and were given greater opportunities to develop alternative allegiances, which were paradigmatically embodied in peer groups (Reiger 1991, 10 ff., 50–51; Reiger 1985, chapters 6–7; Gilding 1991, chapters 2, 5; Zaretsky 1986; Aspin 1994, 28–30).

Fertility rates by that time had begun dropping. The increasing economic burden which children posed to families, with their continuing marginalization in the labour market, and the increasing cost of social reproduction, combined to provide a great incentive to reduce the number of children. When considering the reproductive behaviour of Australians in the late nineteenth century, one must keep in mind that giving birth was then a complex and potentially fatal chore. Birthing posed a considerable health risk, especially at the turn of the century and shortly after when the hospitalization of childbirth increased maternal mortality and morbidity by exposure to infections. (On the other hand, hospitalization reduced infant mortality and morbidity.) Also among the poor, many women who had suffered from rickets (often immigrants from the UK) had damaged pelvises. This made childbirth particularly complicated and painful at a time when effective analgesics were not widely available. Childbirth was also complicated by the tight lacing which was fashionable among women in the late nineteenth century (Reiger 1991, 14; Reiger 1985; Gilding 1991, chapters 5, 6).

The period of early industrial capitalism saw the increase in power of the newly emerging professional elites – State bureaucrats, and experts such as physicians – who came to exercise more influence over the lives of the working classes through the arms of the State. Their training, international professional contacts (especially in Britain, the US and Canada), and ethos transcended the borders of the nation state. These bureaucratic and intellectual elites formed an independent fraction in the dominant class that was motivated by a different ethos from the economic elite who came to be organized around the control of industrial capital. While the moneyed elite remained committed to the distinction between the private and public domains, the experts and bureaucrats espoused an ideology of efficiency and scientific management which was to be extended universally to the family and to reproduction. Under the aegis of the latter, the State, which assumed the role of supporting the vitality of capitalism and the White race, took a great interest in the conditions of the working class (Reiger 1985; Gilding 1991, chapter 6; Grimshaw 1983, chapter 8 ff.; Connell and Irving 1992, chapter 5).

At the time, degeneration was a main concern in European culture, and fears regarding the deterioration of the race reverberated throughout the British world, especially after the Boer War (Pick 1989, chapter 7). Public concern grew further when it became clear that birth rates had been declining since the 1860s. Alarmed savants and mandarins, concerned over the fate of the European stock, were driven by their responsibility to the race, as well as by considerations of social efficiency, to intervene in the management of families, especially working-class families

(Grimshaw 1983, 39 ff.; Grimshaw et al. 1994, chapter 8; Reiger 1991, 13 ff.; Reiger 1985, chapter 5).[2] Women now came to assume primary responsibility for social relations and the emotional well-being of the members of the nuclear family household. Unlike earlier times when the father initiated his sons into an occupation, the increased predominance of the wage economy, coupled with paternal absence from the home, left the mothers – in conjunction with State experts and educational institutions – in charge of socializing their children into work, managing the family budget, and keeping the family together (Gilding 1991, chapter 6; Reiger 1985; Zaretsky 1986, 131).

Public health campaigns touching upon proper child-rearing strategies – having bourgeois ideals in mind, the working-class family as an object, and the working-class mother as a target – came to be a permanent fixture of public life in Australia. One such example was the campaign launched at the turn of the twentieth century to encourage mothers to breastfeed their own children. Another was the concerted effort to restrict the access of women to the labour market in the first two decades of the twentieth century with the explicit intention of encouraging the healthy breeding of more members of the British stock. Such campaigns were quickly replicated by marketers of products whose health benefits were not always quite so clear, such as industrial substitutes for breast milk (Reiger 1991, 14–16; Gilding 1991, 59; Grimshaw et al. 1994, chapters 7–9).

Concerns over the enfeeblement of the British stock in Australia were eliminated in WWI along with 1 per cent of the population. Another historic consequence of the offshore carnage was that for the first time since the European invasion of the continent, the gender ratio was normalized, even in the bush (Clarke 1989, chapter 6).

***

An initial wave of suburbanization took place in the 1880s, especially in Melbourne. A strong building industry had existed in Australia since the 1860s, and homeownership rates were comparatively high in the colonies. Even large segments of the working class could become homeowners. As of the 1880s the proportion of urban dwellers among the population increased steadily. By the end of the nineteenth century the majority of Australians lived in cities (Snooks 1994, 38).

The 1920s saw an even greater wave of suburbanization as increasing numbers of working-class households sought to adopt the trappings of bourgeois

---

[2] Grave concerns over the reproductive under-achievement of White Australian women, and its consequence to the security of the race, continued well into the post-WWII era. The White Australia immigration policy was put in place in part to take out the reproductive slack that was left by Australia's obdurate young and fecund (Grimshaw et al. 1994, chapter 11).

domesticity, and joined others in the race to the suburbs. Inter-war suburbanization followed the paths of public transportation routes which in those days enabled the commute necessary for people who lived more than a walk or a bike-ride away from work. The new suburbs formed endless rows of bungalows set in quarter-acre blocks, broken up by public transportation routes, shops and schools (Gilding 1991, 45). While household production for the market was being supplanted by market forces (as when commercial dairy farms replaced backyard dairy farming), the new suburban arrangements allowed for increased production for use by households, as there was more space for vegetable patches and poultry. This production for use proved very important with the rapid collapse of the markets in the 1930s (Gilding 1991, 61).

Suburbanization was accompanied by improvements in household technology which reduced the demand for servants, so that increasingly households which had previously relied on domestic employees came to rely on the labour of the wife/mother of the family. Thus progressively more married women from further up the social scale were becoming housewives. By the 1940s, live-in servants had all but disappeared from most upper-class households. At the same time, many of the causes of working-class household fragmentation had disappeared: the mechanization of labour in the bush reduced the demand for seasonal labour and for domestic service, and new opportunities appeared for young women in education and in the labour market, which all meant that young women continued to live with their parents for longer periods of time. The piecemeal development of social welfare policy – predicated upon the nuclear family – further reduced the fragmentation rate of working-class households, and with it multi-family households, as fewer people required hospitality from relatives. Thus, the nuclear-family household increased its prominence both up and down the social ladder (Reiger 1991, 33 ff.; Reiger 1985, chapter 1; Gilding 1991, 40–47; Game and Pringle 1983, 83 ff.; Grimshaw 1983, 39 ff.).

This period saw some interesting shifts in the visibility of class conflict. On the one hand, the polarization within the working class became more visible than ever before, as the better-off fled to the new suburbs, while the worse-off stayed put. On the other hand, class differences between women lost much of their visibility. More than ever before women were disconnected from the formal labour market, and with the disappearance of servants and domestics, class distinctions in the privatized, feminine sphere became less stark (Gilding 1991, 61–63).

A new emphasis on the quality of the household and family life spread with the progressive suburbanization of the more affluent segments of the working class. This emphasis centred on the role of the mother of the family. Extended networks of support which once played an important role in childcare, as well as baby-farming, gave way to the mother as the major, and often sole, carer of infants and children, in conjunction with the State apparatus. The home became progressively a domain in which women exercised control and expertise. Those technocrats and bureaucrats – many of them bourgeois women – who concerned themselves with the functions of households addressed their guidance directly to mothers. Their influence was exercised through such institutions as domestic-science classes at school, suburban baby clinics, women's magazines and medical consultations. Women were not passive in the process, and responded quite favourably to such intervention (Reiger 1985; Reiger 1991, 19–21; Game and Pringle 1983, 85–87; Grimshaw 1983, 39–47; Gilding 1991, 56–63, chapters 5, 6; Grimshaw et al. 1994, chapters 8–9). The increased recourse to the State-sponsored clinic and medical services must have been partly due to the further elimination of older, urban, networks and services such as midwives, as a result of the process of suburbanization.

Also in the 1920s, the progressive deterioration of the family-wage system began in earnest. New South Wales (NSW) led the way. Its *Industrial Arbitration (Declaration of Living Wage) Act* reduced the standard family for purposes of the living wage to a childless couple. The State was to subsidize the care of children, a role which began with the NSW Family Endowment legislation. NSW was followed by the Commonwealth. The Commonwealth Arbitration Court's decision of 1931 identified the industry's ability to pay as the main criterion for wage fixing. In the late 1940s the federal government adopted the NSW Family Endowment legislation (Game and Pringle 1983, 86–87; Grimshaw 1983, 42). This was a major step in an ongoing process of consolidating industrial capitalism in Australia, by further socializing its cost while privatizing its profits.

***

Suburbanization was temporarily halted by the Great Depression and WWII, but not for long. The 1950s were a period of strong and sustained economic growth. Credit became more widely available than ever before, and the automobile was for the first time accessible to the majority of Australians. The conditions were ripe for most of the working class to be suburbanized.

A post-war flight to suburbia quickly turned into a flood. Homeownership peaked, and the nuclear-family household achieved near-universality throughout society. The long spell, associated with the Great Depression, of declining marriage rates and rising ages at marriage, ended abruptly immediately after WWII. The result was a rapid increase in household formation, record marriage rates, a drop in age at marriage and, of course, the baby boom.

However, as will become clearer in the next section, many of these dramatic changes in the family of the 1950s were ephemeral, and trends started reversing by the 1960s. Thus age at marriage was increasing in the 1960s and beyond, reflecting cyclical changes, namely the economic slowdown, as well as secular ones such as the arrival of the contraceptive pill and IUD. These latter leaps in copulative technology have all but eliminated 'shotgun' marriages, and contributed to a proliferation of recreational sex both within and without marriage (Game and Pringle 1983, 80–85, 88–89; Gilding 1991, chapters 5, 8).

The forced savings from war-time rationing compounded the increase in disposable household income to fuel consumerism, as bare necessities quickly exceeded mere access to food, health and shelter, and became progressively defined by preference and lifestyle. Consumerism was centred on the home and household, the site of personal individuality and the pursuit of status and happiness. Thus the pursuit of subjective experience – previously the domain of the leisure class – trickled down the socio-economic ladder (Game and Pringle 1983, 81, 87 ff.; Reiger 1991, 35 ff.; Zaretsky 1986, 49 ff.; Gilding 1991, chapter 8).

Ironically, the increased accessibility of food, health and shelter did not result in a parallel decline in the dependency of workers on the labour market. Rather, whole industries emerged to produce, control and amplify consumers' needs (Whitwell 1989; cf. Galbraith 1969). Advertisers and their allies accelerated the consumerist drive through a constant creation of a sense of lack, a need to acquire something in order to achieve fulfilment, happiness and worth. This drive was highly sexualized in form, and related differently to the two genders. The types of needs and satisfaction it offered males assumed a person characterized by aggressiveness, activity and a desire to control. By contrast, females were imagined as passive, narcissistic and receptive (Game and Pringle 1983, 94–95; Gilding 1991, 116–118). This is not to argue that consumerism produced this genderedness. But it definitely reflected and amplified a clearly gendered mode of sociality that is prevalent in Australian households in particular, and their counterparts throughout the White Anglophone world.

Part and parcel of the increase in homeownership and the flight to suburbia was the quick and comprehensive drop in shared accommodation. The Australian home was now well and truly identified with a detached house. The new suburban working-class home was disconnected from earlier neighbourhood networks. Gone were the tradesmen and vendors who regularly visited homes to sell their goods. Shopping malls and department stores came to dominate the retail sector. Increasingly people found themselves commuting to work a considerable distance from where they lived. Leisure activities were domesticated too, with the proliferation of the gramophone, the radio and, eventually, television. Thus the household was further privatized, and much of the social basis of working-class mobilization dissipated (Game and Pringle 1983, 88–89; Reiger 1991, 36–38, 54; Gilding 1991, 37–47, chapter 8).

This is the historical context in which the suburbanized working-class – often referred to as the middle class – achieved dominance. Craig McGregor aptly summed up its spirit:

[T]he middle class in Australia seems to have a persistent drawing power in terms of ethos, image and lifestyle. At its centre is the home, classically a bungalow with its own front garden and backyard in which the middle class lives, dreams, procreates, raises children and enacts a ritual of work/sleep/sex/love/kids/family/death which is at the very heart of the Australian dream. (McGregor 1997, 141–142; cf. Whitwell 1989)

***

The post-war economic growth was accompanied by some fateful structural shifts. Capital increasingly replaced labour in the production process. Especially heavy work and skilled labour were replaced by machinery, thus reducing the capitalists' dependence on the comparatively expensive male labour power, and opening the way for the greater exploitation of cheaper, less-skilled female labour. Furthermore, the relative size of manufacturing in the total economy declined as the tertiary service industry rapidly grew in importance (Snooks 1994, 104–112; Boreham and Hall 1993). These two processes – the development of technology and the increase in service industry – brought about a major realignment in Australia's political economy in the form of a rapid increase in active participation of married women in the labour market.

This shift was driven primarily by changes in the demand for labour. In the manufacturing industry demand increased for non-skilled, light labour. The tertiary and service industries offered jobs that suited women's dispositions. What made jobs feminine was a direct result of the gendered division of labour at home. Thus, jobs were classed as feminine if they involved primarily caring, personal-relations skills, or dealt with children. The main parameters of the feminine-ness of jobs seem to have been established by bourgeois women long before these shifts in the labour market. Hospitality and philanthropy, alongside the maintenance of personal relations, were clear feminine concerns in nineteenth-century bourgeois Australia (Gilding 1991, 49–55; Boreham and Hall 1993).

Feminine jobs tended to be part-time, attract low wages, and demand low skill levels. This was possible because married women were normally second wage earners. The increase in demand for women's labour occurred at a time that household technology changes had enabled women to cut down on the time spent on household chores and increase their time spent in paid labour. Further, the insatiable needs which consumerism had produced made the acquisition of cash more desirable than before. These drives to participate in the labour market came hot on the heels of the dismantling of the barriers to full competition of married women on the labour market, a major retreat from the family-wage system. All this resulted in the increase in women's participation in the labour market, as well as an increase in reliance on household technology. The increase in married women's labour-market participation rate in the 1960s and 1970s was accompanied by a decline in the participation rate of men. Nevertheless, the gendered division of labour did not change much, and men continue to earn higher wages than women, and work longer hours (Game and Pringle 1983, 89 ff.; Snooks 1994, chapter 5; Boreham and Hall 1993; Weeks 1995; Grimshaw 1983, 42–43).

These shifts coincided with the large-scale introduction of household technology and mechanization to the domestic labour process. Household technology costs had dropped considerably in the period 1890–1940, but remarkably the ratio of equipment to household worker dropped even more, reflecting the market stagnation of the period and the decline in household market income. However, with the great post-WWII economic growth which increased household income and the labour market demand for female labour, technology was introduced rapidly, and on a massive scale, into households. Equipment came to substitute a large amount of household labour. This both increased standards of household work and enabled labour time to be transferred from the household to the labour market as married women's participation in the labour market grew. In any event, consumer spending on domestic appliances and automobiles grew rapidly, increasing the dependency of the working-class household on the labour market, and with it, the economy's dependency on consumer spending (Snooks 1994, 53–60; Reiger 1991, 46–47).

As women participated in increasing numbers in the workforce, the status and value of housewifery declined throughout the latter decades of the twentieth century. The new household technology reduced the level of skills required from housewives. Financial income, and its accompanying power and prestige, increased the value of the employed woman, at the expense of the full-time housewife. Double incomes increased the earnings of households, even though the relative value of wages declined, leaving single-income households comparatively worse off than before. In other words, while most households were better off than before, this was made possible by a sharper increase in the total supply of working hours per household to the labour market. In fact, Australia's relatively high level of homeownership was only sustained by dual-income earning (Game and Pringle 1983, 86; Gilding 1991, chapter 8).

There was a strong class logic to the degradation of housewifery. Up until WWII, a full-time housewife and a home in suburbia distinguished those better-off families from the working-class majority. The 1950s saw the popularization of the suburban lifestyle among working-class Australians, but now fractions of the elite were shifting away from the single-income household. The kinds of employment opportunities which were progressively opening up to women were not themselves equally distributed across society, as the well-paid, personally rewarding, high-status occupations were mostly the preserve of the elites. Thus, in the post-war era it was the affluent who spearheaded the charge of married women back into the labour market (Wolcott et al. 1997, 103; Grimshaw 1983, 42–43; Game and Pringle 1983, 92; cf. McGregor 1997, 174; Reiger 1991, 41–43; Gilding 1991, 124; Rapp 1992).

Along with the spread of consumerism and rapid technological development, came an increase in the cost of social reproduction, driven by a rapidly increasing inflation rate in cultural capital – mostly educational, professional and technical qualifications and credentials. This inflation was expressed, for example, in increasing levels of qualifications which were required to enter into prized careers and resulted in higher retention rates of educational institutions (Gilding 1991, 116 ff.; cf. Bourdieu 1986; Bourdieu and Boltanski 1981).

Just as the rise of industry cut men off from women, and reconstituted masculine domination, so did the rise of mass education and mass media create the contemporary form of youth and adolescence. The concentration of youth in and around educational institutions, youth's marginalization in the labour market, and the development of youth-specific mass media, supported the emerging constitution of youth as an imagined community which is united by youth culture. The lag of the family behind mass culture, and the intense separation of experience between the parents at home and the youth in the educational institutions contributed to the emergence of the generation gap as a permanent feature in the contemporary European cultural sphere (Grimshaw 1983, 44; Zaretsky 1986, 53–56).

Youth culture emerged as a significant social reality in the 1950s. This was strongly linked to the booming marketing industry. The extensive use of sex in marketing in those pre-pill days, when contraception was not very efficient, must have contributed to the drop in age of marriage and the rise in marriage rates (Game and Pringle 1983, 92–93; Gilding 1991, 116). This, and the increasing participation of women in the economic and public spheres, intensified the generation gap which exploded in the late 1960s in new cultural and political movements. The family came increasingly under scrutiny by youth, by radical academics and professionals, and by intellectual tone setters. A sense of crisis started emerging throughout the 1970s, and with it the view that the 'traditional family' – in effect the stereotypical suburban family of the 1950s – was under attack, in crisis or collapsing (Game and Pringle 1983, 80; Grimshaw et al. 1994, chapter 13).

One of the consequences of the radicalism of the 1960s and the 1970s was the passage of the *Family Law Act* (1975), and the establishment of the Family Courts system. Divorce was made easier, judges were given greater flexibility in resolving custody disputes (with the child's well-being a primary concern), and homemakers enjoyed greater protection in property settlements. De facto unions also came to be regulated along similar lines (Goodman 1983).

The dramatic economic growth of the 1950s petered out and by the 1970s the economy was slowing down. While the process of globalization saw more manufacturing jobs move offshore, the rate at which new manufacturing jobs were created has slowed down. This has resulted in an increased deterioration in the conditions of labour, as the relative ratio of primary labour-market jobs has dropped. Unemployment rose and remained high well into the 1990s. This process was accompanied by the pacification of labour. The unions were tamed, strike action and industrial disputes dropped along with the real wages of most workers, while the hours workers spent at work increased. The ratio of wages to profit has continuously dropped, as inequality between and within classes has increased (Boreham and Hall 1993; Gittins 1997).

These changes affected Australian society unevenly. Youth unemployment rose sharply. Largely as a result of this, the rate of inflation in educational qualifications accelerated. Teenagers were no longer able to achieve economic independence, and the prospects of people in their twenties achieving economic independence were grim compared with the 1960s. Large numbers clogged up the educational institutions in the hope of getting ahead and securing a competitive advantage in the job market. This was probably the major cause of the generational conflict between youth and adults in working-class Australia. (Bourgeois youths and families have a different relationship with institutionalized education and the labour market – Connell et al 1982.) Welfare expenditure was continuously reduced. External support for family households was cut as the costs of social reproduction were progressively transferred from government and business to households. Tertiary education fees were re-introduced, as were below-award[3] youth wages. Government financial support for students and dependent youth was reduced as was eligibility for sole-parent pensions (McDonald 1995, 28–29; Gilding 1991, 121–122). Inequality grew within the working class, and the fate of those who depend on welfare, like many single-parent families, worsened.

The explosion of generational politics has complicated the process of the collapse of personal life and family into one another. Since the late 1960s, it seems, individuality has been progressively juxtaposed to the family, rather than being identified with it. Individualism was now extended to women and children, as the family came to be seen as a site of domination and conflict.[4] The constant drive towards consumption aggravated the conflicts between breadwinners and dependants within the family. The greater participation of women in the workforce, and the positive work experience of women in the intellectual and professional elites made housewifery look very miserable indeed. Consequently, especially among professionals and intellectual workers, family came to be seen as a potential hindrance to individuality, rather than its site. The goal of marriage has come to be couched in terms of partnership, personal reward and personal growth and fulfilment. Failure to meet such expectations has become legitimate and reasonable grounds for separation and divorce (Gilding 1991, chapter 8; Bittman and Pixley 1997, 64–70).

---

[3] Award wage: 'a wage arrived at by mutual consent or arbitration and fixed by an industrial court, payable by law to all employees in a particular occupation' (*Macquarie Dictionary of Australian English*, second revision, s.v. 'award wage').

[4] When classical English liberalism valorized the individual, English liberals were imagining the male head of a family as that individual, and remained mute about the status of the majority of humans (Zaretsky 1986, chapter 3). This left some serious cracks in the ideological edifice of modern capitalism. These cracks became visible especially after the 1960s, and most acutely in bourgeois liberal circles. Women and children were set to become no lesser individuals than men, and family came to be seen as a potential hindrance to individuality.

Chapter 3

Contemporary Patterns of Family Practice: Historical Continuity and the Myth of Crisis

Currently, at the turn of the millennium, there is a general sense that the family is in crisis; that the institution is facing a major challenge like never before; that the nuclear-family household – the essential Australian institution – may no longer be as viable or as attractive as it once was. This sense of crisis may be seen as the result of various processes.

One is the effect of feminist challenges to much of the rationale which underlay public policy towards the family. Another is the economic squeeze on much of the working class as the cost of social reproduction rises. Yet another is a shallow historical memory which pervades public discourse, and which identifies the family of the 1950s as '*the* family' or the 'traditional family'. Consequently, any changes to the patterns of the 1950s, for instance to the exceptionally high marriage rates, may be seen as a retreat from the family.

The longing for the 'good old days' might also reflect the profound sense of loss and anxieties of some of Australia's 'true-blue' who feel threatened by globalization, secularism, politicization of the personal and the rising profiles of non-Whites in the country.

To this sense of crisis in the family must be added the move away from structuralism in social sciences and the re-discovery of the subject, along with an attempt to adopt a more genuinely multicultural style among large circles of Australia's intelligentsia. Together these factors predispose social observers to discover historical transformations, oppositional styles, subversion, individual agency, resistance and so forth, at the expense of constancy and immutability. Further, the penchant some conservative elements in society have for familism must be at least partly responsible for the zeal with which iconoclasts target the family, exposing its darker sides (e.g. violence) and its mythical nature.

A Historic Juncture?

Capturing the mood of the period, historian Ann Curthoys wrote in *the Australian* daily in 1999:

At the end of this millennium, the family is being remade, yet again. Relationships within it are fluid and changing, and there is no single dominant pattern. Two-income families, single-income families, and one-parent households are all common. Unmarried women have children on their own, and homosexual couples, many with children, are increasingly evident. Too often the old classifications simply don't work, as many families operate in a borderland between single-parent and two-parent households, as separated parents in some way share the care of children, and blended families are formed and reformed. Growing numbers of adults of all ages live on their own, yet adult children leave home at a later age than before. (Curthoys 1999)

The notion that the nuclear-family household is in decline is normally motivated by a number of perceptions. One is that alternative household structures, mostly group households and homosexual families, are rapidly increasing in number. Another is that people increasingly prefer to live alone, resulting in the statistical drop in official rates of nuclear-family households (as defined by ABS) to below 50 per cent of households. Yet another has to do with the increased divorce and separation rates, and the decline in fertility rates. Finally, some take the increase in de facto couples to suggest, too, that the nuclear-family household is in decline (cf. Gilding 1991, 128–130; Curthoys 1999; Bittman 1993). But is this sense of fluidity and change justified? What about the Australian family is, in fact, in flux? And what is not?

A close examination of the form of Australian families and households fails to support the sense of an overwhelming shift, or a major collapse of the nuclear-family household in Australia. The resilience of the nuclear-family household is not surprising, given its historical depth, yet astonishing, given the constant and recently accelerating shifts in the social and ideological contexts in which it is embedded.

Following the historical narrative of the previous chapter, this chapter seeks to provide a snapshot of the current state of Australian family practices, based primarily on aggregate statistical data. The first section deals with the developmental trajectory which makes up the cultural complex of the nuclear-family household, or *The Family*. The following section examines the physical manifestation of this complex, namely the home. Following this, the discussion turns to the patterns of organization of activity within the nuclear-family household by examining its organization of labour, broadly defined. Finally, the discussion moves to examine the relationships between particular families in what is often thought of as extended family networks.

The Nuclear-Family Household

What do the statistical data reveal about family practice and its current historical conjuncture? For analytic reasons that will become clear shortly, I will not take the nuclear-family household to mean a fixed prototypical unit of parents and offspring in a home. Rather, in order to better appraise the historical developments in the field of family practice I will treat the nuclear family as a developmental cycle which comprises the following stages: childhood dependency; leaving the natal household and achieving independence (social and economic); partnering; expansion (childbearing and child-rearing); contraction (as offspring gain independence and embark on their own trajectory); retirement; and singlehood (cf. Aspin 1994: 20–24). Individual agents may move among these stages idiosyncratically, repeating some stages, for example.

Constituting the family as a developmental cycle will make it easier to assess whether some statistical changes (e.g. the increase in sole-person households) are due to a shift in normative family patterns (e.g. people preferring not to marry, and live alone) or merely demographic trends (e.g. the increase in life expectancy and, consequently, the proportion of widows and widowers in society).

Significantly, the nuclear-family trajectory is not in itself historically fixed. The late stages of contraction and prolonged retirement have emerged relatively recently. They first became common in the late nineteenth century, when the increase in life expectancy meant a progressively larger proportion of the population lived past their offspring's period of economic dependency and into retirement (Burns 1983, 50).

While family practices have never stopped evolving, the data suggests that most of the recent statistical changes in the family do not reflect a fundamental transformation in the nuclear-family household trajectory, but rather changes in the distribution of social agents among the different stages. In fact, if we consider all households which are within the developmental cycle I have incorporated into my definition of the nuclear-family household, it will become clear that an overwhelming majority of households are within this developmental cycle, and that the overwhelming majority of householders are involved in such households. Australian Bureau of Statistics (ABS) figures for 1992 have 85 per cent of the population living in family households. Of these, 98.5 per cent were either couple families or single-parent families (85.6 per cent and 12.9 per cent respectively) and only 1.2 per cent were 'other families' (mostly multi-family households). The remaining 15 per cent of the population were divided among those living in institutions (3.7 per cent); those living alone (8 per cent) and those living in group households (3.3 per cent) (de Vaus 1997c, 3–5). Those living alone or in groups are not themselves, usually, outside the normal developmental cycle of domestic units. The majority of those living alone or in groups are either before marriage, after marriage or between marriages. The number of people involved in multi-family households (about 1.3 per cent of households) probably accounts for less than 2.6 per cent of the population. Of these, 79.7 per cent consist of adult offspring and one or more of their ancestors (de Vaus 1997c, 4; Millward and de Vaus 1997, 41–43).

Regarding the 'alternative' household arrangements, the following points should be made. Homosexual couples account for less than 1 per cent of all couples. Whatever rise there might have been in the occurrence of homosexual-family households, these do not numerically undermine the dominance of the nuclear-family household (McDonald 1995, 32). (The shift itself might still be a very significant statistical development within the gay world.)

As for group households, these accounted for 5 per cent of households in 1991 (22 per cent of households were sole-person households, and 73 per cent family households) (McDonald 1995, 19). They are composed primarily of young people who are struggling to match social independence with the increasingly elusive economic independence. Group households are convenient ways for youngsters to negotiate their social commitments in the increasing time gap between social independence and financial independence. The increase in group households thus follows the increase in the age of marriage since the 1960s, but does not indicate the emergence of a new household type. Further, young people who are in the lengthening liminal stage between social independence and financial independence often move in and out of their parents' home, and continue to use their parents' home as an abode of last resort (McDonald 1995, 25–27). In other words, many who live in group households still rely on their family households of origin. Not surprisingly, there is a parallel tendency of young people to live longer in their parents' household than before (see figures in McDonald 1995, 28; Hartley and de Vaus 1997). This lengthening liminal stage between social maturation and economic independence does appear to have recently taken root in the mainstream family trajectory.

The proportion of sole-person households has increased from 10 per cent in 1961 to 21.9 per cent in 1991 (McDonald 1995, 19; de Vaus 1997c, 4). These householders, however, account for only 8 per cent of the population (de Vaus 1997c, 4). Increased divorce rates and life expectancy have all served to increase the numbers of sole-person households as has a drop in marriage rates. But, by far, the ageing of the population is the single most important cause of the increase in sole-person households (de Vaus 1997c; de Vaus 1997d; de Vaus 1997b; de Vaus 1997a). In other words, the recent increase in sole-person households cannot be interpreted as the emergence of a new alternative familial lifestyle or as a normative shift. It is mostly a reflection of changes in the distribution of agents into different stages of the life cycle.

Single-parent families accounted for 12.8 per cent of families in 1991, compared with 9.2 per cent in 1974. This increase in the twenty years before 1991 was due primarily to an increase in divorce rates, and to a lesser extent to an increase in extra-marital births. Sixty-one percent of single parents are divorced or separated. Eighty-eight percent of single-parent families are headed by women (McDonald 1995, 21–22; cf. de Vaus 1997c). In a broader historical perspective, though, the ratio of single-parent families in the 1890s was similar to that of the 1990s, although the proportion of those headed by males was higher (38 per cent in 1891) reflecting the contribution of maternal mortality to single-parenthood (McDonald 1995, 22). Furthermore, for both men and women, for all age groups, remarriage rates are substantially higher than first-marriage rates (even though remarriage rates dropped between 1976 and 1995) (de Vaus 1997d, 20–21). This suggests that divorcees do not reject familism in general, but rather the particular family they were involved in.

Further, the increase in divorce rates from the late 1960s (see Figure 3.1: 'Crude divorce rates and numbers, 1947–95' in de Vaus 1997b, 27) cannot be taken as a reflection of a similar rise in family strife. The modern rise in divorce rates in Australia began in the late 1960s, accelerated during the 1970s, and levelled off during the 1980s (McDonald 1995, 53–54). Comparisons of figures following the introduction and implementation of the *Family Law Act* (1975–76) with divorce figures for earlier periods overstate the rate of family breakdowns. The greater ease of divorce in the period following the introduction of the *Act* means that a greater ratio of separations has been formalized in divorce. By contrast, in the nineteenth century desertion – a common masculine response to financial and familial hardship – was not officially consecrated in divorce (Gilding 1991, 36). Further, the increase in life expectancy during the twentieth century means that the ratio of marriages ending in death has declined, thereby increasing the number of marriages which last long enough to end in divorce, without this increase reflecting any greater likelihood of marital fragility. (Against these two factors, the increase in de facto marriages means that a corresponding increase in marriage breakdowns is masked, because de facto marriage breakdowns are not normally formalized.) Lastly, the late 1970s saw a dramatic increase in divorce rates partly because the backlog of divorce applications from previous years was being finalized, as were many hitherto-informal separations. Given current trends, the actual effects of divorce rates on the long-term distribution of people into the different developmental stages of the household is less than might be expected. Whereas a married couple in the 1990s was less likely to be married after 30 years than couples in the 1960s, a married couple in the 1990s was more likely to be married after 30 years than a couple in the 1890s. It is also important to note that past experience shows that at times of an economic squeeze, marriage rates drop and divorce rates rise. These shifts are part of the general patterns of family life, not a sign of transformation in the family (de Vaus 1997b). Had divorce and marriage rates become insensitive to the changing economic fortunes of society, that would have been a departure from existing patterns.

The quantitative significance of divorce in the general life experience of the population is itself often overstated. Children's experience is a case in point. About 1 per cent can expect to experience the divorce of their parents for each year of life – that is, 10 per cent by the age of ten, and 20 per cent by the age of 20, for example (McDonald 1995, 55). The ratio of children experiencing the separation of their parents is, obviously, greater because not all separations end in divorce. A survey conducted in Western Australia in 1986 shows that three-quarters of children continue to live with both biological parents for most of their childhood (91 per cent of one-year-olds; 85 per cent of six-year-olds; 80 per cent of 12-year-olds; 77 per cent of 15-year-olds) (McDonald 1995, 23). So for the vast majority of Australian children (including children of divorced parents), the nuclear-family household remains a critical and normal aspect of their childhood. Also, due to the high remarriage rates, a very substantial number of children whose parents are divorced end up living with a step-parent in new nuclear-family households.

Another recent development which has contributed to the seeming crisis in the nuclear family is the increase in the age at marriage. The median age at first marriage in 1974 was 20.9 for women and 23.3 for men, and in 1995 the median age at first marriage was 25.3 for women and 27.3 for men (de Vaus 1997d, 14). In the period 1940–70 Australians married younger and at higher rates than ever before in order to commence sexual activity and gain independence from their parents. The expansion of the labour market facilitated this process. Around the mid-1960s, about a quarter of all new brides were pregnant at marriage (McDonald 1995, 30–33; Aspin 1994, 40). The increase in the age of marriage by the 1990s reflects, at least in part, the postponement of the formation of new households. This is the product of various factors. One is the reduction in work opportunities and the inflation in cultural capital, which delay the attainment of economic independence. Other reasons are the increased access to more effective contraception, and the greater financial and social support to extra-nuptial births, both of which have all but eliminated 'shotgun' marriages (McDonald 1995, 30–33). Significantly, the average age differences between newly-weds has remained steady, women being around two years younger than their partners (the median age at first marriage in 1974, 1984 and 1995 were 23.3, 25.1 and 27.3 respectively for men; and 20.9, 22.9 and 25.3 respectively for women) (de Vaus 1997d, 14). Accompanying the increase of age at marriage was a drop in marriage rates. In 1976, 62.9 of every 1,000 unmarried men, and 61.1 of every 1,000 unmarried women, married. In 1995 the figures were 36.7 and 35 respectively (de Vaus 1997d, 14).

Crude birth rates have been consistently declining since the middle of the nineteenth century, with the exception of the baby boom following WWII and its 'echoes' – slight increases in birth rates as a result of the increased ratio of women in childbearing ages at the time when the women born during the initial baby boom reached childbearing age. The boom itself did not reflect a reversal of the trend towards reduced marital fertility. In fact, marital fertility was in a constant decline from the 1880s until the 1950s when it stabilized. (The baby boom resulted from an immediate drop in the age of marriage after WWII, and from an unprecedented level of marriage rates.) The drop in fertility was accompanied by a drop in infant and childhood mortality, so that the effects of reduced fertility on actual household size was mitigated. From the mid-1950s the average issue of existing marriages has stabilized between 2.5 and 3 offspring (McDonald 1995, 23, 44; Grimshaw 1983, 39 ff.; Game and Pringle 1983, 84; Aspin 1994, 35–36; Gilding 1991, chapter 5). A further decline occurred in the 1960s and 1970s, with fertility rates stabilizing in the 1980s and 1990s (de Vaus et al. 1997, 47). Social researchers have ascribed this recent decline to women's increased workforce participation and to a proliferation of effective contraception and abortion (de Vaus et al. 1997, 47; Snooks 1994, 69–73). It probably also reflects the increased cost of social reproduction (e.g. through the inflation in cultural capital).

The drop in fertility rates does not in itself signify a decline of the nuclear-family household. Nuclear-family households have indeed fallen in size, although they still function as nuclear families. Further, the cumulative effect of the drop in family size on people's experience is often exaggerated. From the parental perspective, based on the birth rates of 1988, 32 per cent of women will bear three or more children, 24 per cent two children, 24 per cent one child and 20 per cent will bear none. But the experience of children, based on the very same figures, is by necessity different. Sixty-one per cent will have mothers with three or more offspring, 26 per cent mothers with two offspring, and only 13 per cent will be single offspring (McDonald 1995, 45). Obviously, none will be born to a childless mother. This discrepancy between the two perspectives may account for the pervasive sense among many that the drop in family size between their parents' generation and theirs is more significant than it, in fact, is.

De facto couples accounted for 8.2 per cent of couples in 1991, a low figure which is nonetheless slowly increasing (McDonald 1995, 21). This increase is especially great among persons under 30. In 1986, for the first time, women in the age bracket 20–29 were more likely to live in de facto, than in *de jure*, marriages (Gilding 1991, 122–124). The rise of de facto relationships does not nonetheless signify a major normative transformation in the nuclear-family household. De facto marriages have largely become preludes to *de jure* marriages. Sixteen per cent of marrying couples had cohabited before their wedding in 1975, compared with over 50 per cent in 1991 (McDonald 1995, 21, 34). It is the increased cost of social reproduction that delays young adults' attainment of financial independence and thus brings about an increase in the rate of de facto couples as the two persons involved delay their marriage until such time as they can afford to have children. In addition, current rates of de facto marriages in Australia are still lower than those that prevailed in the first half of the nineteenth century, when the only officially acceptable marriages were Anglican marriages (Carmichael 1988, 2–5; Aspin 1994, 38). In any event, the increase in de facto relationships accounts only in part for the drop in marriage rates.

In the years 1971–91 a gradual rise in the mean age of mothers accompanied the general decline in fertility and increase in age at marriage. There has also been an increase in births outside formal wedlock, although this is largely due to the increase in de facto relationships (McDonald 1995, 46–47; de Vaus et al. 1997, 49–54).

Related to the increase in the age of mothers is a concentration of childbearing in the mothers' late twenties and early thirties (for detailed figures see Table 5.3: 'Age-specific birth rates in Australia, 1971–94' in de Vaus et al. 1997, 49). The ratio of births in both older and younger age brackets has dropped (de Vaus et al. 1997, 48). Researchers explain these transformations as the result of the greater participation of women in the workforce. Childbearing is increasingly delayed until the woman's education and training are largely complete and her career well on its way. After their career is established, women prefer to get childbearing out of the way in a rather short time to enable them to resume employment and boost their income (de Vaus et al. 1997; Gilding 1991, 124–125).

This concentration of childbearing was predicated upon developments in the technology of birth control. The quick widespread use of the contraceptive pill and the IUD marked the beginning of this enhanced control over the number and timing of childbirths. This was accompanied by a drop in the cost of surgical intervention under the increased funding of healthcare by the State. In the 1970s the incidence of sterilization trebled, and abortions doubled. In the 1980s there was one abortion for every four live births (Gilding 1991, 125).

It is very common for women in the childbearing phase of the household developmental cycle to limit their participation in the labour market by opting for part-time or casual work or temporarily opting out of the workforce. The labour-force participation rate of mothers increases with the age of their youngest dependent child (Wolcott 1997, 84). ABS figures published in 1995 show that in couple families with dependent children where both parents were employed, only 42 per cent of mothers were employed full time. Broken down by age of children the figures are 35 per cent of mothers being employed full time in families with children aged under 4 years old; 41 per cent in families where the youngest child is aged 5–9; and 50 per cent in families in which the youngest child is aged 10–14 years old. All this contrasts with the nearly universal full-time labour-force participation of fathers (Wolcott 1997, 85). This concentration of childbearing into a distinct and limited stage, and its separation from the child-rearing phase, appears to be a new shift in the family trajectory. In other words, the last generation has seen the family expansion stage progressively broken up in two between a childbearing phase and a child-rearing phase.

To recapitulate – the nuclear-family household remains the statistically dominant form of household among Australians of Anglo-Celtic descent. This stability and the historical depth of the nuclear-family household in Northern and Western Europe is remarkable. Recent changes have occurred, although they mostly apply to the distribution of social agents among the different stages in the developmental cycle of the household, not to the developmental cycle as such. It is probably in that area – the transition between the different stages of the nuclear-family cycle, that the effects of the State and the market can be most easily seen.

Specifically, in the last generation the ratios of sole-person and single-parent households have increased, but not as a result of the emergence of new types of households. Other changes included an increase in divorce rates, an increase in age at marriage, and a drop in birth rates as well as the increase in de facto unions. These changes reflect transformations in other fields of practice. Although significant, they do not amount to a critical shift in the nature of the developmental cycle I have termed a nuclear-family household.

On the other hand, limited transformations in this cycle do currently seem to be taking place. Among the young adults who are not financially independent a new and more prominent stage is emerging in which social adulthood and financial independence are separated. A prolonged transitional stage has emerged, during which young adults continue to depend to varying degrees on their household of origin. Another phenomenon which may turn out to be a historic transformation in the developmental cycle is the progressive concentration of childbirth in a limited period of time, normally the mother's late twenties and early thirties, and its separation from a more prolonged child-rearing phase. We now need to distinguish between a stage of childbearing – characterized, among the rest, by sharply reduced participation rates of the mother in the labour force – and a stage of child-rearing in which the mother participates in the labour market to a greater extent than during the childbearing phase.

Having discussed the trajectory of the nuclear family, I will now turn to the home – the stage and physical manifestation of the nuclear family. It is ultimately the nuclear family in its home – the nuclear-family household – that forms the prototypical family both among researchers of the family, and among social agents (the prototypical family is discussed in chapter 4.)

The Home

By contrast with the modern home – one of whose main functions is to ensure the privacy of the family and its members – pre-modern European homes of the popular classes typically had very few rooms, normally one. Houses were shared with farm animals, and with servants. Beds were shared, too. The separation of bedrooms from more public rooms, doors and corridors with rooms leading off them, are a legacy of the mid-eighteenth century bourgeoisie. These structures of homes diffused gradually throughout society. The norm of either one person or two spouses per bed has only become universal by the middle of the twentieth century (Bittman and Pixley 1997, 53; Richards 1990).

Suburbia was born in the 1920s when the dominant view of society saw the nuclear family in the family home as the cornerstone of society. State policy, church teaching and professional intervention reflected both the lifestyle of the elites, and their deep-seated phobias. Boys and girls were to sleep in separate rooms, and the married couple themselves were to have their own room. By the 1950s this view and the material means to realize it had trickled down to the bulk of the working class (Reiger 1991, 33–35).

An important characteristic of the suburban home – especially in the outer suburbs – is its distance from services. Modern suburbs are premised on the extensive use of cars and telephones. The corner store and visiting salesmen have been replaced with shopping malls and telephone marketing. Social relations are less dependent than ever on geographic proximity. People 'keep in touch' by phone, and can conveniently visit relatives and friends who live in different suburbs and different towns (Gilding 1991, chapter 8). To Novocastrians, Sydney was within range of regular weekend visits, taking about two hours. Canberra, over a six-hour drive, however, was at a range of special occasion visits, but too far for regular weekend visits.

The vast majority of family households in Australia reside in detached houses. (Wolcott et al. 1997, 103). Flat living tends to be associated with poverty, hence the higher rate of flat living among single parents (Wolcott et al. 1997). The number of what the ABS defines as multi-family households is small. Among non-indigenous Australians multi-family households account for 1.8 per cent of what the ABS defines as family households (73 per cent of total households). This amounts to 1.3 per cent of total households (de Vaus 1997c, 4). A large portion of these are granny flats (see chapter 4 below).

In line with other similar settler societies (e.g. New Zealand, Canada, US), Australian homeownership rates are high. According to ABS figures for 1992, 74 per cent of families owned or were purchasing their homes; 22 per cent were renting; and 4 per cent were boarding or living rent or board free. While homeownership rates have fluctuated since the 1950s, these fluctuations reflect the fluctuations of the political economy, not the importance of homeownership to householders (Wolcott et al. 1997, 102–103; Whitwell 1989).

The capacity to own real estate, and the cost of homeownership, are not equally distributed across society. Living is substantially cheaper for the rich. Real estate is a prime example. The cheapest way to buy a home is by a single payment. Those who have sufficient funds at their disposal will get a house for less than those who need to rely on credit, which is the next cheapest way of buying housing. The greater one's initial deposit, the better terms can one expect on one's loans. This means that those who can make an initial deposit, and whose potential earning capacity is persuasive enough, will be able to eventually own real estate. Finally, those who are too poor to afford an initial deposit receive the worst housing deal. They pay rent which is all too often not less than mortgage payments, but unlike mortgagees, they will never own the home they live in. In fact, this makes it economically viable to the better-off members of the working class to invest in real estate and use the rent they collect to pay off the mortgage. Eventually, the tenants who pay rent buy the house for the landlord, and enrich the lenders in the process.

Although the desire for homeownership is normally accounted for in terms of security, usually economic, this is not a sufficient explanation. Once ownership expenses and opportunity costs are taken into account, it turns out that a substantial number of homeowners lose as a result of their homeownership. In 1991, for example, over 35 per cent of home-owning or home-purchasing families lost over A$1,000 (Wolcott et al. 1997, 104; cf. Burbidge and Winter 1995; Richards 1990; 1985). In other words, homeownership is much more important than simply a strategy of economic utility maximization.

Being the physical manifestation of the family, the home is central to the constitution of the household, and homeownership a measure of control over the family destiny. The home is the backstage, as it were, for the members of the household. As such, it comes to be the physical expression, and experiential paradigm, of both the household and the privacy of the domestic unit.

The home is also the privileged site of female labour, and the area where women exercise a fair degree of dominance. In the nineteenth century, when other family members might move in search of work, it was the mother of the family whose residence defined the family home (see first section of chapter 2). Before the radical increase in the participation rate of married women in the market economy following WWII, the home was the place where the mother/wife was usually found, although with the increase in the participation rate of women in the workforce, and the near-universal involvement of youth in educational institutions, more and more homes came to be empty during the day (Reiger 1991, 44; cf. Richards 1990).

Organization of Labour

The continuous increase in married women's labour-market participation rate is one of the most important transformations in Australia's political economy of the twentieth century (Snooks 1994; for figures see McDonald 1995, 37; and Wolcott 1997, 83.) But no less remarkable than the changes this involved in the gender order are the aspects of the gendered division of labour which have not changed. Especially, the internal division of labour within the household in the 1990s does not differ radically from that which obtained in the first half of the century. The difference is that of degree, not of kind. Also, the division of labour in the marketplace bears all the hallmarks of the gendered division of productive and reproductive labour within the household. In this section I will briefly review some of the data on the division of labour within the household. I use the term labour here in the broad sense, to include activities such as the maintenance of social relations.

The increase in women's labour-market participation did not reflect a radical redefinition of masculinity and femininity. The driving force for the increase was the emergence of jobs and industries which required typically feminine kinds of activity, and the development of unskilled, highly regimented labour processes. This increased demand for female labour in the labour market, labour that was cheaper than men's as men were usually main breadwinners.[1] In other words, in

---

[1] Snooks makes this point in arguing against 'supply side' theories which attribute the increase in women's participation rate in the labour market to a change in women's attitudes, or to feminist action to remove discrimination against women (Snooks 1994, chapters 5, 6). His argument – namely that the proximate cause of the greater participation rate was the change in the economy – seems to be supported by his evidence. However, he is mistaken to argue that his regression analysis – which shows that women's participation rate can be virtually completely accounted for by the change in capital to labour ratios and capital to labour prices – does not rule out a decisive role for feminist action in creating the conditions which enabled women to join the workforce in the first place. Furthermore, it is not at all necessary that the transformation in the market sector should be viewed as the cause, and the participation rate of women as the effect. It is precisely the availability of women as cheap unskilled labour (cf. Weeks 1995) that has rewarded the particular direction that technological development took, by providing the economic incentive and rewards for

some areas of industry skilled men were replaced with unskilled women and machines. At the same time, service industries emerged which provided work that more readily appealed to women. Women's wages increased at the time when the consumerist urge surged more than ever before. The relative value of material capital thus increased, making it more worthwhile for more married women to leave the household for longer periods of time to participate in the labour market. Households sought to replace with capital (e.g. appliances) the labour power which was now transferred to the labour market (Snooks 1994, chapters 4–6; Reiger 1991, 53–58; Game and Pringle 1983, 89 ff.). While the greater participation rate of married women in the labour market might have been an important shift in the structure of Australian capitalism, the default familial arrangement, according to which the man is the main breadwinner and woman the main homemaker, remained largely intact, as did the inventory of tasks that men are better at and prefer to do, along with those which women are better at and prefer to do.

While women were reintegrated into the labour market, the marginalization of youth labour continued. Furthermore, in homemaking, too, children continued to play a limited role indeed compared with their nineteenth-century counterparts. Childhood, adolescence and young adulthood have become dedicated to formal and informal education, training and partnering. Those youths who have no choice but to seek employment (such as homeless youth) are in a very vulnerable position (Parliament 1995).

In general, then, while thinking of the Australian family of the second half of the twentieth century, instead of thinking of men as breadwinners and women as homemakers, it is more accurate to think of most men as primary breadwinners and secondary homemakers, and of most women as primary homemakers and secondary breadwinners, while children are largely unproductive dependants (Gilding 1991, 121 ff.).

There has also been a concomitant narrowing of the gap in time spent on household chores between men and women. This was due primarily to a reduction in the figures for women's time spent on household chores (Bittman 1995; Bittman and Pixley 1997, chapters 4, 5; Wolcott 1997, 88). Such figures, though, underestimate the actual gender difference in time spent on household tasks. There is a greater tendency for women to perform household tasks through the labour market, yet official statistics would classify a woman employed, for instance, in cleaning or caring as being involved in the labour force, rather than carrying out household chores.

Furthermore, the difference in actual time spent doing tasks itself under-represents the genderedness of the division of labour. A different appraisal of the difference is the division of responsibility. Even when the behavioural pattern as measured by time use would suggest an amelioration of the gendered division of labour, an analysis in terms of responsibility would probably align these

the industrial and technical transformations that resulted in a higher level of labour-market participation by women.

arrangements with the broader gendered division of labour. Thus, men who do some kitchen work would normally be *helping* their wives who are responsible for these tasks, rather than taking over responsibility for the execution of those tasks (cf., *inter alia*, Bryson 1985; Richards 1985, chapter 12; Bittman and Pixley 1997, chapters 5, 6; Baxter 1993; Dempsey 1997b; Dempsey 1997a). This reflects the total division of labour in which family maintenance and emotional work are very much feminized (Di Leonardo 1992).

Industrial capitalism has radically disconnected household chores from financial gain. The gendered division of labour thus produces a gendered division of access to material capital. If in pre-industrial times such differences could be narrowed by increased production within the household, the current configuration of the political economy means that the gap can only be narrowed by reducing the gendered division of labour. Further, very often, involvement in the labour market also translates into further training and the accumulation of on-the-job experience. This accumulation of cultural capital lends itself to a further augmentation of earning capacity and increases the capital gap between breadwinners and homemakers.

Since the 1950s it has been the increased participation rate of women in the labour market which is the main reason for the narrowing of the gap in the gendered access to economic capital. According to ABS figures published in 1995, in couple families where both parents were employed full time, women contributed 43 per cent of the couple's earnings. In similar couples in which the women were employed part time, women contributed 27 per cent of the family earnings (Wolcott et al. 1997, 93).

Another manifestation of the continuing gendered division in access to financial capital is the consequences of family breakdown to the financial well-being of men and women. The Australian Institute of Family Studies (AIFS) found that over the period 1984–7 fathers were likely to have an increased standard of living upon separation if they did not have children living in their household, or a standard of living similar to their pre-separation standard of living if they did have children living in the household. The situation for women was different. Women tended to be worse off immediately after separation, and most women remained worse off three years later (Funder et al. 1993, 33–55; cited and analysed in Wolcott et al. 1997, 94–95).

Interestingly, the fate of mothers was negatively correlated with the pre-separation earning level of fathers. Breaking down the patterns into three income-level groups, it transpired that the ex-wives of higher-income earners fared the worst; while ex-wives of low-income earners were best off, eventually improving, on average, on their pre-separation standard of living. This situation may be accounted for in several ways. The wives of men with high income may have a lower labour-market participation rate, which reduces their post-separation earning capacity. They thus may rely more heavily on inadequate maintenance payments. The researchers point out that 'repartnering by mothers tended to be the only way in which adequate income compensation for low maintenance payments was achieved' (Wolcott et al. 1997, 94–95).

This has two major implications. First, it highlights marriage as a viable strategy which mostly women use to convert social capital into economic capital. This strategy is effective enough for the average ex-partners of medium-income men to have largely regained their living standards within three years, and for the average ex-partners of low-income men to have palpably improved their standard of living. The other implication is that by re-partnering, women enjoy the income of their current partners, possibly at the expense of their partners' children from previous unions. As the researchers point out, children of the first family enjoyed a lower share in their non-resident father's income than the children of their father's current family (Wolcott et al. 1997, 95). This puts many women in the position of both victims and beneficiaries of the tendency to spend more on children in one's current household, at the expense of children in other households.[2]

This financial economy should be seen also in the context of the economy of time and social relations. Part and parcel of the division of labour is the division of time spent away from the household, and alienation from the social relationships within the household. The genderedness of different household tasks produces a gendered difference in the distribution of social capital within the family. An important instance of this is difference in time spent and access to children. Generally speaking, mothers spend more time with children, and play a greater role in their lives than fathers do. One survey (Bittman 1995) found that women spent over three and a half times longer in the care of children.

It is important to emphasize that the gendered patterns of labour-market participation cannot account for the gender difference in time spent on childcare and household chores. An ABS survey of time use among Australians published in 1993 indicates that partnered women who have children under 15 and who work full time spend 22 per cent of their day (5.1 hours) on household activities, as opposed to men in similar situations who spend only 11 per cent of their day (2.5 hours) on such activities (Wolcott 1997, 87). Were the gendered division of domestic labour a response to the gendered patterns of the formal labour market, we would expect such men and women to be equally engaged in household activities.

This would rather suggest that the gendered division of labour in the family is the cause, rather than the effect, of the gendered nature of labour-force participation, and the gendered structure of the formal economy. This conclusion is further supported by the fact that the majority of women with children say that they

---

[2] This might explain why most women I spoke with, as well as most men, did not share the views of most researchers, to the effect that child support which non-custodian parents are required to pay is insufficient, and that the enforcement of these regulations is inefficient. The only exception were single mothers I spoke with who felt disadvantaged by their post-separation arrangements. (I will discuss these attitudes of my informants in chapter 5 below.)

prefer part-time employment, regardless of whether they are employed full time, part time or not at all (Wolcott 1997, 85; Baxter 2000; Baxter and Western 1998; Baxter et al. 1996, cf. Hakim 1996 – I return to these issues in greater depth in chapters 7 and 8).

Another measure of the gendered difference in the quality of social relations within the household is the custodial arrangements which follow marital breakdown. In well over 80 per cent of instances, it is the mother who becomes the custodian parent, not the father. Approximately 87 per cent of 'single-parent families', that is households of a parent and his/her dependent children, are headed by women (Aspin 1994, 129; Funder et al. 1993).

Put more generally, while the gap in actual access to the labour market might have narrowed, the gendered nature of the division of labour and concomitant distribution of capital continues – men tend to dominate material capital, while women tend to dominate social capital. Youths remain marginalized in the labour market and in access to material capital.

Extended Family Networks

Family-ness not only organizes the relationships within nuclear-family households. It also shapes relationships between separate households of related people. For various reasons, these networks were not widely studied. To make up for the gap in quantitative sociological data, I will rely in this section on ethnographic data, including my own.

Extended family networks in White urban Australia normally comprise the households of adult siblings and their parents, and occasionally might be extended further to uncles, aunts and cousins, normally on an ad hoc basis. Such networks are occasionally referred to as extended-family networks. This is somewhat misleading in that it suggests a principle of familial organization other than the nuclear family. A more accurate rendition than *extended-family networks* (with a hyphen indicating networks of extended family) is *extended family networks* (without a hyphen, indicating extended networks of family). In principle, what connects households to one another is the fact that members in the different households are still members of the same family, as is most typically the case with independent adults and their parents or siblings (see chapters 4 and 6 below). Such networks often operate as mutual aid and support networks. They also greatly overlap with ceremonial kindred groupings, such as the descendants of elderly people who might get together at Christmas.

The volume of aid which flows, or is exchanged, in extended family networks is considerable, and normally occurs outside the formal economy. The main types of transfers and exchange among households can be categorized as material (money, goods, emergency shelter or use rights in goods and capital), physical (labour power), emotional (love, counsel), legal (guardianship) or spiritual (religious duties) (McDonald 1995, 16, 25–27; Millward and de Vaus 1997; Millward et al. 1997).

Incidentally, a quantitative measure of actual transfer among households would grossly underestimate the value of these networks. Often these networks function as an insurance, as it were – a solution of last resort which is 'always there'. There are also other similar links, such as between non-custodial parents and the households in which their children live. The volume of support which flows in networks of the latter kind has increased considerably since the 1960s (and is regulated by the State in a way that other extended family links are not).

Collateral relationships were not nearly as stable as lineal ones. Furthermore, most of the aid was transferred down generations lineally rather than collaterally. Among the families I studied the independence of households did not seem to be compromised by transfers down the generations. Parents gave their adult children gifts because 'times are harder now' as one elderly man explained, and 'to help with the children – it's very expensive to bring them up today', as an older woman explained. (This latter quote shows some of the ambiguity that can be imposed on any transaction within the family – the gift was given by the woman to her adult daughter and son-in-law, but was construed as support for their children, her grandchildren.) There was also a great deal of transfer of resources among siblings' households, although this took the form of reciprocal exchange in contrast with the acceptable unilateral nature of transfers across generations. So, for example, sisters or sisters-in-law would exchange child-minding, or otherwise would more generally exchange favours. In one instance a couple relied on the wife's sister (who was a single mother) to do casual childcare work in return for money. This was construed as solving their need for reliable casual childcare and her need for some extra cash. When financial aid was transferred among siblings it was virtually invariably in the form of loans (even when it was not at all clear if they would be repaid). Such transfers were rarer than intergenerational monetary assistance.

The same gendered patterns of practice within households also mark extended kin networks. As part of the overall gendered division of responsibility, the responsibility for maintaining the household functioning is clearly gendered. This holds true throughout anglophone metropolitan and settler societies. Women generally assume the responsibility of ensuring and maintaining orderly social relationships both within and without the household. Extended family networks are therefore largely managed by women (Millward 1993; Short n.d.; Millward and de Vaus 1997, 40; Di Leonardo 1992; Rapp 1992, 56–58; Yanagisako 1977). The domination of women in the maintenance work of networks of related households has been noted in many segments of urban society (summarized in Di Leonardo 1992, 252–253). In Newcastle women were clearly more actively engaged in, and more adept at, maintaining and managing social relationships. This is part of the specialization of women in the accumulation of social capital.

The domination of women over family network maintenance work seems to have increased under capitalism with the emergence of the separation between the public and the private (Zaretsky 1986; Collier et al. 1982). This is partly so because factors which would have supported strong masculine ties among relatives have disappeared. These include, among working-class Australians, the formalization of vocational education at the expense of paternal initiation of sons into trades, the highly diminished tendency for sons to follow in the occupational footsteps of their father, and finally, the weakening of industrial trade unions and the closed shop which institutionalized nepotism in labour recruitment.

In line with British data (summarized in Yanagisako 1977, 220) and equivalent Australian data (Stivens 1974, chapter 6; Martin 1967, 50–51), there was much greater emphasis among Novocastrians on intergenerational ties between mothers and daughters. Typically, mothers would be the main driving force behind keeping their offspring in touch. They did so normally by enlisting the collaboration of their daughters or daughters-in-law. Sisters Hildred and Phyllis were, by their own admission, pretty close as a direct result of their mother's efforts. Their mother would strive to bring her daughters and granddaughters together, often instigating shopping mall excursions with both her daughters and granddaughters.

Men took remarkably little initiative in these issues. In fact, women among my informants played a large role in managing and maintaining the networks of their husbands. Adult sons and fathers owed much of their concrete contact to occasions organized by women. In several families I came across the maintenance of relationships between male siblings was quite often heavily managed by their wives.

But the effects of women's domination of extended kin networks can have the opposite effect, too. For example, two brothers I met had their relationships sour as a result of conflict between the two wives. The brothers did not harbour any ill feeling towards one another, but explained that the conflict between the wives made their actual contact minimal. The wives themselves supported these views. While I have heard a few stories of men – either related or friends – whose relationships were badly affected by tensions between their wives, I did not encounter a single instance in the field in which relationships between related women suffered substantially as a result of tensions between their husbands. Furthermore, whereas I have heard repeatedly of men being caught up in struggles between their wives and mothers, I did not hear of women who were in strife as a result of conflict between their husbands and fathers.

This situation contravenes somewhat the description of women's networks as networks of solidarity. While solidarity, such as argued by Maila Stivens (Stivens 1974, Part 2; Stivens 1978), is definitely part of the picture, it is not the whole picture. In focus groups and interviews Novocastrian women construed their relationships with their mothers and mothers-in-law as potentially stressful, and often motivated by a sense of obligation. Whereas in conversations and interviews a few women identified their husbands as their best friends, or a close female friend, only one identified her sister as a best friend, and none identified her mother as her best friend. Interestingly, a study in north London found that adult women and their mothers were not very intimate and close, and that it was sisters who formed 'very close' relationships (O'Connor 1990). Among my informants, relationships with sisters were construed as voluntary and free from obligation, and therefore potentially closer and more intimate. They were therefore also more volatile and more variable. Some women were not at all close to their sisters, whereas others were very close. There did not seem to be the same variation in relation between adult women and their mothers.

Rather than solidarity as such, it seems to me that women enjoyed a heightened all-round intensity of emotional relationships compared with men. When they were close, they could be more intimate; when they were in conflict, they could be more acrimonious; and when they felt obligation they could move and be moved by senses of guilt and shame to an extent greater than men. This reflects their greater investment – social, emotional and otherwise – in social capital. The stakes in social relationships in general, and in familial organizing in particular, were higher for women than for men. I would therefore interpret women's domination of the familial domain as an expression of an internalized predisposition to invest more of themselves in social relations. These dispositions run the gamut of emotional, aesthetic and intellective dispositions (I will further explore the genderedness of subjectivity in chapter 7 below).

Conclusion

The brief historical review in the previous chapter situated the changes in the Australian family within the broader transformations in the social order. In line with the historiography of the Australian family which underlay that synthesis, the profound changes in the Australian family were highlighted. However, not only changes need to be accounted for. Continuities are no less important. In fact, much of the history of the family is a story of remarkable continuity and immutability of the family structure in the face of profound historical transformations.

As a preliminary step towards assessing both transformations and continuities in kinship practices, the nuclear family was re-conceptualized as a life trajectory. As it turns out, the nuclear family remains very much the dominant practice. The main changes seem to be in the distribution of agents in the different stages of this life trajectory (e.g. an increase in single-person households as a result of the increase in life expectancy). Nevertheless, there have been changes in the way people relate to the family (expressed, among others, by increased divorce rates and average age at marriage) but the extent of the change is often overstated. Some of the magnitude of change is artificial (e.g. many marital breakdowns which now end in divorce would before 1975 have ended in mere separation); so too the influence these changes have on experience is often exaggerated (most children of divorced parents, for instance, do live out most of their childhood in nuclear families); and much of the change seems to reflect a retreat to normalcy from post-WWII idiosyncrasies, rather than a novel trend. Alternatives to the nuclear-family household trajectory remain remarkably rare.

Two new changes in the nuclear-family household trajectory appear to be taking place. One is the growing liminal stage between social adulthood and economic independence, characterized by low income, marginalized labour-market status, involvement in educational institutions, and dependency to varying degrees on the household of origin. The other is a growing differentiation of childbearing and child rearing into two distinct stages with different patterns of labour-market participation by women.

When reviewing some of the data on other kinship practices I argued that homeownership is significant beyond mere economic rationalism.

The genderedness of the division of labour within the home is proving to be resilient. I associate this division of labour with the general differences in internalized dispositions and distribution of capital (social vs. economic), a theme I will take up in later chapters. The total division of labour – social, material, emotional etc. – inside the household is mirrored in the feminization of broader kin networks. Women dominated the social and emotional maintenance work within families and between families.

The reality that this chapter explores is the reality of Australian family practice – a practice typical of anglophone settler societies. The rest of this book is dedicated to theorizing the normative and cultural aspects of this practice. Drawing on contemporary approaches in the sociology of practice, cognitive sciences and phenomenology, I will reconstruct the logic of the practice of the social agents, whose aggregate conduct has produced the patterns that have just been discussed.

The next chapter takes the preliminary step towards analysing the historical resilience of the nuclear family by highlighting its cultural and cognitive dominance, which greatly complements its statistical dominance.

Chapter 4

The Doxic Family

The previous chapter argued that the nuclear-family household, conceived of as a trajectory, remains statistically dominant, and is undergoing some limited transformations. This chapter turns to the cultural and normative levels of social practice. It offers a preliminary exposition of the culturally and socially dominant notions of family. The next chapter will broaden the analysis by focusing on divergent non-standard practices in order to better understand the nuances of family practice and the dynamics of the historical evolution of the nuclear family form.

But before considering alternative practices, the 'normal' family must be presented, and its peculiar cultural position understood. To do so, I will take up Bourdieu's tripartite typology of practice – doxa, orthodoxy and heterodoxy. Briefly, doxa is that aspect of the lived world which is taken for granted. Even though it is culturally constructed and mediated, it is experienced as natural and unmediated reality. It is often invisible by virtue of its ubiquity. Orthodoxy refers to all those practices – of judgement, of physical action, of thought, and so forth – for which alternatives are conceivable from a social agent's perspective, but which are still the dominant practices. Heterodoxy denotes alternative practices which are not the dominant ones (Bourdieu 1977, 159–171). Armed with Bourdieu's typology, this chapter identifies the prototypical family and interrogates its status of cultural dominance.

Family as a Realized Category

The nuclear family is the prototypical family in the Northern and Western European cultural sphere. It is *the* family par excellence – the unmarked variant that functions as the standard against which all other variants are compared. What makes other social arrangements 'family' is the fact that they resemble this prototype of family in some fundamental way. But while what makes a social relationship classifiable as family is some critical trait it shares with the nuclear family, there is not one substantive characteristic that is common to all arrangements which are 'family'. Still, social arrangements which have insufficient in common with the nuclear family will not be experienced, understood or perceived as family.

Thus, a monogamous, childless couple of gay men may be considered family, as would a single heterosexual mother and her daughter. Those two different social units have precious little in common which distinguishes them as family, except for the fact that both are variations on the theme of the prototypical family. It is this variation which enables them both to be understood as family, albeit idiosyncratic varieties thereof. By contrast, two pugilists who are sparring partners, or a woman professor and her female postgraduate student might form relationships which are very similar to the gay couple or the mother-daughter unit respectively, much more similar than the two family arrangements are to each other. Yet the relationships of the two pugilists or the two academics would not be included in the category of family, because they lack the critical resemblance to the prototypical family. This would hold even if the two pugilists had sex with one another, or the two academics shared an apartment.

Significantly, what constitutes the critical resemblance which forms the precondition for social arrangements to be experienced as family is situational and depends on many variables. This amorphous critical resemblance cannot be defined *a priori* or in formal terms, yet competent social agents seem to negotiate the category of family quite easily with little recourse to explicit, reflexive contemplation.

In other words, the universe of family practices is structured as a radial category. It has a central subcategory – or prototype – and various non-central extensions which are variants of the central subcategory. The variants are not deducible from the central category by recourse to a formally articulated rule of deduction. Rather, they all resemble the central subcategory in their particular ways, although each non-central extension may be essentially different from other non-central extensions (cf. Lakoff 1987, chapter 6).

The prototypical nuclear family functions as what Bourdieu has dubbed a realized category (Bourdieu 1996). It is more than a cultural value, an imaginary mental construct, or 'merely' a word which is being used by social agents and social, political and cultural agencies to understand the world and thereby impose itself on social agents. It is also at one and the same time a social reality, the reality in which people live their lives. It is a *nomos*, a 'tacit law […] of perception and practice that is at the basis of the consensus on the sense of the social world (and of the word "family" in particular), the basis of *common sense*' (Bourdieu 1996, 21). It is integrated into the habitus – that is, the socially conditioned dispositions – of social agents. It is a principle which organizes both people's apprehension of reality in particular and their action upon the world in general. Put differently, beyond the statistical prevalence of the nuclear family, the category of family organizes much of the social agents' lived world. The harmony between the internalized category and the category as it is manifest in practice is what makes the world appear natural and self-evident (Bourdieu 1996, 21). It is important to emphasize that such an internalized category is not only an intellective construct but also an affective and emotive construct; that is, it orchestrates a whole range of emotional states as well as intellective representations.

The nuclear family as a realized category forms a gestalt which incorporates many specific cognitive models. Such models include the division of labour within the family, the convergence of social and biological parenthood, dependency of children on parents and so forth. 'Unpacking' this gestalt into its constitutive parts would yield components which are formally simpler yet cognitively less basic than the whole gestalt. In other words, the gestalt as a whole is cognitively efficient and practically 'grammaticized'. Grammaticized concepts are distinguishable from ungrammaticized concepts in that the former are used rather than pondered; automatic rather than controlled; non-conscious rather than conscious; effortless rather than effortful; fixed rather than novel; and conventional rather than personal (Lakoff 1987, 320; cf. Keesing 1990; for a full discussion of levels of categorization see Rosch 1978).

For example, the gestalt includes a mother who is the genetic mother, the birth mother and the social mother. These more specific maternal models when taken on their own are cognitively not basic-level models, though. They are hyphenated maternities, as it were. They are, in a sense, idiosyncratic maternities. Maternity par excellence, the unmarked maternity, is embodied in a woman who is a genetic, birth and social mother.

Those aspects of family life which deviate from the prototypical nuclear family are what makes people's families different, what is unique and remarkable about them, what is noteworthy in dinner-table conversations, parties, gossip and ethnographic interviews. Those aspects of persons' lives which do completely comply with the prototypical nuclear family are what people share with the 'collective', with 'everybody else' as it were. These aspects are remarkably unremarkable, and are unlikely to be elaborated on in such conversations or gossip exchanges. The doxic aspects of the family which are taken for granted and experienced as universal escape unarticulated in mundane discourse. Orthodoxies are also not particularly interesting topics of familiar discussion. They do explicitly emerge, nonetheless, in the context of comparing, assuming, analysing and judging heterodoxies.

The transparency of normalcy, that is, the fact that it passes unnoticed and remains un-interrogated by public opinion, is part of the privileged position it has acquired, the right to question and not be questioned, the authority to contemplate others but not be contemplated. Against the visibility of the aberrant, which always invites judgement, the transparency of the normal conveys the presumption of innocence, the immunity from prosecution, having no case to answer, as it were. This is the root of the symbolic privilege which accrues to the universal norm. It is hard to imagine somebody leaning over and whispering in the ear of an interlocutor 'X is heterosexual', or 'X is a monogamist', or 'X and Y, who are married to each other, have sex together'.

There are occasions in which normalcy grabs the limelight and makes itself plainly visible, as for example with one couple who celebrated their golden anniversary and basked in the glory of not having separated or divorced, unlike so many others. The man, looking around at his children, grandchildren and their spouses who had gathered for the occasion, proclaimed his happiness and pride at having been married to the same woman for all those years. At least one of the members of the younger generation perceived it as an injunction, as 'a statement of this is how things should be; this is an example you should follow'. This visibility is specifically that of orthodoxy, not doxa. It is also a visibility of a different order from that of the constant visibility of the aberrant. It is the visibility of the witness for the prosecution, as it were. It is normalcy asserting its possibility and its existence, thereby shifting the gaze back to the aberrant which is yet again called upon to justify itself. In other words, that golden anniversary was as much a statement about marital breakdown, as it was about marital longevity, and a very particular statement at that.

It is thus by merely being normal that the normal places a demand on the aberrant. People are required to either conform, or take a risk and stand accused. The normal, by virtue of their normalcy, come to possess a certain element of symbolic capital. Their sense *is* the common sense (cf. Bourdieu 1996, 22–23). This forms the basis of the advantage of conformity.

The invisibility of the doxic makes it impossible to provide an immediate, exhaustive, systematic description of the constitution of the realized category of the family. In fact, giving visibility to the invisible, thinking the un-thought, to use Foucault's terminology (Foucault 1974), is to do violence to the ontology of the doxic, to its invisibility. This, though, is essential to the anthropological project.

The mapping out of doxa requires a complex movement in two directions. One way of doing so is to map out the visible – orthodoxy and heterodoxy – and thereby approach the invisible and the taken-for-granted. Whereas extrapolating the invisible from the visible may well turn out to be the more accurate way of approaching the subject, some tentative, positive approximation of the doxic is still required, if only to create an initial set of references. This is in a sense an intuitive and suggestive projection of elements from one ontology onto another.

Ethnomethodologists and other micro-sociologists have specialized in exposing the underlying foundations of social interaction. In his analysis of the family Bourdieu summarizes the properties that they have found in the family. I propose to use this summary as a point of departure.

> First set of properties: through a kind of anthropomorphism in which the properties of an individual are attributed to a group, the family is seen as a reality transcending its members, a transpersonal person endowed with a common life and spirit and a particular vision of the world.

> Second set of properties: definitions of the family are seen as having in common the fact that they assume the family exists as a separate social universe, engaged in an effort to perpetuate its frontiers and oriented towards idealization of the interior as sacred, *sanctum* (as opposed to the exterior). This sacred, secret universe, with its doors closed to protect its intimacy, separated from the external world by the symbolic barrier of the threshold, perpetuates itself and perpetuates its own separateness, its *privacy*, as an obstacle to knowledge, a private secret, 'backstage'. One might add to this theme of privacy a third theme, that of *residence*, the house as a stable enduring locus and the

household as a permanent unit, durably associated with a house that is endlessly transmissible. (Bourdieu 1996, 20)

These quotes reflect a certain universal trait of European metropolitan and settler societies. In Anglo-Celtic Australia, as elsewhere in the Northern and Western European cultural sphere, the 'dominant pattern' of family structure, indeed *The Family*, is a nuclear family that resides in a delineated household, and includes two monogamously intertwined adults – male and female – and their offspring. This is the default notion of the family. When applied differently, to extended families for example, it is in a sense a figurative, modified or borrowed usage.[1]

The Nuclear Family, the Person and the Container Schema

The two main elements which are captured in Bourdieu's summary are the corporate nature of the family and the emergence of the domestic/private domain. By corporate nature I mean that the family becomes an entity in its own right which exists apart from its individual members. If family members cease to exist the family may still exist, as when a family member dies. Still, if all family members die, the family ceases to exist. By the same token, families might cease to exist while family members continue to exist, as when a childless couple divorces. When thought of in relation to a specific group of people, the family does not reside in any particular individual but in the set of relationships among them.

In other words, the family is constituted as a person in its own right, and the experiential construct of personhood acts as a schema which metaphorically structures family. The corporeal self is a fundamental, culturally specific construct. It is predicated upon the commonsensical ascription of a unified identity to a body as it transforms, and is transformed, throughout time and space; and upon the constitution of the person as somehow transcending in its essence the specific situations and the webs of relationships in which the person is embedded. The application of the metaphor of the person to the family carries many entailments. Families are given names (e.g. the Simpsons) and a distinct identity. The family bond encloses the family members within a clearly bounded symbolic space, like the skin encloses the internal organs which make up the body of the person.

This discreteness which the family shares with the individual person is part of a broader practical metaphor, namely the container schema. Lakoff and Johnson see

---

[1] Incidentally, in Newcastle at least, pets are not thought of as part of the family. The majority of households I studied did not have pets, but a significant number did, invariably cats or dogs. My informants never mentioned them when asked about their family members and they were not a main source of preoccupation. This stands in contrast with Bruce Kapferer's expectation (Kapferer 1988, 158). Kapferer argues that pet-loving and masculinist mateship are inherently linked in their underlying cultural logic, and that both are integral to working-class Australian culture. Later in this chapter I will argue that also mateship is not a key aspect of my informants' daily lives.

the container schema as one of the very basic structural metaphors which they ascribe to the pre-conceptual experience of the body, especially to the division between the interior of the body and the outside world, both of which are separated by the surface of the body (Lakoff and Johnson 1980, 29–32). While pre-conceptual schemata emerge spontaneously from the bodily experience of the young human organism in the ontogenetic process, the effects of the real world vary cross-culturally with variations in experience, and are mediated by the pre-existing conceptual structure (Lakoff and Johnson 1980, 154), as well as by social structures.

The container schema clearly demarcates inside from outside, and constitutes the inside as essentially integrated and qualitatively distinct from the outside (Lakoff and Johnson 1980, 14, 24, 29–34, 56 ff., and see below under 'Resolving Metaphorical and Structural Contradictions'). This is the image schema that underlies the metaphorical extension from the person to the nuclear-family unit. It is also the common metaphor which is used to conceptualize property or place, like home, country and so forth. In other words, this schema runs through the many facets of the gestalt of the family, making it coherent.

This metaphorical extension is clearly motivated, but by no means inevitable. Other schemata are also anchored in the human experience of the body and they too could organize the abstract realm of the family. The core–periphery schema, for example, is also very common.

An artistic expression of the core–periphery schema is given by Roman Polanski in his 1976 movie *The Tenant*. In it, the drunk, unhinged protagonist (played by Polanski himself) mumbles as he is being undressed by an eager young woman (played by Isabelle Adjani):

> He: 'Tell me, at what precise moment does an individual stop being who he thinks he is?'
> She: 'You know, I don't like complications.'
> He: 'If I cut off my arm, right? I say me and my arm. If you cut off my other arm, I say me and my two arms [...] Take out my stomach, my kidneys, assuming that were possible, and I say me and my intestines. Do you follow me? And now, if you cut off my head. What do I say? Me and my ... Me and my head, or me and my body? What right has my head to call itself me? What right?'

As it happens, the phrasing of the question, 'if you cut off my head' rather than 'cut off my body', underscores the fact that it is, in fact, 'me and my head', rather than 'me and my body' which is the correct answer.[2] In any event, in this

---

[2] The peripherality of the head relative to the torso holds throughout the European cultural sphere. Hence the headless chook (chicken) is a meaningful image for Australian idiom, but a bodiless chook is not. This is also why upon seeing Alice, the Queen of Hearts could scream 'off with her head' rather than 'off with her body'; why (regardless of whether at the hand of French revolutionary republicans or English reactionary monarchists) condemned people were commonly beheaded (or decapitated) rather than bebodied (or

conception of self which Polanski uses for the ruminations of his paranoid antihero, the core of the corporeal self lies firmly in the torso, with the limbs and head being peripheral members of the body. On the other hand, quite clearly the head is less peripheral than arms or legs. This indicates how the core–periphery distinction can be gradational, rather than a qualitative break between two discrete categories.

This core–periphery schema is one mode of experiencing the corporeal person, and is inherently no less suitable to organize family-ness. The difference between the two metaphors – the core–periphery schema and the container schema – may be linked to their effects. The core–periphery schema lends itself to highlighting the content of the core. The core's extension into the periphery depends on this content. The container schema highlights the exclusion of that which is outside. It stresses the boundary which clearly encloses and demarcates, over the actual essence of that which is enclosed and demarcated.

The cultural significance of the container schema may be linked to the historical organization of the possession of land in Europe, a paradigm for the capitalist estate more generally. This is epitomized, among others, in landownership which in common law came to be constituted as the right to exclude others, with little regard to what use if any one makes of the land from which others are excluded. Thus, the landowner's ownership is expressed in a right to fence off the land.

The same distinction, which I have applied paradigmatically to landownership, seems to obtain in the cultural construction of family. The container schema which organizes Western and Northern European family stresses the boundaries which enclose the essence. Thus, when applied to sexual access, my informants thought of marriage as creating a boundary which excludes extramarital affairs, so that having any amount of extramarital sex was improper. By contrast, my informants did not seem to have a notion of how much sex should be had between spouses. Not having sex, as such, was not a violation of familial propriety the way engaging in extramarital sex was. Furthermore, my informants did not conceive of marriage as the sole context for having sex, and thought of premarital sex as both common and legitimate. Premarital sex was the norm rather than the exception (especially in the last few decades when age at marriage has increased, as has access to relatively reliable contraception). In essence, in Newcastle as elsewhere in mainstream Australia, marriage is less about providing people with sexual access to others (i.e. spouses), and more about restricting sexual access between those married and others. Marriage's major function with regard to sexual access is thus the creation of a boundary around the married couple, and not the fixing of the relationship between them.

Similarly, when it came to disciplining children, there was a great deal of variation in discipline policy, but one thing that all parents I talked to seemed

---

decorporated); and why in a state of panic someone might 'lose his/her head' but not his/her body.

to agree on was their objection to people other than themselves and their partners disciplining their children. That included the children's grandparents. Some grandparents I spoke with were reluctant to overstep the mark and encroach upon the exclusive territory of the parents. They also saw it as an advantage – they could take a relaxed and forgiving attitude towards their grandchildren, leaving the unpleasantry of discipline to their grandchildren's parents.

Interestingly, this attitude extended to children too. One teenager whose mother had re-partnered stated that she did not think her mother's new partner had the right to discipline her or tell her what to do. She volunteered the observation that her opposition was one way of driving home to her mother's partner that he was not fully part of the family, and that he would have to put in an effort to win and maintain her approval. A man who had moved in with his partner and her adolescent children said that the best survival strategy for him was to leave all discipline problems to his partner.

The nuclear family is thus qualitatively demarcated rather than fading away into extended kinship networks. This conception is made up of clear boundaries which make qualitative distinctions between fixed, mutually exclusive and mutually defining entities. It is part of a broad, atomistic, indigenous European structuralism of mainstream Australia.

While the container schema is crucial in structuring the nuclear family, the core–periphery schema does play a limited role too in structuring family relations. It may be used to organize one's mental structure of one's extended kin network. Some relatives are closer than others, and some relatives are distant. Further, the formal system of reckoning relationships with degrees of relatedness and removal (e.g. second cousin once removed) is based on a gradational extension from an inner core to a periphery.

On the face of it, this might appear to contradict the argument that the container schema structures family-ness. But this contradiction does not emerge in practice, as the two schemata organize somewhat different contexts. The container schema organizes the inclusion/exclusion of people from the category of family. At a secondary level, the core–periphery schema organizes the universe of relatives who are within the kindred, but outside the immediate family. (I will return to these themes in chapter 6 when discussing relatedness.) This particular configuration of practical metaphors is the product of a historical process. It was not inevitable.[3]

---

[3] The container schema and the core–periphery schema are not the only structures of household and families around the world. Brad Weiss describes a sub-Saharan pattern of social organization in which inside and outside are oriented towards one another rather than qualitatively separated and opposed (Weiss 1996).

The Nuclear Family and Private Time and Space: Further Extensions of the Container Schema

In its practical, daily deployment, family is a polysemic concept – it can denote, and thereby combine, any of a number of theoretically distinct categories of social relations. The concept operates metonymically. It pertains to a set of genealogical relationships, a particular group of social relationships, a physical space (home), a certain type of social relationship (suspension of explicit economic calculation), a certain element of corporate economic activity (household), a physiological function (reproduction), and more. Here I will expand on a few of these intertwined facets.

The Household

Family and kinship provide the practical idioms which organize both the internal structure of the household and some of the relationships between households. The cooperation among members of family households is formally free from obligation of direct material reciprocity. Family involves the suspension of impersonal economic calculations, an active misrecognition of the material aspects of the social relations within the family, in contradistinction to the outside world. Hence the enchanted economy which operates within family households, and certain networks of households, is motivated by familial relationships. In fact, my informants rarely if ever used the term household spontaneously. They would normally use the words family or home to refer to household.

One of the bases of this misrecognition is the organization of the family as an elementary unit – an atom, as it were – of which individuals are organic components with differential functions. Thus, family members are not fully interchangeable. Families, on the other hand, are nominally equivalent to one another and are structurally interchangeable. They therefore require an element of reciprocity in relations between them.

Ironically, perhaps, it is because the family becomes an embodied individual of sorts at a higher level of abstraction that it allows within its boundaries the relaxation of some of the physical boundaries which mark off the person of its individual members from one another. It is precisely because the nuclear family is sometimes perceived to be an ontological equivalent of the individual that this violation of the person of its individual members is possible; just as it is precisely because within the boundaries of the nuclear family the atomistic nature of the individual is suspended that the family can be transformed into an individual of sorts. The ultimate suspensions of the boundaries of the individual include sexual intercourse, explicit dependency, licence on physical punishment and physical proximity, and above all, the facts of sexual reproduction and birth which are blatant, but unavoidable, biological violations of the very atomism ascribed to the person of the individual.

As Rayna Rapp put it,

> The family is the normative, correct way in which people get recruited into households. It is through families that people enter into productive, reproductive and consumption relations. The two genders enter them differently. Families organize households, and it is within families that people experience the absence or presence, the sharing or withholding, of basic poolable resources. 'Family' (as a normative concept in our culture) reflects those material relations; it also distorts them. As such, the concept of family is a socially necessary illusion that simultaneously expresses and makes recruitment to relations of production, reproduction and consumption – relations that condition different kinds of household resources based in different sectors. Our notions of family absorb the conflicts, contradictions, and relations that households hold to resources in advanced capitalism. (Rapp 1992, 51)

Interestingly, the misrecognition of economic calculations involves both a doxic and an orthodox element. It is doxa when applied to lineal relationships. It is orthodoxy when applied to collateral relationships. Inequality in lineal relationships such as parent–child relationships is, in fact, an integral aspect of the quality of those relationships. Collateral relationships, as part of their seriality, require equity and parity. Parents I interviewed went to great length to stress that they treated their children equally. Some, however, pointed out to disparities in the way they and their siblings were treated by their own parents. When it came to such complaints, people showed a remarkable capacity to calculate and compare. One woman, for example, put figures on the financial assistance her brothers got when they left home, to show how disadvantaged she was. These calculations went beyond financial capital. Differential treatment in freedom of movement, harshness of discipline, and so forth were all brought up and calculated. The difference between the calculability of serial relations, and incalculability of lineal relations is part of a broader difference between these two types of relations, a difference I will take up in chapter 6 below.

The nuclear-family household is an experiential paradigm that is replicated spatially in the institution of the family home, and temporally in the distinction between time at work and 'after-hours'. This paradigm may be manifest in many other situations, too, as social agents transfer similar logics from one context to another.

Space

The family home in Newcastle, and throughout most of urban Australia, is a spatial equivalent of the social unit of the nuclear-family household. Architects normally design residential units for a heterosexual adult couple and two or three children. These units are constructed as separate from other family units around them. The family home is clearly demarcated from the rest of the world. There is no sense in which urban design allows for units greater than the nuclear family. There is no sense in which a cluster of houses, a street or a suburb form a distinct, socially coherent unit.

Very few of my married contacts in Newcastle lived in an apartment, although some apartment blocks were available. Apartments were normally occupied by impoverished families, and by people in transition – students in particular, and young people in general.[4]

A common pattern was to move into a house before marriage, or upon marriage, and to start paying off a mortgage on the family home. Homeownership was perceived as an anchor for the family, the way to ensure stability in the future and an ability to 'leave something' for the children. This explains the fact that homeownership in Australia exceeds the levels that would obtain if ownership were merely a strategy of economic utility maximization (see chapter 3).

The family home itself can be divided in different ways between front stages and backstages depending on the context and various attributes of the persons involved. These distinctions are secondary applications of the inside vs. outside or the private vs. public distinctions, which marks the container schema's organization of space. Significantly, each such distinction is not nestled within a broader distinction. Rather, those various divisions intersect with one another. (This is in contradistinction with the Berber house where each division was encapsulated by a similar distinction at a higher level – Bourdieu 1990c, 271–283). The lounge room (an Australianism for living room) or dining room can become a front stage when somewhat distant guests are invited in, and the kitchen may become the backstage. The kitchen is more often than not the backstage for women, who are usually those responsible for cooking.

Thus in one of the families I was familiar with, the woman would normally entertain her friends in the kitchen, as opposed to the man who would sit with his friends out in the yard. When I interviewed him at home, normally at a time when his wife was home, we conducted the interview either outside or in one of the rooms which was being renovated upstairs. When I interviewed her at home it was normally during the day when he was at work, and we would normally sit in the kitchen. This pattern replicated itself in other families. In one other family, for example, when I was invited to dinner with a few other guests – a rather formal occasion – we sat around the heavy dining-room table. But when I just dropped in for a coffee or a beer, we would sit either in the kitchen around the counter, or out on the porch in the back yard.

For children, their rooms would often constitute a backstage and an area where they are allowed to have more control over the use of space and their time. Very often this is not necessarily a matter of greater power on the part of the children, but rather a means of exclusion which enables the parents to more comfortably

---

[4] Not all apartments in Newcastle were aimed at the lower end of the housing market. There were a few upscale units with harbour views in the gentrified inner-city suburbs. But they were uncommon, and seemed to be geared mostly towards professionals who had come from out of town.

dominate the rest of the home. 'Misbehaving' children are often sent to their rooms to cool off.

A main bone of contention between adolescents and their parents was the care and tidying of the adolescents' rooms, a matter of freedom and basic human rights for the children, and of elementary hygiene and responsibility for the parents. At issue were the parents' surveillance rights. The different forms of power that children and parents could muster to assert their position were always contingent and reflected the state of the field of the family at the time.

The parents' bedroom constituted a backstage to the non-familial world. Infants, toddlers and prepubescent children normally enjoyed greater access to this room, and might be allowed to sleep there with their parents, but by adolescence this practice became rare, and adolescents would rarely find reason to enter their parents' bedroom, especially at night. An integral aspect of this sanctity of bedrooms was the centring of sex around the nuptial bed, and the privatization of sexuality and its confinement to that particular backstage within the family home. It would be deemed inappropriate for parents to engage in sexual intercourse or in erotic exchanges (such as explicitly erotic caressing and 'deep kisses') in the presence of their children. One woman recounted to me the story of a woman she knew who did not believe in locking doors or knocking, until one day, in the middle of sexual intercourse, she noticed her seven-year-old son standing near the bed and looking. The storyteller did not feel the need to elaborate on the reason why the presence of the seven-year-old was a problem. This was self-evident. To my informants sexual activity in front of one's children would border on the incestuous and the sexually abusive. (The only exception would be infants who might be sleeping in the master bedroom and who were presumed to not perceive what was happening.) The avoidance of the parents' bedroom was thus part of the broader incest avoidance. Anxieties related to the confounding of parent–child relationships with erotic relationships were further expressed by some people with whom I raised the issue who admitted that it was hard and uncomfortable for them to think of their parents as sexually active beings. (Breastfeeding was another potential source of anxiety over confounding the erotic with the parental – see chapter 7 below.)

Whereas the internal separation of backstage and front stage was contextual, the house boundaries were fixed and clearly demarcated, forming the backstage for the family members as family, against the world. In accord with the container schema this boundary was clearly defined and demarcated two qualitatively opposing entities – a set of binary oppositions. It was particularly consonant with an atomistic view of the world, namely one that sees society as composed of or as divisible into a set of distinct, autonomous, equivalent elementary particles in the form of individual persons or families.

Time

This structure is also manifest in the way time is experienced in Anglo-Celtic Australian society. One example is working-class daily time management. Wage earners sell their labour power to their bosses for a clearly defined period of time. During that period of time they are supposed to leave all their concerns behind and dedicate themselves to the job. This ends when the working day ends, and as the workers commute back home, they are supposed to leave behind their working concerns and resume family concerns. This boundary is a major stake in the struggles between employers and employees. A common complaint among salaried staff was that they had less control over time, and that their private time was always in danger of being invaded by work. Workers who were forced to work at night or during the weekends for no extra remuneration felt wronged. They felt that work at irregular hours, that is, time which is by rights that of the private domain such as night shift ('dogwatch'), should be compensated for. By the same token, employers are rather sensitive to their employees' use of work time to deal with their own private affairs. After all, that time does not belong to the worker to dispense of as s/he pleases, but rather is the property of the employer.

Commuting can be approached as a ritualized spatio-temporal boundary in which one leaves one space, social role and persona, and adopts another one. To my largely working-class informants commuting often conflated a transition between workplace and home; between a dominated position and a dominant position; between time in which one is controlled by others and time which one controls oneself; between a situation in which one's presence is contingent upon one's use value and productivity, and a situation in which one is inherently valued.

The ritual of the commute smoothes over the transition from the private domain of the household to the public domain of the workplace. It is a spatio-temporal separation of two different contexts in which social agents adopt different personas. It clearly demarcates private time and space – private in that it is not under the control of State or market agencies – from the time and space which 'belong' to others, employers for example. Commuting allows for the two spheres to be kept apart both physically and symbolically.

Generally, weekends, afternoons, evenings and nights were private times which were rightfully dedicated to 'non-work' activities, primarily to families. For parents of children, night-time was often a backstage from daytime when the children are around and require a measure of propriety in adult conduct. The physical exclusion of children to their room was often paralleled in curfew hours which ensured that the later night hours are free from children and become the parents' own time. This extended beyond sexual activities. Topics of discussion which children should not be privy to were raised in those times, as well as other activities like sharing a joint with friends.

Resolving Metaphorical and Structural Contradictions

So far I have argued that the basic schema which organizes the realized category of the family in Northern and Western European metropolitan and settler societies is that of the container. But the metaphorical extension of this schema entails further configurations, contradictions and conflicts.

One is the issue of the permeability of boundaries. Thus, young adults find themselves often in a liminal space, not quite in, but clearly not out. The negotiations surrounding these liminal spaces often bring much of the underlying doxa into sharp relief.

For instance, the intensity of the enduring link between independently living single persons and the homes of their parents, is clarified in the story of Franz. His parents separated when he was roughly 17 years old. For a while he lived with his father. It was his choice, as he blamed his mother for the marital breakdown of his parents. (His mother had had an extramarital affair, and eventually left the family home to live on her own and continue her relationship with her lover.) He then moved in with his mother in order to patch up the relationship. Shortly thereafter they had an altercation and he decided to move out. His father, who was anxious that the son should maintain his relationship with his mother, would not let Franz come back home until he sorted out his differences with his mother. Franz decided to leave his mother's home nonetheless, and the following day moved in with his ex-girlfriend's family. At the time he and his ex-girlfriend had already broken up their romantic relationship, although they remained friends. By moving in with his friend's family Franz incurred the wrath of his family of origin, including his older brother and sister who had left home a few years before. As he put it, 'When I decided to do that, move out and live up with them [his ex-girlfriend's family], my family cut me off completely … didn't want to know me.' When I asked about his siblings, he said that his elder brother

> … would talk to me. My sister, she talked to me. I've seen her up at Green Hills [a shopping centre] […] I've seen her up there one day. She has [sic] seen me and she said, ah, if I see you on the street and that I will still talk to you and all that, 'cos you're still me brother, but, she said, mum and dad doesn't [sic] want anything to do with you while you're living with them [the ex-girlfriend's family], so, all that time I was looking for another place to live, and I found that one [where he lived at the time of the interview] in the paper. Now I get on great with dad again. And mum as well.

When I asked what exactly was the problem his family members had with his moving out of his mother's place, whether they objected to his having left his mother, he answered,

> Ah, yeah, or they kind of like put it like I moved out of there to live with another family, and they kind of like felt betrayed that I was going to another family and lived with them. But I didn't see it like that. I just wanted to get out, get away from mum.

But having learned of the way his act had been interpreted, Franz quickly moved out on his own. Obviously, Franz had inadvertently violated some of the conventions of practice. By relying on the home of a different family he broke the boundary of the household which includes all members of a nuclear family, including those who are living on their own. By rights he should live either with his family of origin, or on his own (possibly sharing a flat with some flatmates), or set up a new family household of his own.

When a couple becomes 'a couple', they establish an exclusive relationship which removes them from the domain of their families of origin and forms the basis for the creation of a new family. This has some very practical significance. For example, before one is clearly involved in one's own family of orientation, one may make claims on the home of one's family of origin. This, however, changes when one creates one's own family of orientation. Thus, unattached single people would quite commonly move into their parents' home for short periods of time, such as during periods of financial distress. Another area in which unattached singles relied on their families included use of washing machines and cars. This reliance is reduced as the new family is formed. In fact, to most informants the achievement of a measure of economic independence was a prerequisite to marriage.

In my informants' world marriage entailed neolocal, conjugal co-residence. In fact, co-residence is what distinguishes between de facto marriages and the relationship of boyfriend–girlfriend which are of lesser commitment. Hence, for a boyfriend and girlfriend to 'move in together' is a major transition on the way towards terminal monogamy. Once cohabiting, partners are no longer likely to move back in with their families of origin unless their relationships break down. Reliance on the homes of origin was ephemeral among my partnered informants, and generally reserved for situations of last resort or unusual circumstances. Clifford and Hildred, for example, moved in with his parents for a few weeks after they sold their old house and before their new house was complete. They said things were fine, but they were glad that they did not have to stay there for long.

The creation of a new family as children leave their home and make their own families is itself a source of structural tension. The creation of a new family by marriage (*de jure* or de facto) marks the transition of a person out of one family household and into another. (This could either be an immediate transition as one person marries and moves out of his/her family of origin's household into his/her own family household. More commonly this transition is the culmination of a process that began with moving out of one's parents' home.) Obligations relating to the family of origin become secondary to one's obligation to one's 'own' family (family of orientation). A great deal of effort is then exerted to prevent conflicts from arising between the demands of the family of origin and those of the family of orientation. This negotiation is one of the main concerns of family politics.

Particularly fraught with potential difficulty is the relationship between the two families of origin which come to stand in a state of structural conflict. Indeed, one of the main concerns of a new family is to define the relationships with the two old ones, and to balance their interaction to avoid a situation of favouritism. This is not to say that the two families of origin are in a state of active conflict. The structural conflict can express itself in a great deal of social labour, including goodwill, being exerted in order to avoid conflict. The structural conflict does mean that when things do go wrong between in-laws, people understand why. It means that if someone strikes a very good relationship with one's in-laws, that feat would be noteworthy. This can be contrasted with the structural complementarity of husband and wife, a complementarity which need not imply that those relationships are necessarily peaceful and cooperative. It does mean that when husband and wife do get on together, it makes sense and is unremarkable. If conflict ensues, the grapevine will start generating information and interpretations as to 'what went wrong'.

Some rituals like the wedding or the honeymoon are used to symbolically create the structural separation between persons and their families of origin. At the same time, the organization of the wedding, the reception and the like allow the two families of origin to get involved in the new family and cooperate with one another, thereby establishing a pattern of interaction that would enable them to continue in a positive way later. A common pattern, for example, was for the family of the bride to organize the wedding and the family of the groom to attend to the liquor. In any event, the planning of the wedding often brought together the parents of the two spouses-to-be, especially the mothers, to coordinate the ceremony, including such critical aspects as the list of invitees.

This is particularly important at first marriages when the spouses are still young, when they are well and truly leaving the domain of their families of origin. It was very common in second marriages or the marriages of people who had been living out of home for many years to downplay the significance of the wedding and to invest less effort and resources in it, or to forego the formal wedding or the elaborate ceremony altogether.

Sometimes a fierce competition between families of origin may ensue without taking the form of open hostilities, but the form of matching each other's investment in the new couple in what is reminiscent of the potlatch. Financial support flowing down the generations, for example, can be used to out-do the other family of origin. Some grandparents kept themselves informed about the Christmas gifts the other grandparents of their grandchildren gave. Many grandchildren from a young age master the arts of manipulation and playing off grandparents against one another as well as parents against one another. Lucy recounted how her son, Max, would play up the gifts he got from one set of grandparents when talking to the other set of grandparents, and sometimes even lie about the gifts he got. Mary Catherine, a young woman of 18 whose parents divorced when she was a young adolescent, said that she noticed that she and a few other children of divorced parents would get more gifts than other children, because of the competition between parents and grandparents. 'It's like they are trying to buy us with all these presents', she said.

But the container schema is static, while families are dynamic entities. The formation of new families and movement of persons from the family of origin to the family of orientation contravenes the boundedness and internal coherence of the family unit. This contradiction requires additional cognitive elaboration. It is at least partly resolved metaphorically by further entailments of the metaphorical structuring of family as person. The emergence of new families is structured along the schemata relating to birth and maturation, whereby new entities emerge from existing ones and, once emerged, they are separate containers which nonetheless may contain essentially the same substances.

Indeed, biological and social reproduction is a core facet of the ensemble of models which combine to make the gestalt of the prototypical family. 'To have a family', to my informants, means to reproduce within the family. As one informant explained, 'until you have children, you are not *really* a family. You are just a couple.' When my informants talked about 'settling down' and 'having a family', the settling down referred to marriage in anticipation of children, and having a family referred to reproduction. The reality of birth and production of new persons becomes a practical metaphor for the emergence of the new family out of two old ones. Just as within the family the mother and father combine to produce a new person which still shares an essence with his/her parents, so do the two members of a new couple combine to make a new family which is distinct, although it still shares a familial essence with the two previous nuclear families. And just as the relationship between parents and their offspring is construed as direct, unmediated, unseverable and 'organic' (by blood), so the relationships between the new family and its families of origin are experienced as direct and enduring; and just as the relationship between mother and father is construed as always contingent and potentially terminable, so too the relationship between the two families of origin are experienced as contingent and weak, in contradistinction with their relationships with their offspring's families of orientation. (See chapter 6 for an elaboration of relatedness and the experience of personhood.)

Not only the emergence of new families forces the boundaries around the family into the foreground. The prospect of collapsing such boundaries has a similar effect. One context in which the separation between family of origin and family of orientation comes to the fore is the granny flat. The granny flat is a solution for conflicting pressures at particular conjunctures. Such a situation arises typically when for some reason it makes sense for an adult couple to share a house with one or two parents of either spouse. Such situations may arise as a result of financial pressures; or when an older person's spouse dies and that person prefers to move in with his/her adult child. A different reason might be the deteriorating health of the spouse's parent, who requires more constant attention.

Such situations give rise to conflicting pressures. On the one hand is the requirement to share a house among three generations. On the other hand there is the exclusive barrier around the nuclear-family household of the younger adult's family of orientation. Both older generation and younger generation are concerned about their independence. The younger adults seek to defend their control over their own destiny as adults, and are wary about the possible interference on the part of the older generation. The older person is equally concerned to secure his/her control over his/her own destiny.

The granny flat is created when the house is physically divided into two households – the major one and an additional small one, the granny flat, which is often devised by closing off a balcony or a garage, or by getting a caravan and parking it in the yard. It is a way of maintaining a balance between proximity and independence, and reducing possible causes of tension between the generations.

For example, Eleanor had gradually become a carer for her mother and her mother's partner in the years before my fieldwork. She and her mother never got on terribly well together, she said. In the first few years the mother and partner lived in the same house as Eleanor. Eleanor described that period simply as 'hell'. She described her mother as a 'control freak' who would try to manipulate everybody around her, especially Eleanor. Eleanor was performing her caring tasks out of her sense of obligation by her own account, although, by her own admission, she had also become dependent on the carer's pension which was paid by the Commonwealth government. A couple of years before my fieldwork, she had her house split in two, and a small portion of the house was converted into a granny flat, so that there are two separate households. This, she said, enabled her to regain control of her own life, and enabled her to interact very minimally with her mother if she so chose. She said she did not know how she managed before the house was split in two.

The Mate

One theme that has been developed in the anthropology of the Australian family threatens to undermine my analysis of the family as a bounded entity. This theme is the 'mate' and his role in the family. Thomas Ernst went as far as to argue that there is a distinctly Australian atom of family which includes the mate as well as the conjugal couple (Ernst 1990). This theme was also touched upon in Annette Hamilton's analysis of the once-popular children's book by May Gibbs entitled *The Complete Adventures of Snugglepot and Cuddlepie* (Hamilton 1975).

The attraction of the institution of the 'mate' to Australian researchers is augmented by its being a quintessentially Australian institution. Since the 1960s a certain element of nationalism has flourished in Australian social sciences and humanities. Mateship, central as it is in Australian national(ist) mythology fits in nicely with this ideological frame of mind.

Curiously, nothing in my experience with intact marital partnerships in Newcastle suggests that the mate has any role whatsoever in the family. In fact, the friendship networks of my male informants were very restricted. A few told me that they had no friends. This is very much in line with the interview responses and cultural analysis in Don Edgar's treatise on the Australian family (Edgar 1997, chapter 3) and with the situation in the English working class as reported by Graham Allan (Allan 1979, 69 ff.).

This situation is also very similar to that described by Maila Stivens for a middle-class suburb of Sydney in the late 1960s. For all men involved in her study, family formed the core of their social network. There were some differences between men of different class positions, though, namely 'in the extent to which kin relationships formed a central part of their social contacts. For the more "private reserved family people" of the lower middle class and the working class, "family" was central. Professionals had more friends, but even the most sociable did not replace family with friends and their most intimate relationships still frequently involved kin' (Stivens 1985, 30).[5]

There does not seem to be much support for 'the mate' (singular) as an integral part of the Australian family in research, although the significance of 'mates' – peers of the husband – has been observed in some social studies of families. In her study of a mining town in the 1970s Claire Williams has operationalized belonging to mateship cliques as follows: 'if a husband mixed with his mates socially without his wife more than twice a week, he was deemed to belong to a clique' (Williams 1981, 137). Williams found, based on this definition, that 45 per cent of men belonged to mate cliques (Williams 1981, 137).

Significantly, women socialized with other women on a much larger scale (Williams 1981, 144–146), although to Williams this did not become an issue of equivalent significance to males' socialization. This is partly due to the fact that working-class male mateship has become an item of interest to social scholars, and partly due to the fact that males' extra-conjugal socialization is a source of controversy among spouses, in a way which female extra-conjugal socialization may not be (given that normally women organize social relations). Stivens, too, when writing about the extra-familial social pulls that men experience referred to men's social drinking, especially on the way home from work, and women who complained about that practice (Stivens 1985, 28–29). When writing about women's social networks researchers generally assume that such networks support women and, *ipso facto*, the family.

In any event, frequent interaction in social networks like those described by Williams was not very common among my married informants in Newcastle. They rather saw the kind of mateship and bonding between males which is antagonistic with family relationships as something of an anachronism.[6] Both married men and married women often identified their spouses as their best friends (as did Edgar's interlocutors – Edgar 1997, chapter 3). Obviously, the exclusivity of their conjugal intimacy incorporated amity in addition to copulation. Moreover, married couples most commonly socialized with other couples rather than with individuals.

---

[5] The situation appears to be different in rural Australia (Dempsey 1992; Oxley 1974).

[6] It should be noted that attitudes towards mate cliques even among Williams's informants themselves were by no means uniform, and a few of her male interlocutors held a dim view of mateship circles (Williams 1981, 136–139).

Still, the single friends of married persons tended to be of the same gender as the married person. This is part and parcel of a general tendency towards gender-specific social networks. Men tended to associate with men, women with women (and couples with couples). My impression is that women were more vigilant in maintaining this gender segregation. In one conversation I had with a couple the man said that even though his friends were generally male, and his wife's were generally female, he did not think it would be a problem if he had female friends and she had male friends, and that he was sure his wife felt the same way. However, as it turned out, she did not, and proceeded to say that she would find it very hard to understand if he had a female friend, and that she did not think she would have a male friend. She then explained that between men and women 'there is always the sex thing', and that in any event, men and women like doing different things. Another woman who claimed she and her husband were best friends also said that she would feel awkward if her husband formed intimate, even if non-erotic, friendships with other women, and that she expected him not to.

Also when associating as couples, men would normally interact primarily with men, and women with women. While such a norm was not articulated spontaneously, my observations were confirmed to me in response to my questions.

On the whole, then, for my married informants, friendships outside the family circle tended to be contingent, non-committal, fragile, voluntary. This was both their attraction ('you can always choose your friends, but not your family'), and their weakness. The most comfortable friendships that married people formed were with other married people as one couple with another. Otherwise, old friendships from before the couple's marriage depended for their continuation on the spouse accepting the friend and joining into the friendship, turning the one spouse's friend into 'a friend of the family'. The closest to mateship I found among married informants were strong friendship bonds among women, rather than men, especially those women not in full-time employment who often used the time when their partners were at work to socialize and carry out domestic activities together (shopping, child-minding, etc.).

Several explanations may be offered as to the differences between the prevalence of mateship cliques among Williams's informants and their relative insignificance among mine. One has to do with a change in leisure practices among working-class Australians between the mid-1970s, when Williams conducted her fieldwork, and the mid-1990s, when I conducted mine. Factors which might have contributed to such a putative generational change include the collapse of working-class consciousness and workers' pride, the embourgeoisement of working-class culture and the strengthening of the ideology of familism.

Another explanation may be found in the difference between the social dynamics of remote mining towns, like Williams's Open Cut, and those of established cities like Newcastle. In company towns people often come from various places for a limited amount of time, and are situated both spatially and socially in a liminal space, something akin to what Victor Turner has called 'liminal state' (Turner 1969). According to Turner, participants in liminal states will develop 'communitas', and create strong bonds between each other as the individualizing and distinguishing features of each individual disappear. Significantly, mateship cliques among Williams's informants were rather specific to occupation types (e.g. mechanics with mechanics), supporting the proposition that the bond which tied such cliques had to do with similarity in working and living conditions.

Yet another potential source of discrepancy between Williams's findings and mine is that her sample was heavily weighted in favour of young couples, presumably in their twenties, with pre-school children (Williams 1981, 135), while most of my married informants were in their thirties and beyond, often with older children. The discrepancy between the findings might therefore partly reflect the different life stages of our informants. In chapter 8 I will discuss the transformation in masculine style from larrikin masculinity to respectable masculinity which typifies working-class male life trajectories. It could be that the transition between the two is accompanied by a transition of orientation from a youthful orientation towards peers, to an orientation towards one's family.

There remains the question of the discrepancy between Ernst's and Hamilton's presentation of The Mate as a central figure in Australian family life, and the argument of Stivens, Edgar and my own (echoed for England by Allan) to the contrary. The discrepancy, I propose, is the product of a confusion of two kinds of analysis. While the mate is an essential aspect in Australian mythology, it is not an essential aspect of Australian social practice. This confusion occurs when analysis of the content of national mythology, such as Ernst's and Hamilton's, are presented or read as analyses of social practice.

Conclusion

The prototypical family, then, operates as a realized category. It is at one and the same time a cognitive structure and a structure of social practice. As such, it joins with similar structures to organize the social experience of agents in its broadest sense; that is, the physical, intellectual and emotional aspects of the lived experience.

The family, an abstract cultural construct, is constructed to a considerable extent by the cultural construction of the embodied individual. More specifically the image schema of container, which is rooted in the pre-conceptual embodied experience, is metaphorically extended to organize family practice.

Family, as a realized category, is polysemic. It metonymically structures various spheres of practice such as household and home. This is because the unity of family with household and home are part of the gestalt of the nuclear family. Thereby the image schema which originates in the person and is reproduced in the family comes to structure the home and the household, as well as other facets of the socio-cultural complex such as time.

While the container schema is salient in organizing the nuclear family and is metaphorically extended spatially (home) and temporally (weekend, for instance), the core–periphery schema does play a limited role in conceptualizing extended kin. The latter may be graded by degrees of kin proximity. (Kinship will be explored in greater depth in chapter 6.)

For different reasons neither mateship nor extended kin networks conflict with the analysis of the family as a clearly bounded entity. The former was not as significant in practice among my informants as some analyses might have suggested. The latter not only does not violate the structural principles of the realized category of the family – in fact, it adheres to them and reinforces them.

Chapter 5

Doxa, Orthodoxy and Heterodoxy

The previous chapter considered the prototypical family and began analysing its cultural dominance. This chapter broadens the purview of the discussion to include heterodox family arrangements. The evaluation of these will allow for a more nuanced understanding of family practices and their historicity.

But first it would be useful to recapitulate the tripartite typology of practice. To the extent that agents' dispositions match the prevailing patterns and regularities of practice, so would the agent experience the world as self-explanatory and self-evident. In other words, when the structures of the world as they are incorporated into the subjectivity of social agents (that is, habitus) match the social structures at large, the arbitrary social order is experienced as natural, as self-evident, as an integral part of the mundane order of things – simply, the way things are. This mode of justification bypasses logic and reasoning, ideological contemplation or any kind of explicit consideration. Things are simply the way they are and could not possibly be otherwise for the simple reason that this is the nature of things. Such taken-for-granted things are what Bourdieu calls doxa (Bourdieu 1977, 164 ff.).

By contrast, orthodoxy refers to all those practices – of judgement, of physical action, of thought, and so forth – for which alternatives are conceivable from an agent's perspective, but which are still the dominant practices. Heterodoxy denotes alternative practices which are not the dominant ones (Bourdieu 1977, 164 ff.).

The complex which is the realized category of the family is made up of both doxic and orthodox elements. The core of the family remains doxic. Its visible margins where changes might be afoot are orthodox. In this chapter I initially discuss the anatomy of a few heterodox alternatives. Subsequently the analysis is broadened into a discussion of heterodox challenges in general, and the relative historical resilience of the realized category of the family.

Heterodox Challenges

Homosexual Families

In both personal interviews and focus groups, homosexual families were among the first examples that Novocastrians cited to demonstrate that the Australian family is in a process of profound change. Such families were viewed as a novel, significant and radical alternative to the prototypical family. This view of the homosexual family as a radical alternative was shared across the spectrum of attitudes towards homosexuality and the homosexual family.

Significantly, homosexual lifestyles which were not familial were not raised as instances of novel, subversive family arrangements. It was those homosexuals who strove to be recognized as a family, with full parenting rights, whom my informants cited as challenging the social order. Neither the stereotype of the promiscuous, sexually active homosexual, nor that of the celibate homosexual living alone, were perceived as equally radical. These were rather seen as idiosyncrasies – usually benign although some Novocastrians considered them abomination – but not more.

What is radical is not homosexuality as such, but rather the demand for recognition of homosexual unions as marriages of the same status as those of heterosexual conjugal couples. That this should be seen as an overwhelming transformation in the nuclear family is remarkable precisely because of the great similarity between the notion of homosexual families and the nuclear family. Homosexual families, or more specifically, homosexual marriages of the kind that my informants felt to be radical, were those which involved exclusive monogamy and which would incorporate children in a position that is commensurate with the mainstream nuclear family.

The logic which has homosexual families – but not unfamilial homosexuality – as a radical shift has its equivalent in heterosexual practices. Inherent to the ideology and practice of the nuclear family is a separation between a public appearance of adherence to legitimate standardized behaviour and the possibility of contravening it in practice. Thus, adultery does not in any way challenge the notions of the nuclear family. Adultery might have detrimental ramifications for a particular family, but not for the nuclear family as a realized category. It would be adultery which refused to be seen as such, an open relationship that is symbolically and publicly asserted between a married person who is still involved in his or her marital family, and a sexual partner other than that person's spouse, which would challenge the nuclear family. By the same token, homosexuality does not challenge the standard nuclear family so long as it does not seek to advance publicly sanctioned legitimate alternatives to any of the nuclear family's constitutive parts.

I should stress that the arena of public appearances here is not that which is confined to lawyers, politicians and the like. It is the level at which things can be said freely without worrying about who knows what, the level at which knowledge is explicit and for universal consumption, the level which is 'for the record' as it were. It is the level at which one can choose to operate if one wants to ignore what really happens and focus on what should, in fact, be happening. This is in contrast with knowledge for exclusive circulation or consumption, which in its broadest sense is the 'public secret', the instance in which the entire public moves, as it were, to an 'in-camera' sitting of the 'committee of the whole'.

What the homosexual family specifically challenges when it demands recognition is the identity of the procreative union with the family, and the biological reproductive basis for parenthood (Weston 1995). Challenged is the nuclear family's inclusion of the two sexual partners who produce the children involved. To be prototypical parents, a couple needs to be a complementary union of both sexes. This is contravened in the homosexual couple.

By posing as a radical alternative the homosexual family accomplishes three things. What elements it shares with the realized category of the nuclear family it further reinforces by glossing over them at the very moment of taking them for granted. The association of the family with the main tasks of rearing children, the association of the family with an enduring, sexually exclusive union of two adults, the identification of the nuclear family with the household, the exclusion of non-nuclear family members from the nuclear family, are all reinforced by the homosexual family, and are further secured as doxic by this very challenge. So is the overlap of romance, eroticism and marriage.

The second accomplishment of the homosexual family challenge is to put forward some alternative practices to current ones, thereby exposing orthodoxy to the possibility of change. The exposed elements of orthodoxy include the heterosexual character of the nuptial arrangement, the strong preference to confound, whenever possible, 'social' and 'biological' parenthood, and so forth. Much of this is not unique to the homosexual family. For example, the homosexual family joins with feminism to elevate the gendered character of the spousal relationship from the security of doxic ubiquity and obscurity, to the focused position of orthodoxy. Consequently, this gendered character of the family becomes a clearly and explicitly defined set of practices to be defended, attacked, measured, evaluated and reformulated.

The third – and more general – accomplishment of the homosexual family is its further promotion of the underlying logic of its heterodox challenge. This logic – of serial individualism – is a significant organizing value in the ethos of Australia's (and indeed the world's) currently dominant elites. Seriality refers to a logic which constitutes positions as fully interchangeable. Thus, rather than highlighting a gendered division of labour among spouses, serial logic would constitute these positions as equivalent, and therefore interchangeable (cf. Sartre 1976–91; and see the adaptation of Sartre's ideas in Metcalfe 1988). This logic is expressed in the rhetoric constituting the marital dyad as partners, a terminology closely associated with the struggle for emancipation of women and the transformation of the gendered division of labour. The serial aesthetic is closely associated with the individualism of liberal reformers as well as with the tenets of economic 'rationalism'. It is inherent in the rationalist, modernist European ideological project.

Single-Parent Families

Single-parent families are also commonly thought of as a novel lifestyle. I came across several single-parent families in Newcastle. Most were mother-headed, a fact consistent with the figures across Australia (see figures in chapter 3). Some of these families resulted from unplanned pregnancies or the death of a parent, although the majority resulted from divorce or separation. All single parents I interviewed indicated that they would rather be partnered, but not at all costs. None held single-parenthood in its own right to be an ideal situation.

Single parents reported they did seek romantic liaisons in the hope of re-partnering. The expressed reasons ranged from loneliness, a desire to be 'normal' and give children a 'normal' life, the desire to share the pressures of parenthood, and the economic burden of single-parenthood. Thus, single-parent families remain an unstable unit because of the explicit possibility, even hope, of forming a two-parent nuclear family. The prototypical family remains the stable and preferred unit.

Other than in the number of parents involved, single-parent families seemed to differ in several ways from double-parent families. The fence of exclusion around the single-parent family is more permeable in two ways. One is the legitimacy of sexual access of adults outside the family to the single parent. The other is the greater access of relatives, especially female, who take over some of the care responsibilities and assist the single parent. This applies both to the mother-headed families, and to the one father-headed family for which I have some information. A common complaint of single mothers was that their relatives tended to interfere in their affairs in a way which they would never have done when they were married. (They did also admit, though, that they also relied on these relatives to a greater extent.)

For example, Phyllis, a mother of an eight-year-old girl, like all other single parents I interviewed, did not originally intend to become a single mother when she fell pregnant. In her case it was an unplanned pregnancy which happened when she had a boyfriend. When she became pregnant her boyfriend proposed to marry her, but she told me she turned him down because she knew he only proposed because she was pregnant. In the period that followed, as a result of her refusal, they were drawn apart, and eventually he left town. Phyllis had not seen him for years, and did not know where he lived.

Phyllis was in daily contact with her mother, and relied on her for a great deal of support, both with finances and with childcare. She did not always appreciate her mother's presence and greater involvement in her life. At times she needed to resist her mother's interference. Phyllis had one married sister. She, too, was a source of support. The married sister was employed full-time, and at times relied on Phyllis for childcare or chores around the house, an arrangement which served both the sister's need for help and helped Phyllis financially. Also in her relationship with her sister, Phyllis felt a measure of weakness. At times she felt that her sister was also trying to dominate the way she was conducting her affairs. The economic disparity was an element in that power differential. She needed the financial support from her sister, but she felt that that support was the basis for her sister overstepping the mark and meddling in her affairs. By contrast, the married sister experienced greater autonomy in her relationship with the mother and other relatives. This was partly the result of her economic position, and partly a recognition of the fact that she shares her life with her husband, and is therefore not as open to her relatives' intervention.

The fact that fathers can function as single parents may itself be experienced as a heterodox stance in that it challenges the gendered division of labour. It is normally the woman who gains custody over the children following a marital breakdown. For men to assume the primary caregiving role was seen as more strained and more difficult than for women to function as primary breadwinners (I will return to this point in chapters 7 and 8 below). In practice, this radical gendered situation in lone-father families may be attenuated in many ways. Lone-father families had a heavy involvement of female relatives of either living or dead spouses. In one such family I encountered in Newcastle the eldest daughter, in her mid-teens, also took on some of the domestic roles.

While I do not have any quantitative data to suggest that women outside the family are involved in lone-father families to a greater extent than in lone-mother families, I can report that there was great concern in social circles surrounding lone-father families regarding the capacity of the lone-father to manage; greater, it seemed, than over the capacity of a lone-mother to manage. Moreover, both men and women acquaintances of a lone-father of three girls expressed admiration at his ability, as a man, to cope with his daughters' needs during adolescence, or else were concerned that it might be too complex a task for a man. I did not encounter a similar level of concern regarding lone-mothers of boys in similar ages. In any event, the reproduction of the prototypical gendered logic of the division of familial labour in these networks of female to support reduces from the radical difference that lone-father families exhibit. At the same time, through the strain that all those involved undergo, the single-father families do strongly reinforce the doxic supremacy of the biological, parental links which tie parents to children in bonds of familiality and mutual responsibility.

But the reinforcement by single-parent families of the realized category of the family runs deeper than this. None of the single parents I interviewed or spoke with ended up as single parents intentionally. It was rather that something went wrong on the way towards the nuclear family. Even if by default they remained pretty stable, single-parent families were always experienced as a temporary arrangement because of the possibility and hope of re-partnering on the part of the single parent. Thus single parents did not reject the rationale or superiority of two-parent families. Children of single parents were acutely aware that eligible adults in their parents' social network were potential partners to their parents.

By struggling to survive and balance the requirements of paid work with the demands of caring, single-parenthood further amplifies the doxic aspects of parenthood, which place the responsibility for the welfare of children on the shoulders of those who bore them. These doxic aspects are experienced as love, and are accompanied by an orthodox ideology of social responsibility which is predicated on the presumed intentionality of the act of parenting.

The single-parent family has been normalized as a family type in Australia. This is expressed in various ways. ABS and AIFS have defined this arrangement as the lone-parent family[1] and have proceeded to measure its manifestation. State agencies and academic knowledge producers have increasingly turned this type into an object of contemplation, consideration and action. Finally, in cultural production for mass consumption there is an increased representation of the single-parent family as a deliberate strategy, rather than the result of a prematurely terminated marriage. This attests to the legitimacy this family type has acquired among Australia's cultural elites.

Remarkably, and contrary to ubiquitous perceptions, the ratio of single-parent families is not unprecedentedly high. The rates were comparable in the late nineteenth century, albeit for different reasons (see chapter 2). In other words, the shifting significance of single-parent families as a heterodox challenge cannot be simply accounted for by shifts in its statistical occurrence. Again here, to understand why such practices emerge as an established heterodoxy, it is important to bear in mind the prevalent concerns among the cultural, professional and bureaucratic elites in redefining gender roles, in the emancipation of women and the incorporation of working-class women into the workforce, as well as the redefinition of the legal rights which are involved in marriages. Put differently, it is not the increase in the incidence of single-parent families as such, but rather shifting political and ideological agendas that combined to turn the single-parent family into a family type and a policy issue.

De Facto Marriages

De facto marriages are also often thought of as expressions of the current crisis or shift in the family. On the whole, de facto marital arrangements that I encountered followed the pattern of *de jure* families except the spouses were not formally married and did not share a surname. Significantly, while 'de facto' is a universally recognized term, its counterpart, *de jure*, is not in daily use. Unless explicitly designated as 'de facto', nuptial arrangement are taken to be *de jure*. In other words, the de facto tag still designates it as heterodox, while the lack of an equivalent tag for the *de jure* couples underscore their orthodox, unmarked nature.

De facto marriages are flexible arrangements which lend themselves to manipulation in presentation quite easily. Existing de facto marriages were described to me by informants as families which exist to the same extent that nuptial families do, the only difference being 'the piece of paper'.

This presentation is not completely accurate, though, as often the level of commitment involved in de facto marriages is less than in *de jure* arrangements. For example, it is commonly agreed that dissolving a de facto arrangement was easier than *de jure* arrangements, primarily because of the relative freedom from

---

[1] Lone-parent family is defined as 'A person aged 15 years or over who does not have a usually resident spouse (i.e. married or de facto partner) but has at least one usually resident child (natural, step, adopted, fostered or otherwise related) with no spouse or child of his/her own' (de Vaus and Wolcott 1997, 136).

judicial formality. Moreover, whereas previous *de jure* marital arrangements always need to be remembered and recounted in one's biography, de facto relationships can be easily glossed over, and relegated to the lesser commitment of a boyfriend–girlfriend relationship. This was most apparent when collating biographical data from different informants. In a few cases the number of previous relationships they reported for themselves and their spouses did not tally, and when I further investigated the matter it normally transpired that some did not count de facto relationships while others did. Interestingly, married women were more likely to downplay and overlook previous de facto relationships than were their husbands.

I encountered mainly two kinds of de facto relationships. One was of a couple living together as a prelude to formal marriage. This would normally last from several months to a few years and culminate in a wedding. It was a way for a couple to have a trial run, as it were, without upping the ante by undergoing the expensive nuptial arrangements and the social obligations which are involved in a wedding, and the greater difficulties in dissolving the union should the need arise. To many it was a way of reducing the stakes, emotional as well as material, until such time as procreation begins, the stage by which arrangements need to be formalized to match the new stakes which are involved.

A different type of de facto relationship I encountered was that in which the adults involved, or at least the wife, were past their first marriage. In these instances a formal wedding was not forthcoming. Part of the rationale for this arrangement was the reduced urgency for the wedding. The first wedding seems to function, especially for women, as a rite of passage that signifies full adulthood, and is no longer critical for subsequent familial arrangements, especially if there were children involved in the first marriage. Another reason cited by once-married people for de facto arrangements is that having gone through the travails of separation and divorce once, and being painfully aware of the risks of marital breakdown, individuals are seeking to lower the stakes in their relationships.

Weddings are not the only ceremonial aspect whose urgency is attenuated in remarriages. Surnames are also less of a concern in such situations. It is common for the woman to revert to her maiden name, and for the children to maintain their father's surname. One woman I interviewed retained her surname from her first marriage because she thought it was too much of a hassle to do anything about it.

In any event, in all these instances of de facto arrangements the extent to which the full complex of the prototypical family is, in fact, challenged is very limited indeed.

Non-Types

Some heterodox practices appear as mere idiosyncratic ad hoc arrangements and are therefore not recognized as alternative types by social agents. These tend to be much greater departures from the realized category of nuclear family than typed heterodoxies.

One such example that I encountered in Newcastle comprised a concrete set of relationships which had evolved over time as a set of ad hoc steps. This arrangement involved Ruth and Margaret – two un-partnered adult women living in separate homes a good 20-minute drive away from one another – and eight-year-old Michelle. Ruth presented Michelle as her quarter daughter. Quarter, she said, because half of what a person is passes on through the genes, and half through the environment. Michelle was not her biological daughter, so she only considered herself responsible for half of the environment which is half of what makes a person, hence, a quarter. Margaret, Michelle's birth mother, was credited by Ruth with half the child (half the genes and half the environment), and Michelle's genetic father, who had only seen his daughter three times in the eight years since she was born, was credited with a quarter of the child by virtue of his contribution of half her genes. Indeed, Ruth is a mathematician by training – she was employed at the time as a consultant in a chemical industrial complex in Newcastle. But the quantification of parenthood carries more significance than might at first appear. I will return to this point shortly.

Margaret, for her part, was very quick to clarify that she and Ruth were not lesbians and had never been romantically or sexually involved with one another. Their arrangement started when Margaret fell pregnant unexpectedly – she was not partnered at the time. Her natal family lived in a different part of the country. This is significant because both women asserted that had Margaret had relatives around, especially women of the same generation, their arrangement would probably have never emerged because it would have been those women who would have had 'a better initial claim', as Ruth put it, over Michelle and over the responsibility to assist Margaret through the pregnancy.

Margaret turned to Ruth, her best friend, for support. Late in her pregnancy she was diagnosed with cancer. It was too late for an abortion, and Margaret required surgery. Ruth helped her out throughout the period, and also accompanied her to prenatal classes.

Margaret was still ill following childbirth and relied on Ruth for assistance with childminding. Shortly after returning home, a severe storm struck Newcastle, and Margaret was left without running hot water. (The versions of the story differ here. Ruth claimed Margaret had never had hot water in her apartment and following the storm had no running water whatsoever. Margaret insisted that she had had hot water before the storm, and only lost it during the storm.) Michelle was ten weeks old at the time. Immediately following the storm, Michelle stayed at Ruth's as Margaret commuted between Ruth's and her own place to fix it up.

Margaret resumed paid employment very quickly. Her work included contract work at times, and there was a period in which she did night shifts. Ruth minded the baby, at first at Margaret's place, and progressively at her own place. The triangular relationship continued developing. Margaret enjoyed the time off, and Ruth enjoyed the role she played in Michelle's life and Michelle's role in her life. This arrangement became gradually routinized.

When Michelle was three the two women formalized the relationship legally, and Ruth was granted guardianship over Michelle. At least part of the consideration was the concern Margaret had over what would happen in case she died. This also allowed Ruth to play a greater role in Michelle's life as now she was empowered to sign various school forms and other documents which require the approval of a legal guardian.

Margaret thought her own childhood experience might have facilitated the emergence of this arrangement. She explained that she and her brothers were the only children in their extended family of parents, grandparents, aunts and uncles. She remembered spending a lot of time with her two favourite aunts and her grandmother, all of whom 'mothered' her. This might have prepared the grounds for the arrangement that later emerged with Ruth.

At the time of my fieldwork their routinized residential pattern had been in place for quite some time. Michelle had her own room in both homes, and would normally spend the first half of the week at Margaret's, and the second two to three days at Ruth's. Holidays, weekends and so forth were determined on an ad hoc basis, although Margaret had Michelle more often on such occasions.

Although this arrangement had evolved over almost eight years, it was still tenuous in many ways. For one, the power relations between the adults are such that Margaret can unilaterally terminate Ruth's relationship with Michelle at any time. Possible partners, especially of Margaret who was more prone to form romantic attachments, always threatened to throw the arrangement out of balance. Margaret was very sensitive to this situation and took great care to introduce male friends to Ruth and try to eliminate possible complications. But this did not change the tenuous position of Ruth.

This arrangement is heterodox in many ways. The two adults are not romantically or sexually involved with one another, nor have they ever been. They live apart, and are not consanguineally related to one another. Both lay claim to Michelle as a daughter. The women consider their relationship with one another that of friendship, not family, but their relationship with Michelle as familial.

Inevitably, though, this heterodoxy overlies a profound doxic and orthodox basis. This is evident in Margaret and Ruth's use of doxic notions of parenthood and familism. It is important for both that their families of origin did, eventually, accept their arrangement. Ruth's parents had once attended a function for grandparents at Michelle's school. Margaret's parents had also accepted Ruth's parental role. The importance placed on the acceptance of the other partner by both women's families of origin, and the sense of relief that this arrangement was, in fact, accepted, and that Michelle was accepted by Ruth's family, all resemble the family politics surrounding the formation of a blended family.

More profoundly, the societal experience of maternity and the construction of maternity are being strongly reinforced within this heterodox arrangement. This doxic articulation of parenthood expresses some fundamental aspects of the affective and intellective experience of parenthood. I mentioned above Ruth's quantification of parenthood according to which she can claim a quarter of the child, and Margaret can claim half. This is more than a mathematical manifestation of pop developmental psychology. It is also an expression of the culturally constituted and experientially validated significance of 'biological' parenthood. This is reinforced in the very dynamics of the relationship. Thus Margaret – responsible for half the child – enjoys greater authority than Ruth who lays claim to a quarter only. Margaret remains the ultimate authority over Michelle. She is the one who retains exclusive care and control rights. And if the arrangement were to collapse, she would be the one to be left with Michelle. Both women acknowledge that if somebody would need to give up her career to look after Michelle if she were to become severely ill or incapacitated, it would be Margaret who would do so. (Indeed, Ruth's family of origin were at first concerned at such possible outcomes and the hurt it might cause to Ruth, but they became more confident as time passed by.) Margaret – being the 'biological' mother – retains the ultimate responsibility for Michelle. Also in terms of the division of time between the two homes, Michelle spends more time at Margaret's home. Although Ruth attends school events and activities of the Parents' and Citizens' Association events if they interest her at the time, Margaret is the one normally mostly involved in these affairs. In essence, Ruth's rights in Michelle do not in any way reduce Margaret's supreme rights and responsibilities which are grounded in her being the 'natural' mother.

Once identified as parents in whatever quantifiable capacity, the implications are again articulated in doxic ways. Ruth, for example, insisted that 'if you're going to have a child, if you produce a child, you have a responsibility you cannot ignore. If you choose to get involved [as she did] you acquire a responsibility you cannot ignore.' The responsibility towards the child is especially important in the period before it can look after itself. An important aspect in the acceptance of Ruth and Margaret's arrangement was the legitimation of Ruth's discharge of parental obligations, such as attending with Michelle school birthday parties and similar events which are designed for children and their parents. Here, again, the heterodoxy of Ruth carrying out parental roles is only enabled by reinforcing the doxic relationship of responsibility that parents, as carers, have towards children.

The very models and concepts the women use to account for their relationship carry within them the doxic basis of this heterodoxy. Ruth compared their arrangement to the situation which prevails with divorced families in which children have two homes between which they rotate, only in this case the parents had never been married and never split up. As such, maternity and parenthood are confirmed. The ultimate responsibility of the producers of children for the welfare of the children is upheld. Also, the desire of the un-partnered Ruth to partake in the parental experience further conforms to a (highly gendered) experience of adulthood which stresses the joys of parenting, the satisfaction derived from caring for a helpless and dependant young person. Another set of doxic relations which are reinforced in this double-familial situation is the overlap between the family boundary and co-residence. Michelle's belonging to two families, as it were, is manifested in her permanent residence in two households. In both women's homes she had her own room. The fact that the two adult women are not familially linked to one another is spatially reflected in their separate residences.

This doxa notwithstanding, this arrangement is obviously highly heterodox. But it is precisely because theirs was not a 'type' of family, that Margaret, Ruth and Michelle's arrangement did not become a full-blown heterodox challenge and remained just that – Margaret, Ruth and Michelle's arrangement. Thus, even people who knew them personally, and who were familiar with their arrangement, did not spontaneously mention them as an example of changes in the family. I will return to this point below.

The marginalization of this specific arrangement was helped by the fact that both adults occupy an unusual position within the Novocastrian social space. Margaret, being an artist, and somewhat bohemian, might be expected to be a bit different. Ruth had lived in Newcastle since infancy but, her father being a scientist with BHP, she had always been consciously different from the people around her. When asked about class differences she denied they existed as such, but added quickly that her family was different from other families around in their philosophy and style. For one, they were staunchly atheistic. At school she was therefore exempt from attending Scripture classes. Her family also stressed education and sciences. Both her parents were professionals in full-time paid employment, her mother being a psychologist with the local hospital. Ruth remembers eating out a lot as a child, another difference from most of her peers around her. Ruth had wanted to be a scientist since she was very young, which was the reason she chose to study mathematics. But these differences amount precisely to class differences in style, although significantly it was experienced as individual idiosyncrasy by Ruth herself. The fact that both women could easily be classed as different helped their own arrangement to be perceived as part of their own idiosyncrasies, rather than an innovation or an alternative to the normal scheme of things.

The Symbolic Politics of Family Heterodoxy

Classifying practices or elements of practice as doxa, orthodoxy, or heterodoxy is an analytic step that should assist in evaluating the state of play in a continuously evolving field of practice – the universe of family practice at the present instance. This cultural universe is a product of the practice of many social agents over time. It is dynamic. In the process of historical evolution, orthodoxy can become heterodoxy and vice versa. Doxic elements of practice can be forced into full view as orthodoxies, and orthodoxies can become entrenched as natural and taken-for-granted, that is, they can become doxa.

Based on the previous chapter and this, the cultural universe of family types can be described as follows:

1. The nuclear family is the basic-level family, the most cognitively simple gestalt, the unmarked construct, the default notion of the family.

2. Different familial arrangements combine to form a graded category. Gradation, or extent of centrality, means that some variants are more typical and less idiosyncratic than others. In other words, the different variants can be ordered according to their relative deviation from the prototype – the central category – in this universe. The realized category of the family forms the prototype that defines this universe.

3. The different family arrangements form a universe with a radial structure (cf. Lakoff and Johnson 1980; Lakoff 1987, especially 91 ff.). The variants do not have any substantive characteristic in common throughout the universe of family structures. What makes them all family is the fact that they resemble, albeit in different way, the central category of the family – the prototype. Thus we can conceive of the universe of family arrangements as a set of different practices which are organized around the prototype of the family, and linked to it in their various idiosyncratic ways. Of course, the extent to which variants approach the central prototype is an empirical question regarding the cultural construction of these variants.

This is the snapshot of the field of practice. But is it possible to use this snapshot to identify some of the dynamics of historical evolution which underlie it?

In previous chapters some transformations to the field of family practices were identified. These appeared to be mostly a response to changes in the political economy. But more remarkable than the changes was the apparent continuity in the universe of family practices. Historical studies now suggest that the prototypical family structure in Northern and Western European families has been stable for well over a millennium. What is it about this prototypical family that makes it so resilient to change? Or, which amounts to the same thing, what hinders the radical power of alternative practices? This and the next few chapters will suggest some answers to these questions.

A close look at the snapshot of Novocastrian family practices may point at some of the conservative dynamics of the universe of family practices. First, there is the irony of heterodoxy.

In order to enter the universe of family practices, a practice must be recognizable as a family practice. It is some form of resemblance to the realized category of the family which constitutes a practice as a family practice. A practice which lacks any meaningful similarity to the realized category of the family would simply not enter the cognitive universe of family practices.

This necessary similarity is part of the irony that, in order to qualify as a challenge to the orthodox form of family, a heterodoxy must share some substantial aspects with the prototypical family, and consequently reinforce these aspects. Moreover, the more powerful the challenge of a heterodox practice, the more it would share with the orthodoxy of the prototypical family. In other words, the most viable alternative practices, and the most likely to spread and become accepted, are those that deviate the least from dominant practices. The more radical its alterity, the less likely is a heterodox practice to become established orthodoxy.

But this irony of heterodoxy is not the only conservative dynamic that supports the status quo. Often, heterodox pulls can be fragmented and contradictory, thereby attenuating pressures towards change. Contradictory heterodox pulls may reflect, and become embroiled, in broad social divisions. Shortly I will explore one such example, where the fragmentation in social structure militates against the emergence of an explicit, coherent and powerful heterodox challenge.

But the social dynamics which underlie the changes at the cultural level have other influences too. In order to enter the field of possible alternatives, a practice must be named and made to exist. The most powerful way a heterodox practice can be stifled is by not being recognized and nominated as a practice. Through their cultural power, social elites act as gatekeepers, as it were, thereby further restricting the scope of the cultural politics of family practices. One critical area where the cultural power of the social elite becomes visible is their capacity to constitute their own partial views of the field and its alternatives as the exclusive set of impartial views. Below I will exemplify how critical it is for a practice to be recognized as such by the elites in order to become a viable alternative practice in the universe of family practices.

Related to this containment of the radical effect of heterodox practices is another form of containment, the tagging of practices as alien or foreign; in other words, as belonging to a different arena, and therefore excluded from the familiar universe of practices.

Different Heterodoxies Pull in Different Directions

The dilemma of the feminist opposition to the division of labour between men and women is an example of orthodox elements which are challenged from different heterodox quarters, but seem to survive by virtue of the conflicting positions of the heterodox challenges. The reality of the 'traditional family' which feminist critics seek to destabilize is that in which men are the main breadwinners and have the main or exclusive access to economic capital. Women's activity is centred around the home and is devalued by the structure of capitalist production.

This state of affairs is being challenged from two conflicting angles. One is that which sees the division of labour between men and women as the root of women's oppression in advanced capitalist society. People who follow this line of reasoning argue that housework is stupid, boring, unsatisfying and oppressive (e.g. Bittman and Pixley 1997; Baxter 1993; Dempsey 1997b). This line of argumentation seeks liberation for women through participation in the paid labour market. This position shares with the 'traditional' political economy of family the devaluation of homemaking and housewifery.

This position is, typically, class-specific and common in those segments of society where work is associated with notions of a career and self-actualization. By contrast, to large segments of the working class, work is an unpleasant experience, engaged in out of necessity, with very little in the way of self-fulfilment (Donaldson 1991, chapter 1). Furthermore, the practice of some classes of relegating household chores to members of other classes, mostly women, through the labour market, largely escapes the critical gaze of the 'liberation through labour' camp (but see Bittman et al. 1999).

An alternative position, more common among my working-class informants, accepts the broad outline of the gendered division of labour. It is rather the differential value of women's work vs. men's work which is seen as unfair to women. This ideology reinforces the gender stereotyping of work, and thereby contributes to the maintenance of gender stereotypes in the broader division of labour. This view is expressed, among others, in a preference (both articulated and enacted) of women for a limited involvement in the labour market (e.g. Baxter 2000; Baxter and Western 1998; and see chapter 3).

The merits of each position as such, and the question of whether they are by necessity mutually exclusive, are outside the scope of this analysis. For the purposes of the current discussion it should be pointed out that these two opposing strategies of women's liberation are, to a point, mutually antagonistic in the practice they engender. The latter seeks to support women in their domestic roles, the former seeks to extricate women from these roles. The difference in the class location from which these different perspectives are espoused turns the contradiction into a symbolic class conflict.

The different strategies women adopt – integration into the labour market vs. specialization in homemaking – may come to stand in direct conflict with each other. The women who pursue the one may, in fact, interfere with the strategy of those who pursue the other. This conflict greatly reduces the potential push for change in dominant practices.

For an example of how the antagonism of these two strategies manifests itself in practice one may reformulate the argument of P. England and B.S. Kilbourne who tried to model marital relationships in economistic terms. England and Kilbourne argue, among the rest, that men and women tend to make different types of investment in marriage. Men invest in their career and education. These investments are easily transferable to other marriages. Women, in focusing on children and relationships within the family (e.g. with in-laws) at the expense of promoting their careers, make relationship-specific investments which are not easily transferred to other marriages. As a result, a woman's value on the marriage market is reduced compared with that of her male partner, placing her in the dependent and weaker bargaining position in the family, and him at a position of great advantage (England and Kilbourne 1990; cited by Bittman and Pixley 1997).

This is a typical argument in favour of liberating women through involving them in the labour market. As it stands, though, it is flawed. It misconstrues both the motivation of practice and its socioeconomic ramifications. With some modifications, however, it can serve to highlight the set of political economic rewards which affect practice, although not necessarily in the way England and Kilbourne had intended. Given the virtually exclusively heterosexual nature of the marriage market, women do not compete with their ex-partners for mates. Rather, women compete with other women, and men with other men. Therefore, to understand how investments of spouses affect their position in the marriage market, spouses should not be compared with one another. Rather, a woman's investment should be compared with the investment made by other women, and the man's investment with that made by other men. It is quite possible for a man to invest exclusively in his career, but still see the value of his assets on the marriage market drop because of the more efficient investments of other males, while at the same time his wife might invest moderately, and still improve her position by keeping ahead of the average returns on women's investments on the market. In other words, the marriage market pits primarily men against men, and women against women.

It follows, then, that men who under-invest in their careers will suffer a great set-back in their relative ranking in the male hierarchy. This might help explain the behaviour of some men in the labour market, such as taking on massive amounts of overtime work. More significantly for the issue at hand, though, women who make extensive investments in their own career and other transferable assets devalue the transferable assets of all other women on the marriage market as the latter are pushed further down the female hierarchy by the former. The stakes here are even higher than intra-gender competition on the marriage market. The increased earnings involved in double-income family arrangements allows double-income families to invest more economic capital in their children, that is, in social reproduction. In other words, the higher the earnings of some women, the more devalued would be the assets of the offspring of other women. The same holds true for men, of course.

Significantly, career-investment opportunities for either males or females are not equally distributed across society, but rather favour the dominant classes and ensure a diminished return to working-class women for participation in the paid workforce, to the point where the financial costs of participation in the labour market outweigh the possible gains. In other words, the strategy of greater integration into the labour market disproportionately benefits the women who are better positioned to exploit this market, at the expense of women whose labour-market investment potential are low-yield. In essence, then, some women's strategy of full employment pits them against other women, so that feminist strategies of the dominant class may, in fact, hurt the interests of dominated-class women.

It is probably in light of this challenge that among my informants some women who had no careers felt threatened and challenged by bourgeois feminists and by career women. When I left for 'the field', I had just read Janeen Baxter's 1993 book, *Work at Home: The Domestic Division of Labour* (Baxter 1993). To my surprise, I found myself embroiled in a symbolic class struggle when during a conversation with a close informant I quoted a passage from this book and raised with her the prospects of her oppression. Perceiving (more so than I did at the time) the symbolic class aggression in the implicit criticism of her lifestyle, she responded to my provocation quite angrily. The friendly tones transformed somewhat as my interlocutor embarked on a tirade against 'the feminists'. She followed by stating that she thought that if a woman chose to have a career, she should have the same opportunities as men, but if a woman chooses to stay home and look after the children, she should have the right to do so. (At the time my interviewee was home after having her second child. She resisted her partner's pressure to go back to work, and intended to stay out of the labour market for a few years yet, dedicating herself to her children.) The point should therefore be made that this woman had the opportunity to return to paid employment. Her decision not to was not forced upon her by external coercion, and her statements were not an attempt to rationalize an externally imposed inferior position.

Rather, the best way to interpret this reaction is as a conflict of values surrounding the different experiences of femininity in different classes, and as an expression of the inequality in the distribution of economic opportunities across society. Significantly, quite a few women I spoke with felt pushed against their will into the labour market. In individual interviews, in discussions and in focus groups, women generally advocated a pragmatic approach combining the right to be a homemaker with equal employment opportunities. Like the interviewee just cited, they said they thought that a woman should be allowed to choose if she wanted to participate in the workforce. If she chooses to participate in the paid workforce, she should be treated in the same way as men. If she prefers to stay at home with the kids, though, she should not be disadvantaged either. In practice they gravitated towards the latter. Many said they liked their jobs, but preferred to be the main carers for children and be those who stayed at home. In general, the women who worked full time accounted for their full-time employment in terms of economic necessity, and not in terms of personal fulfilment. Self-actualization, or liberation, through labour was a contradiction in terms in blue-collar, and most of white-collar Newcastle.

All these rationalist calculations are predicated upon a gendered political economy of motivation and desire. It does not explain why and how some socioeconomic roles are feminine and others masculine. Rather, the logic of interest calculations only makes sense because some roles are feminine and others masculine. To understand the gendered structure of the political economy one needs to delve deeper into the ways gendered subjectivities are lived. These critical themes will be pursued in chapters 7 and 8 below.

In any event, this class-based conflict of the feminist critique of the division of labour and its consequences has the effect of fragmenting potential challenges to the status quo, and playing the challenging forces against one another. Tax incentives for women to join the workforce were experienced as unfair by those who did not wish to take up the 'opportunities' the political economy was 'offering' them. Two of my informants blamed feminists for such tax policies which they felt had greatly disadvantaged them. By challenging the status quo from two opposing perspectives, the effect of such heterodoxies is greatly diminished. But this situation in which heterodox gender critiques pull in different directions and ultimately fix orthodoxy is only part of the secret of the longevity of the status quo.

The Power to Define Agendas, Types and Non-Types

A critical manifestation of the domination of the dominant class is its ability to impose its interests, agendas and concerns by making them appear as the general concerns and interests across society. Working-class Novocastrians, for instance, believed that the Australian family was undergoing a profound process of change, and that new forms of family were emerging in Australia. In this they were echoing the concerns of large segments of the cultural elites, including politicians, academics, bureaucrats and journalists. It was then, and still is, one of the major preoccupations of the mass media.

Novocastrians readily identified homosexual families and single-parent families as the main new forms of family, again in line with the public agenda as set by the media. This is interesting because very few, if any, of those I questioned knew homosexual families first-hand. (In fact, the incidence of such arrangements is very low – see chapter 3). At the time the media were preoccupied with the homosexual family, and more generally with the status of homosexuals and homosexuality (e.g. Horin 1995).

Also, the concern with single-parent families should not be taken at face value. My informants could not point to a significant increase in the phenomenon of single-parent families in their familiar social environment. In fact, Novocastrians over 60 years old that I spoke with said that they did not really think there was a great deal of change in single-parent families, and that such families were quite common in their childhood, no less than in the 1990s. The figures I cited in chapter 3 also demonstrate that single-parenthood is not at historic record levels. The fact that this family type was identified as being unprecedented in magnitude or significance clearly reflected the preoccupation of the mass media at the time.

While arrangements like homosexual couples and single-parent families have been constituted as family types, not all heterodoxies enjoy this status. Ruth and Margaret's arrangement is indeed a radical one which would challenge many of the basic doxic tenets of the realized category of the nuclear family. Their arrangement is much more heterodox than the other two, yet its potential challenge is contained in a very elementary way. People who were familiar with this arrangement invariably saw it as unique, as something which attests to the idiosyncrasy of the persons involved as well as to the uniqueness of their situation at the time. Remarkably, those who were acquainted with this arrangement, and not with specific homosexual families, still recognized homosexual families as an alternative form of family arrangement, but not Margaret's and Ruth's arrangement. Moreover, Margaret and Ruth themselves thought of their arrangement as essentially an idiosyncratic adaptation of theirs, rather than a systemically significant event. So long as it remained experienced as an ad hoc situation, and was not elevated to the status of a 'type', its heterodox efficacy would remain negligible, and the potential relevance of this arrangement to the question of what is a family would remain obscure.

The first point that this raises is that to understand why some heterodox variants are picked up by the cultural agenda setters, and not others, we need to focus on shifts in the cultural elites. (Earlier, in chapter 3, I speculated about some of the concerns of the cultural elites – including academics and journalists – which predispose them to identify changes, shifts and crises in the family.) In other words, the inherent nature of particular heterodox practices, or shifts in their statistical distribution, cannot, in and of themselves, account for their recognition as heterodox types. Rather, it is the interaction between their inherent nature and distribution on the one hand, and the predispositions of the cultural elites on the other, which explains the timing and manner of the emergence of particular practices as recognizable heterodox types.

More generally, though, this situation reflects the symbolic power differential between Novocastrians, and the makers of national agendas. The Novocastrians who knew Ruth and Margaret were neither predisposed nor empowered to recognize, name and typify alternative family types. It is the political power to recognize individual arrangements as a type, or as a phenomenon, which transforms ad hoc arrangements into recognizable alternative arrangements. This power is concentrated very much in the hands of segments of the bureaucratic and intellectual elites (e.g. ABS, AIFS, government departments that administer social services, media) who are entrusted with the power and authority to identify social phenomena and to judge them. So long as it remains unrecognized in the national agenda, the nuclear family would be safe from Ruth and Margaret's challenge, even in the two women's own eyes. Their arrangement would remain just that, their arrangement. Unnamed, invisible and non-existent. A still-born heterodox challenge.

Tagging Heterodoxies

There are other means by which heterodox challenges become contained. Some alternative arrangements are stigmatized by association with marginalized or otherwise distinct social categories, turning an attachment to normalcy as an expression or embodiment of social identity. At a certain stage I asked Clifford about three-generational households. He and his wife, Hildred, were both in full-time paid employment. At the time they were expecting their second child. The cost of childcare was a major concern with them, and one way they reduced incidental childcare costs was by relying on Hildred's mother or Hildred's single sister. Clifford himself, by his own admission, was getting on very well with his mother-in-law. This was independently reiterated by his wife. Why, then, I asked him, not have a three-generational household, thereby enabling both parents to participate in the workforce and alleviating child-care concerns? Clifford's response was glib: 'The "Europeans" have large families like that. We don't.' He proceeded to describe the difficulties involved in the relationship between adults and their parents, stemming from the incommensurability of relationships between adults on the one hand and those between parents and offspring on the other.

Here I would like to focus on the laconic comment regarding the 'Europeans' in response to my question. It was probably biased by our conversation, in which we had also discussed the way things are done in other parts of the world, although we did not focus specifically on 'Europeans'. Still, it was the kind of statement in which the obvious gets mentioned, is put on the record, and requires no further elaboration in its own right. They do it. We do not. That is the way things are. Now all that remains is to either explain why, or work out the advantages or disadvantages of both ways. To the extent that Clifford needed a moment's pause for thought before this matter-of-fact statement, it was to determine how best to describe the groups to which he referred as 'European', in this context a euphemism for 'wog' or 'dago' – people from southern Europe, the Balkans and the Middle East. What was remarkable was the fact that by being tagged with being 'European', this specific mode of doing things no longer needed to be considered as a viable alternative to the way things were done. *We* – that is 'True-Blue' Aussies (that is, Anglo/Celtic Australians) – just don't do it that way. And there was nothing more to it. That one sentence summed it all up.

Similarly, another person I spoke with said she wished she had had a 'wog wedding', with all the many distant relatives dancing and having fun, rather than the kind of wedding she had in fact had, in which formally dressed guests were seated around dinner tables in a well-organized fashion and speeches were made in a very sedate and respectable manner. But her wish for a wog wedding was not the kind of wish for something she wanted to happen to her. It was more along the lines of 'there is something more authentic/charming/special about the way *they* do things, alas I am not they, and we do things differently'. At no time during the process of preparing her wedding (which had taken place a few years before my fieldwork), was the possibility of a 'wog wedding' ever brought up. They were not wogs. Therefore, they did not have a wog wedding.

These examples underscore the way practice is implicitly constructed by identity at the same time that it constructs it. Things are done a certain way, and not another, because of who we are, but who and what we are is as much determined by what we do. 'We' have 'respectable' and 'composed' weddings, and stick to nuclear family household arrangements because 'we' are 'True-Blue Aussies'. At one and the same time such actions show that 'True-Blue Aussies' are composed and civilized people, and have certain loyalties and relationships.

It is in light of this that wishes, like my informant's for a 'wog wedding', should be interpreted, as should other statements made by various informants concerning the superior family relations in 'other cultures' or the greater authenticity of past generations. The speakers were making observations about what made them, as part of an imagined group, different from other such groups. This was often done in the spirit of respect and multiculturalism, a spirit which is as much a product of the specific situation of the ethnographic interview conducted by an 'ethnic' anthropologist, as it was a reflection of the current mood. Still, whatever respect for others such statements might imply, or whatever genuine or otherwise self-deprecation might be involved, these statements do not reflect an intention to do things differently. Rather, they are statements about the nature of groups and the character of their members. As such they provide a rationalization, rooted in pop psychology and experiences of 'cultural' difference, for the arbitrary distribution of social practices among groups, or at least for the perceived distribution of social practices among groups. But it does not challenge those patterns of distribution.

The identification of particular practices with specific groups serves to reduce the power of the heterodoxies which become associated with such groups; and at one and the same time serves to marginalize the groups which are defined by their adherence to heterodoxy. By the same token, once heterodox practices became associated with marginalized groups, their corresponding orthodox alternatives may come to define the mainstream, and thereby become entrenched. This is yet another dynamic which militates against radical change in the process of historical evolution.

It is perhaps such a dynamic that also facilitates the acceptance of the homosexual family as legitimate by so many of my interviewees. It is seen, ultimately, not as a chosen lifestyle so much as the enactment of family in a clearly demarcated social group, namely homosexuals. If people who were not identified, and did not identify themselves, as homosexuals were to form such unions, the subversive potential of the homosexual family would no doubt have been substantially magnified making it much more subversive, both politically and culturally.

Summary and Conclusions

This chapter has focused on various alternative practices to the prototypical nuclear family in order to further understand the nuclear-family household form and its historical stability.

The prototypical family, by virtue of its status as a realized category, embodies criteria by which practices must be defined in order to qualify as family heterodoxies. That which heterodoxies share with the prototypical family is the doxic basis of family practice. Furthermore, heterodox practices, even as they bring to the fore various aspects of the prototypical practice, and turn much doxa into heterodoxy, do not necessarily destabilize the dominant practice. Various dynamics, such as the contradictory pulls of different heterodoxies, may in fact serve so as to further entrench dominant practice.

The limitations of heterodox practices like those I have described above go some way towards accounting for the historical inertia of the family. They also highlight that continuity and change are not mutually exclusive. In fact, change is always necessarily partial, and dynamics of change are at one and the same time dynamics of stasis. Thus, for example, the homosexual family is one heterodoxy which has elevated much that was doxa into the realm of visible orthodoxy, and has destabilized much of the orthodoxy of family practice. However, precisely as it was doing so, it was also reinforcing and further cementing other elements of doxa. The situation is similar with other heterodoxies that were discussed above, such as Margaret, Ruth and Michelle's arrangement.

But the inherent limitations of heterodoxy are, of course, only part of the explanation of historical inertia. The fact that the nuclear family has existed for so long is reflected in the embeddedness of the family in entire webs of meanings and sets of social relations. Intuitively, it makes sense that such an embeddedness would support the reproduction of the family throughout the generations, and militate against radical shifts. This is so because presumably the other social relations continuously reinforce the cultural base they share with the family.

All this does not mean that radical historical change is not possible, of course. Although such evolutionary faultlines are rare, both their paucity and the conditions for their occurrence need to be elaborated.

The next few chapters further situate the family within the complex overlapping webs of meaning and signification which make up the lived world. Specifically, the discussion will focus on broader notions of kinship, relatedness and person; on gender; and on political economy. The next chapter focuses on personhood, self and relatedness.

Chapter 6

Structural Aspects of Kinship

The last two chapters focused on the nuclear family that lies at the core of my informants' kinship system culturally, normatively and behaviourally. But there is more to kinship than family, and in the next few chapters the horizon of the analysis will be broadened to include the kinship system at large, within which the nuclear family – family in the narrow sense – is nestled. The discussion will be extended to include the system of kinship terminology, associated practices, and the worldview they embody. Specifically, I will focus on the distinctions and categorization that are implicit in the kinship system and structure it at the very same time as they are being reinforced by it.

Filiation and Kindred, the Building Blocks of Novocastrian Kinship

Roger Keesing defined descent as 'A relationship defined by connection to an ancestor (or ancestress) through a culturally recognized sequence of parent–child links (from father to son to son's son = patrilineal descent, from mother to daughter to daughter's daughter = matrilineal descent)'. This stands in contrast with filiation which is a 'Relationship to or through one's father and one's mother, or the basing of rights on this relationship' (Keesing 1975, 148).

As with other contemporary Northern and Western European kinship systems, descent does not appear to be a meaningful principle of ordering the world in Newcastle. Rather, filiation is the essence of relatedness.

Links of filiation are derived from the model of reproduction that constructs the nuclear family as a group of people whose relatedness is unmediated, 'by blood' that is. As one woman commented about her family of origin, 'We're a pretty close family. I mean, we might hate each other's guts, [but] we're still a pretty close family, you know, the blood ties are pretty tight.' The relationships within the family are not voluntary so much as obligatory. But this obligation is one which is actively sought after and reconstituted as voluntary. Love is the label affixed to this voluntarily sought-after obligation. Extended kin are related through chains of people who are themselves fellow members of single nuclear families, and are therefore essentially linked in an unmediated fashion.

The rationale for the relatedness of extended kin is their common consanguineal relationship to common ancestors or intermediate collaterals.[1] Moreover, siblings are prototypically related by virtue of their descent from a common parent or parents; and spouses become securely related – a family in the full sense of the word – by virtue of their common consanguineal link to their offspring. Consequently, effective kinship relationships which transcend the boundaries of the nuclear family are mediated through a succession of filial links. Of course, close contacts between relatives, such as grandchildren and grandparents, cousins and so forth, may create personal relationships beyond the kinship basis of these relationships.

Depending on the context, the kindred members – families of origin, uncles, aunts, cousins, grandparents – may also be recognized as family. This, however, does not negate the argument for a clear boundary around the nuclear family. Relatives who are included in one's extended kin network are deemed to be related by virtue of being primary kin of primary kin, that is, having been within the nuclear family of members of one's own past or present nuclear family. Thus one is related to one's grandmother because she is one's mother's mother. Conflict between granddaughter and grandmother would be felt by the woman in between, the connecting link, whose allegiances might be challenged.

The organizing principles of practice – normally both ubiquitous and invisible – make themselves visible when adjustments need to be made in novel or unusual situations. When Lucy was unexpectedly deserted by Alfred (following a few extramarital affairs on his part, one of which culminated in pregnancy) such a situation emerged. Her family of origin lived in Darwin, and she suddenly found herself on her own in Newcastle, destitute with an infant. Following the separation she stayed with Alfred's parents for a few months. It was uncomfortable but she could not afford not to. Once she had time to make some alternative arrangements, Lucy set out on her own. She re-partnered a few years later. Alfred's parents continued to maintain a relationship with Max, their grandson, even though Alfred had no interest in maintaining any contact. What is important for the matter at hand is that once Lucy moved out, Alfred's parents did not provide any further meaningful support to the household, nor were they expected to. Moreover, Alfred's parents' interest lay primarily with Max, and their contact with Lucy was focused on managing their access to him. While Max might go over and stay with them for occasional weekends, Lucy did not have much to do with them. This situation shows the remarkable significance of filiation in connecting extended kin. Alfred was the connecting link, and his renunciation of the relationship with Lucy and Max threatened the latter two's relationship with his parents. Moreover, quite clearly the grandparents were more interested in Max – direct descendent and therefore directly consanguineally related – than in Lucy who is a collateral and

---

[1] By collateral I mean a consanguine who is neither a direct ascendant nor a descendant (or, as Keesing put it, 'The siblings of lineal relatives (parents, grandparents) and their descendants' – Keesing 1975, 148).

whose blood connection is indirect and mediated through Max. Furthermore, when the story was related to me, the lack of contact between Lucy's household and Alfred's parents was seen as self-explanatory, and was not elaborated on spontaneously. The only matters which received spontaneous elaboration from Lucy and others were the circumstances surrounding her residence at Alfred's parents' place immediately after her marriage broke down, the continued contact between Alfred's parents and Max, and the lack of any contact between Alfred and Max. These were the remarkable aspects of the story that required further explanation: either instances in which contact was maintained without an intermediary who is a member in both nuclear families, or instances in which the contact between erstwhile members of the same nuclear family (Alfred and Max) was severed.

In other instances, the father's desertion of the family effectively meant the severance of contact with grandparents. Thus, Michelle, the young daughter of Margaret and Ruth, had no contact with her father's parents. Nor did Phyllis's daughter, Camilla, who also had no contact with her father.

More generally, in focus groups women pointed out that once they had children, their position of power vis-à-vis their mothers and mothers-in-law improved because they became the link between grandparents and grandchildren. They acted as gatekeepers.

Similarly, extended kin networks which might get together for events such as Christmas during the life of the apical ancestors very often cease this practice once the connecting ancestors are dead. This marks the bifurcation of one extended family into two families once the connecting filial link is effectively terminated.

In a different situation, an informant who sought a place to stay for a short while in another city where he had relatives, asked his mother to get in touch with her brother (his uncle) to see if he could stay with them. The rationale was that the uncle and nephew were not very close, but the mother, the uncle's sibling, was closer and could more comfortably ask for favours. That informant had a right to expect hospitality by virtue of the mere fact of being the son of the uncle's sister. There were other instances too when intervening relatives were mobilized to facilitate interaction between relatives, most commonly parents between grandchildren and grandparents.

In all of these instances the rationale according to which the intermediate genealogical link mediates the relationship between extended kin was taken for granted. Not a single informant saw it necessary to explain why this should be so. These practices reflect an ideological construction of relatedness.

In short, the initiation and creation of effective kin relationships are based on filiation, which is the ideological rationale for inclusion of persons in the extended family. Novocastrian kinship is kindred-based; that is, it is egocentric – relatives are included in one's list of kin because of their relationship to ego rather than because of their descent from some common ancestor.[2] This was graphically illustrated when people were charting their family trees: they would normally start with their generation or their parents, and move up and out from there through a series of filial links. In a sense that notion of a family tree does produce a figure of a tree, seeing that one starts with ego and branches out upwards.

Kindred, however, functioned as a social category, not as a social group with a clear internal organization and common goals (cf. Freeman 1961, 202 ff.). While membership in kindred formed a basis for cooperation and collaboration between people on an ad hoc basis, the only enduring, effective kin-based social group remained the family. The range of kindreds among my informants was typical of British and other Northern and Western European metropolitan and settler societies (Freeman 1961, 207), where people could identify and normally had some contact with first cousins, many of them with second cousins, and hardly any with third cousins. As a matter of preference, kindreds were normally exogamous (cf. Freeman 1961, 207–209). I came across only one married couple of first cousins in the field. It was a fortuitous discovery during an interview with Rodney, a youth organizer, about issues facing young people in Newcastle. When I presented my research topic, we briefly discussed his family. He described his extended family as being 'very close,' and then added, 'Well, I'm actually married to my cousin, so the extended family, we are very close, on both sides of the family.' 'There are places where it's actually a common practice to marry your cousin,' I commented. 'That's right,' he replied, 'and in other places it's against the law. Yeah.' 'It does make it hard to say nasty things about your in-laws to your parents,' I said. 'Yeah,' he laughed. He said that where this caused some difficulty was with his kids.

> It does bring up all sorts of things, and also I've been in trouble with the school because they [his kids] have only got three sets of great-grandparents and everybody else has four sets of great-grandparents, so you know, they say your family tree is wrong. It shouldn't be like that.

I should stress that Rodney and his cousin wife are not members of an ethnic minority, but rather Australian-born, Anglo-Celts (of mostly Celtic ancestry) from a comfortable, white-collar, working-class background. They did not participate in my research as informants, and I am unable to relate their story in further detail.

In general, it was considered undesirable to marry one's cousins, and unacceptable (indeed illegal) to marry one's nieces, nephews, uncles, aunts and closer relatives.

---

[2] Kindred was defined by Keesing as 'A social group or category consisting of an individual's circle of relatives, or that range of a person's relatives accorded special cultural recognition' (Keesing 1975, 150).

Genealogies and Models of Relatedness

When interviewing my informants about their genealogies I usually used the terms 'relatives', 'extended family' or 'family tree' to describe what I was interested in. It was through the use of these terms that I found it easiest to convey to my informants my notion of genealogy. Among my informants, such information was clearly gendered cultural capital. It was invariably the domain of women. Men could answer most of the questions on relatives, but would refer to women for confirmation of their statements, as well as for details regarding the distant relationships which were not in practical use. Women were the acknowledged experts on these matters, and the ultimate repository of kinship knowledge. Women were also generally more interested in such matters than men. They were the ones who seemed to keep track of relatives and hold the information regarding distant relatives. This is part of a much broader total division of labour between the genders, which assigns social skills and social authority to women.

The one exception was a long-divorced man in his seventies who had been keeping an alleged family tree going back to Tory Island. His fantastic stories, including those of a young female cousin he had on Tory who was destined to marry him, and various others, were taken by all those who knew him as pipedreams. At any rate, he was abnormal, and was perceived and categorized as such by the people who knew him. Otherwise, in my experience, relatedness and kinship knowledge were overwhelmingly a feminine concern.

Genealogies and family trees contained knowledge that was used in normal daily life for various purposes. One was to trace the relationship between the living individuals who comprise the extended kin. This information was used in very specific situations in which decisions regarding the extended kin needed to be made. Typically, these included Christmas-card lists and invitations to special events (such as annual events for people who trace their descent to a common extant ancestor – Christmas day gatherings; or irregular events like weddings which might require a broader distribution of invitations).

Since the 1970s, with a wave of patriotism and Australian nationalism, it has become fashionable among Anglo-Celts to find convict ancestors or to trace back ancestry to a specific location in the British Isles. However, my informants had never themselves engaged in a prolonged and systematic search for their ancestry, and most of the information they gave me was based on their own first-hand knowledge and on family traditions, usually passed down the generations, typically from mother/mother-in-law to daughter/daughter-in-law. It is quite possible that systematic searches for one's ancestry are more common in other social environs such as the dominant class.

Questioning my informants about their genealogy – 'family tree' or 'extended family' – I had little trouble getting across what information I wanted. More than Evans Pritchard and his Nuer informants, both my informants and I shared the notions of what a family tree was, and what it should look like. The great agreement of doxic experiences of kinship and family made these interviews more likely to elicit the data requested, and less likely to illuminate the nature of these data. Still, with a measure of reflexivity it is possible to make explicit some of the underlying implicit assumptions in the constructions of family trees.

Family trees among my informants were constructed upwards, but read downwards. This demonstrates a two-phased operation of kinship reckoning – one is tracing relatedness, a process beginning with ego and connecting people through the shortest possible genealogical link. The other is accounting for relatedness, which is prototypically based on common ancestry (and, of course, extendable as necessary by circumstances e.g. to adopted relatives).

An interesting inversion is already implicit in the contradiction between a family tree – the concept – and the graphical presentation of families. Trees are rooted in the ground and grow upward. Still, when showing the movement along generations the temporal progression is downwards, the earlier relations being placed at the top of the page, their direct descendants having been placed immediately below them, and collateral relatives to their side. (This can be contrasted, for example, with the Rotinese practice of reading genealogical trees upwards rather than downwards – see Fox 1988.) As the terms themselves suggest, this two-dimensional spatial arrangement of relatives tallies with the anthropological common sense (for a description of the emergence of the family tree as an organizing principle in Europe, see Fox 1988; and Bouquet 1996).

Thus, even though once constructed, one's roots (a term used, among the rest, to refer to ancestry) are at the top of the page, the process of constructing the family tree on the page proceeds very much in line with the metaphor of tree from bottom to top, normally starting from ego, and then moving to ascendants and collaterals they link to. In fact, the stress on lineality at the expense of collateral relations (which is in line with the significance of reproduction and procreation as the idiom which organizes kinship) will produce a tree-like diagram, in which ego resembles a trunk, that combines the branches above the ground and the roots below the ground surface.

Normally the extension backwards in time (upwards on the page) is comparatively shallow. Rarely did my informants trace family trees further back than the relatives who were part of the living memory of their own parents, with the exception of particular relatives who needed to be remembered for particular purposes. Such ancient ancestors might still be remembered if they were those who had immigrated to Australia, in which case they would locate the family ancestry in a particular British Isle or European country, thus anchoring it in a particular ethnic group; if the ancestor was a convict; or if the ancestor was a member of a royal family (I encountered one such claim) or of the nobility. In fact, often the ancestors would not be remembered by name, only the specific details about them would be recalled and the grandparent on whose side that distant famous relative was.

An interesting aspect of the genealogical memory is genealogical amnesia, or repression. The only category of relations which I found to be actively forgotten, as it were, was that of potential indigenous Australian ancestors. Once I was told by an informant that she thought that she might have had Aboriginal ancestors, but that the old female ascendant who knew the details refused to talk about it. It is instructive that she, as well as other informants, felt it was obvious why her family members were reluctant to keep such information on the record or make it public. She mentioned this genealogical repression which she did not condone, and did not think there was any need to state the obvious and explain why her older relatives were not forthcoming about the Aboriginal aspect of her genealogy.

The presentation of lineal relations along the vertical axis, and the collaterals along the horizontal axis, is also significant. The graphic presentation by which one moves 'down' the generation from 'ascendants' to 'descendants' (although my informants did not use these two terms spontaneously) is quite clearly embedded in the language and imagery used to imagine, and experience, kinship. It is probably related to the fact that informants tend to think of their own immediate families and tend to extend their presentation from there to include ever more distant relatives. Within the circle of immediate kin, categories like older, bigger, higher-ranking and authoritative all seem to be related to the up:down dichotomy on the 'up' side, while their counterparts (younger, smaller, lower-ranking and un-authoritative) tend to be equivalent to the 'down' side.

The up-down idiom of constructing kinship charts is part and parcel of the ethno-science of relatedness. The shared essence of relatives, epitomized in the notion of relatedness 'by blood', flows down the generations lineally, just as fluids naturally travel when left to their own devices. Thus people 'pass down their genes' to their offspring. At a deeper level, it seems that fluid is what mediates the relationships between solids, such as the bodies of the individual persons (or, which amounts practically to almost the same thing, the person experienced as an individual body). Solids are bodies whose structure is imbued with a certain inherent permanence, and which are clearly demarcated and distinguished from other solids. The fluids establish contact between such bodies, as epitomized paradigmatically not only in blood relatedness, but also in breastfeeding, sexual intercourse and other practices which evoke it like the deep, wet kiss. In other words, the experience of the person becomes comprehensible through the image schema of a container, with the perimeters of the body acting as the container, and the essence of the individual, transmitted as fluids, as the substance which is contained within that body.

The individual, structured through the container metaphor, is the atom of my informants' kinship system and vision of social division. It is a unit abstracted from the various contexts in which it is embedded, and from the flow of time in which it changes. By extension, corporate bodies like the nuclear family are construed by such a metaphor. As I mentioned in chapter 4 above in relation to the nuclear family, the metaphor of an independent atom of society runs into difficulty when confronted with the realities of reproduction. As with the reproduction of families, the reproduction of individuals violates the notion of a discrete container. This is metaphorically resolved by viewing blood relationships as relationships of essence, as I described above.

The core idiom of kinship and family, that is, the key organizing structure of kinship and family, is reproduction (by which I mean the cultural construction of the physiological and social processes of reproduction, cf. Keesing 1990). The paradigmatic example of a relationship of relatedness is that of parent and offspring. It is a relationship that is natural, in its ethno-scientific construction, and engenders feelings of obligations on the part of both sides towards one another. Built into these relationships is an essential element of inequality. The senior relative, the parent, is up; the junior one, the child, is down. The parent is altruistic, the child submissive (cf. Finch 1989, 162 ff.). The prototypical gender roles of the model of reproduction form the basis of the parental primacy of mothers. One of my male informants admitted that he could never have the closeness to his children that his wife enjoyed. She carried them and nursed them. It is this unmediated physical connection between mother and child which lends itself to the construction of maternity as prototypical parenthood, and paternity as secondary parenthood.

Going back to the analysis of persons as solids whose relationship is mediated by fluids, one can see how at this intuitive, symbolic level the wife/mother becomes the mediator of transfers of essence between father and offspring. Sexual intercourse connects the husband to wife; while pregnancy and lactation connect mother to offspring. Hence the transfer of essence (fluid) between father and offspring is mediated through the mother/wife.

The linear, downward flow of relatedness is a paradigm, a practical metaphor, for other social practices. A person feels obliged to pass on property downwards, lineally. Children have a greater moral claim over the inheritance of their parents than do the parents' siblings. Similarly, grandchildren have a greater claim than do nephews and nieces. In a sense, seeing the relationship of children to their parents' property as a 'claim' is substituting a legalistic perspective for the experience and practice of my Novocastrian informants. The transfer of economic assets down the generations normally occurs incessantly from childhood, and is not delayed till death. Rather, inheritance upon death is the final act in the long process of transfer from one generation to the next, beginning with the very transfer of life. This made intuitive sense to my informants because relations of filiation are not deemed to be a relationship between completely independent and different persons. Children and parents share an essence, which is unquantifiable and indivisible. ('Your child is part of you,' as one female informant exclaimed.) In addition to the idiom of blood relations, it can be seen in the physical similarity that people find between children and their parents. Children become the manifestation of their parents in the next generation. This sharing of essence makes them not quite a different, fully separate, person (although they are by no means the same person). Therefore, the property of the parents is, in fact, the property of the children too, and the transfer which occurs throughout life is different in nature from a market transfer between two independent and equivalent persons.

The ambiguity of difference and identity is brought together in names given to individuals. Given names are unique. The surname unites the family. Interestingly,

I did not come across instances of the practice of naming sons after fathers. I did encounter, albeit rarely, the practice of using names which are 'in the family'. This practice involved the use of the names of dead ascendants as the child's second name. I did not investigate the issue systematically, so these observations must remain tentative and impressionistic.

While lineal relations were deemed to be natural, and therefore obligatory, collateral relations were experienced as voluntary, freer, and involving fewer obligations. Mature siblings were the point at which lines diverge. My informants, who believed that their notions of relatedness followed scientific or natural closeness, were surprised to be told that a person is equally genetically related to his/her nephew, niece, uncle and aunt as to his/her grandchildren and grandparents. To them the latter relationships were much closer. Persons were also deemed to be more closely related to their offspring than to their siblings, again in contradistinction with the equality of the genetic coefficient of relatedness. This surprise emanated from the fact that their notions of relatedness were those of an essence passed down the generations, and not a divisible and quantifiable coefficient of relatedness.

Very much in line with the bifurcation of family with siblings is a phenomenon which is a by-product of my informants' kinship terminology system. Full siblings – the prototypical siblings – share a common perspective of the ascending generations in their kinship universe. But spouses, rather than siblings, share a common view of the descending generations in their kinship universe. In other words, full siblings share the same parents, uncles, aunts, grandparents and so forth, whereas it is spouses, rather than siblings who share children, nephews, nieces, grandchildren and so forth. This seemingly trivial point reinforces the transition from family of origin to family of orientation, as well as stresses the tensions between the two.[3]

My informants' family trees included only consanguines and their spouses. Affinal relations were not otherwise included in one's family tree. One reason is, perhaps, the graphical requirement to trace two parents for every single consanguine who is mentioned in the family tree. More significantly, though, it seems to me that spouses were included primarily because they seem to enjoy the status of a quasi-consanguine. Since both spouses were consanguines of their common children they do share an indirect consanguinity of sorts. As far as my informants were concerned, affinal links were not enduring links of relatedness. Spouses become related, indeed turn from a 'couple' (a potential family) into a 'family', only once they have offspring. It is only through the children – common blood relatives – that they become familially related.

---

[3] In other kinship systems the situation may be quite different. Full siblings among the Yolngu share a view of both ascending and descending generations (Keen 1994; Morphy 1984).

The Logic of Kinship Terminology

I am not interested here in the analysis of an abstract system of kinship terminology for its own sake. Rather, I will focus on kinship terminology in use, as part of social practice. For example, formal English reckons cousins with degrees of relatedness and removal (as in second cousin once removed). Although my informants are aware of the existence of this system they do not normally use it, and are not familiar with its usage. This English-language view, as it were, of kinship is an integral part of the official domain. Mastery of this 'correct' way to deploy this kinship system is an instance of cultural capital which is unevenly distributed across society.

Among my informants, standard terms of reference were resorted to by people in formal occasions. Bureaucracies were liable to inquire about the details of one's father, mother, one's mother's maiden name and so forth. In familiar settings the terms of reference and terms of address tended to coincide. In fact, the choice of which term to use is one element which would constitute an interaction as either more familiar or more official. Talking about 'my mother' is more official than talking about 'mum'.

Standard terms of reference, rather than terms of address, have traditionally been the focus of anthropological kinship studies. However, terms of reference are probably the less significant to understand the 'native point of view'. Among my informants, individuals acquired their particular view of their kinship universe very early as children, using the familiar sets of terms of address and reference. The automatic use of the familiar system, and the fact of its ontogenetically earlier acquisition indicate that it, rather than the official system, is the cognitively basic level of kinship terminology (Rosch 1978; Lakoff and Johnson 1980; Lakoff and Kovecses 1987).

Among my informants, imbuing children with the correct kinship perspective is a deliberate and collaborative effort in which all adults cooperate. It is quite common for adults to refer to and to address one another using the appropriate terminology to the youngest generation present. For instance, a married couple of parents might refer to each other as 'mum' and 'dad' for the explicit benefit of their children. Similarly, grandparents might also refer to each other by the terms that would be appropriate to their grandchildren. This adoption of the new terms of reference and address for the sake of the children in itself becomes quite often a ritual which signals to the new parents and grandparents and others that they, themselves, have changed their status. Some couples might resort to their children's or even grandchildren's kinship perspectives even when the latter are not present; and explain it, if asked, as the force of the habit.

In the informal system parents are normally referred to as Mum and Dad. Grandparents pose a bit of a problem because usually one is faced with two sets which need to be distinguished. Normally one set of grandparents would be called Grandma and Grandpa. The other set of grandparents would often be referred to as Nanna and Pop. The term Nanna has some variants, too, such as Nain (see Goody

1962, for an account of the evolution and usage of the term Nanna and its variants in England). Another way to distinguish maternal from paternal grandparents in families in which one side springs from a non-Anglo background, is to use the foreign terms (e.g. Oma). When asking among my informants I was also told once of a family in which the grandparents were referred to by their title and given name (e.g. Grandma Diane), thereby bypassing the problem. In another instance I encountered, the grandparents were distinguished by their surnames (e.g. Grandma Goodall). But such solutions were unusual. The normal practice among my informants was to use different kin terms for the two sets of grandparents. The decision as to which set of grandparents would be called what is normally negotiated during pregnancy and before the birth of the first child. Factors which are taken into account include the question of whether a set of grandparents is already designated as Grandma/pa, or as Nanna/Pop by any other grandchildren. In general, everything else being equal, the mother's parents would be more likely to be called Nanna and Pop, a designation which is, to my informants, less formal and more familiar. This makes sense because usually one's mother's parents are younger than one's father's parents. Also, the focal role that women tend to play in running and maintaining family ties would normally imply a greater access of a mother's mother to her grandchildren. While most of my informants concurred with the fact that there is a clear tendency to designate maternal rather than paternal grandparents as Nanna and Pop, there was one family who insisted that there was no such bias, and that either set of grandparents could be Nanna and Pop without any clear preference. In any event, once the terms are decided for the first-born child, his/her siblings follow and use the same terminology.

The distinction between the two sets of grandparents is an obvious deviation of the informal kinship system from the formal perspective embedded in the bureaucratic view of kinship, which distinguishes by gender, generation and degree of lineality, but which does not differentiate between the matriline and the patriline. The informal distinction between lines, though, does not indicate an ideological distinction between the two lines. Uncles, aunts and cousins are not differentiated by lines. Rather, this distinction between the patriline and matriline is the by-product of the need to individualize all effective kin (the kin with whom one has contact). Uncles and aunts are differentiated by using epithet and given name (e.g. Uncle Ralph), and cousins are normally referred to by their given names alone. Whereas given names individualize aunts, uncles and cousins, the use of given names to address or refer to lineal ascendants is generally shunned, requiring alternative strategies, such as the use of terms like Nanna and Pop, to distinguish between the different grandparents.

'Uncle' and 'aunt' are commonly used as classificatory categories which include siblings of ascendants and their spouses. The prototype or basic-level examples are a person's parents' siblings. Cousins are a classificatory category which applies to one's parents' sibling's children as prototype and is extended to other relatives through common descent. In more official situations, as when questioned systematically by anthropologists, distinctions might (somewhat reluctantly) be drawn between one's own uncles/aunts and great-uncles/aunts, or mother's/father's uncles. More precise distinctions were very awkward and unnatural to my interviewees who tended not to be entirely sure about the 'proper' terminology to use for such persons. The automatic, default daily use does not distinguish among aunts, among uncles or among cousins.

This deviation from official kinship terminology is significant. Official kinship which distinguishes generational and genealogical distance from ego (such as great-aunt, third cousin twice removed) is based on a gradational core–periphery model centred around ego. There are degrees of relatedness among extended kin. My informants, though, tended to organize their extended kin by recourse to a qualitative break between in and out, in line with the container metaphor. This can be modelled by two concentric circles – the inner one circumscribing the nuclear family, and then the area between the inner and outer circle including the extended family, leaving the rest of the world outside the outer circle. Uncle, aunt and cousin, in my informants' classificatory usage means a relative, but one who is not a member of the nuclear family. This may be interpreted as an imposition of a container model on what might once have been organized by a core–periphery model; or as an embedding of the nuclear family within a broader container of the kindred – the extended family. In either event, this designation of relatives outside the nuclear family with classificatory terms ends up replicating the container model in the organization of the kindred, in that it divides the world according to a permanent binary choice between in and out of the kindred.

In the ascending generations the distinction between lineal and collateral relatives is reinforced in several ways. The terms for collaterals (uncle, aunt) are usually applied across the board to ascendant collaterals. Kinship terminology relates all ascending lineals to one's parents by ascribing a modified parental category to them (grandfather or grandmother). Unlike collaterals, the exact generational difference is always indicated – grandfathers were never referred to as fathers. This reflects the critical difference between the parent–child relationship and the grandparent–grandchild relationship. Similarly, great-grandfathers were never referred to as grandfathers or as fathers.

Compared with its formal counterpart, the informal kinship terminology stresses more forcefully the distinctions between grandparents and parents. The terms used for grandparents like Grandma and Grandpa or Nanna and Pop are different from mum and dad or even mother and father.[4] The informal kinship terminology thus draws a greater distinction between parents and grandparents while distinguishing between lineals and collaterals. The informal kinship terminology system further distinguishes collateral from lineal kin terms by adding given names to collaterals' epithets (Uncle Bob, Auntie Matilda), a practice which is not normal for ascending lineals. The fact that the informal kinship system is the

---

[4] Unlike some North American usages, 'Ma' and 'Pa' were not used among my informants to designate mother and father. Further, 'Pop' never referred to father among my informants, again unlike North American usage (Schneider 1980).

one to which children are exposed from early childhood on a regular basis would suggest that it more accurately reflects and inflects the internalized structures of kinship. Also, the greater independence of the informal kinship system from formally constituted bureaucratic definitions makes it more immediately responsive to social change than is the more formal kinship system.

As a system in practical use, the informal kinship system must come to terms with ambiguities and contradictions. It inevitably incorporates a flexibility of use which lends itself to creative manipulation when necessary. I have mentioned above that ascendant lineals are referred to by epithet alone, and ascendant collaterals by epithet together with a name. Where the age gap between niece/nephew and uncle/aunt was small, or when the relationship was more relaxed and egalitarian as the niece/nephew reached adulthood, the epithet might be dropped, and the uncle/aunt might be referred to by his/her given name alone. This was a mark of familiarity when used in the right context. The use of the first name without epithet was normally reserved for people of the same generation as ego, or of descending generations. This would normally include cousins, nephews/nieces, offspring, and the further generations down the track. (Normally genealogical level and relative age are closely linked due to the limited genealogical extension of families and the small number of offspring in any given family who tend to be born within a particular and limited period of time.) Even if there was a considerable age gap between them, siblings referred to each other by name alone.

Some complication is introduced into the use of kinship terminology by marital breakdowns and blended families. Standardized kinship terminology seems to relate to the prototypical nuclear family situation, leaving their relationships improperly classified. Here kinship terminologies were used somewhat creatively. Thus one girl would use the term 'father' for her mother's first husband who was her genetic father, and the term 'dad' for her mother's second husband. In another situation a woman referred to her mother's de facto partner by his first name, explaining that he moved in with her mother when she herself was no longer a child, and that he was never really like a father to her. Both these instances are significant in that they allow a glimpse into the creative working of habitus. The agents involved do not borrow practices from a pre-determined system of cultural units. Rather, they use familiar models to confront or structure novel situations. The girl who referred to her genetic father as father and her mother's husband as dad is an interesting example. Unfortunately, I only recorded the term of reference she would use, and do not know what term of address she uses for her genetic father. He, however, had been absent from home since she was about two years old and had been living in Sydney for most of that time – spending little time with his daughter. Her mother's current husband was the adult male who had been living in their home most of her life. (At the time of my fieldwork the girl was around 12 years old.) Furthermore, the man she called dad was her sister's genetic father. Thus both sisters, in line with the prototypical model, referred as dad to the same man who was living at home, was in a monogamous relationship with their mother, and was the genetic father of one of the girls. In the other instance, the woman used, quite explicitly, the prototypical model of father to rule her mother's partner out of that category, opting then for the practice which denotes familiarity, voluntarism and egalitarianism, of using his given name. This signifies also the fact that she saw herself unbound by normal commitments of obligations which tie offspring to parents. In fact, her relationship with him was contingent upon her mother's relationship with him.

Another area which does not have clear-cut terminological injunctions is that of in-laws. Upon marriage my informants might assume their spouses' position when addressing their spouse's parents, that is they would call their spouses Mum and Dad. Alternatively they might adopt the terms of address which their children are being trained to use (e.g. Nanna and Pop). More commonly, though, they would address them by their first name, or, in a few instances, by no-naming,[5] that is, by avoiding the use of any term of address; and in formal circumstances (like recorded anthropological interviews) they would refer to them as their spouse's mother or father, or as their mother- or father-in-law, or simply as their in-laws.

Having discussed some aspects of my informants' kinship terminology, I now turn to some of its intrinsic structuring distinctions, as a means of further exploring its underlying worldview.

The Differentiation in the Kinship Terminology System

> Thus, practical mastery of the rules of politeness and, in particular, the art of adjusting each of the available formulae (e.g. at the end of a letter) to the various classes of possible recipients presupposes implicit mastery, and therefore recognition, of a set of oppositions constituting the implicit axiomatics of a given political order: oppositions between men and women, between younger and older, between the personal, or private, and the impersonal (administrative or business letters), between superiors, equals and inferiors. (Bourdieu 1990c, 293, endnote 4)

The sphere of kinship terminology to which my informants are exposed from birth contains a worldview which is structured in specific ways. This sphere – which is structured by the social environment in which my informants live, and which in its turn structures that environment – distinguishes between individual persons, between two sexes/genders, between lineal and collateral relations, between consanguineal and affinal relations (in-laws), between generations (ascending, co-generational and descending), in one particular context between patriline and matriline (by distinguishing the terms of reference and address of father's parents from mother's parents) and between familiar and formal settings.

The analysis of the fit between the social structure as embodied in kinship terminology, and the social structure as it appears in social agents' lived world, runs the risk of assuming a coherent terminological system and a synchronic

---

[5] The concept of no-naming was first suggested by Erving Goffman to Schneider. No-naming is, in Schneider's words, 'the zero form of address' (Schneider 1980, 84).

agreement between the world and its perception, while losing sight of processes of change which might be afoot. In other words, the distinctions that are built into the kinship system may not necessarily reflect the distinctions that obtain in the contemporary social world.

For instance, practices of surnaming reflect an ideological commitment to patrilineality that is rather obsolescent. Surnames and their transmission were perceived by my informants as containing strong patrilineal and patriarchal elements. It is the father's surname which was still normally assumed by the wife upon marriage, and subsequently by the progeny of the union. This was seen by my informants as a legacy of times in which the man was the clear head of the family and women were confined to housewifery. The historical accuracy of this account is less important than the general sense that this practice is a relic of past practices. My informants did not seem much concerned about this issue of surnaming in their daily life. Surnames were normally used only in bureaucratic contexts. A few had given some consideration to the issue upon marriage, or when they needed to determine the surname of their first child for the birth certificate. Otherwise, surnames were seen as rather inconsequential.

This experience of surnaming practices as obsolescent probably reflects the influence of the feminist movement. Generally negative attitudes towards the patrilineal nature of surnaming and its patriarchal implications seemed to me to be more common among my younger interlocutors (people in their thirties as opposed to those in their fifties, for example). It seemed to be closely correlated with more general gender-egalitarian attitudes, at least as they were verbally expressed in public.

Interestingly, most informants who saw this surnaming practice as obsolescent still conformed to the practice upon first marriage. Of the others, it was common for the woman to retain her maiden name as well as take on her husband's name, but the husband would not assume the wife's name, and the children would assume the father's name. The complete 'double-barrelling' of surnames whereby both spouses and their offspring would bear both surnames is more typical of Australia's intelligentsia and cultural elites. The latter, being imbued with the ideology of the bureaucracy of which they are an integral part, take the symbolic implications of bureaucratic practices very seriously indeed. Furthermore, the imperative to improve society in general and engage in symbolic protestation is part of the logic of the dominant, those who take a magisterial, sovereign perspective of society, who are interested in the way society as a whole operates and the abstract principles which govern that operation. The burden of social responsibility towards the rest of society is one of the postures that emerge from this position. Such considerations loom much smaller among members of the dominated classes to whom the social distribution of political consciousness allots a concern with their immediate interests. Rather than identify with the State and Society, they face the State, Bureaucracy and Society as an 'other' of sorts.

An unusual set of circumstances that exemplifies this logic which prevailed among my informants was that of Lucy whom I had mentioned earlier. She had been married to Alfred prior to my fieldwork. Upon marriage she adopted Alfred's surname. The marriage did not last long, and finally broke up shortly after her first son was born. The break-up was rather acrimonious. The ex-husband severed all ties with his son and with Lucy. Different accounts of the marriage depict him as a horrible, selfish, disloyal character. Since the breakdown of the marriage Lucy formed a de facto relationship with Meyer, with whom she had one daughter during my fieldwork, and another one shortly after. Lucy still used Alfred's surname. When I asked her why, she explained that at a certain stage shortly after the divorce she was going to change her surname and revert to her maiden name. She looked into it, and quickly decided it was not worth the trouble, given that so many agencies, like banks and so forth, would need to be notified, and the whole process would entail much dreaded paperwork. This combination of reluctance to deal with red tape, and a lower urgency to deal with officialdom, was rather common among the people I had contact with in Newcastle, and seemed to be itself inversely correlated with a particular agent's position within social space.

In any event, the important point is that surnaming practices were perceived by my informants to reflect practices which were obsolete. There has been a growing deviation in surnaming practices from older conventions, although my informants would be first to admit that they are not leading the way.

Implicit in my analysis is the assumption that schemes of naming and categorization normally lag behind practice, as part of the general lag of incorporated structures behind current 'objective' structures (cf. Bourdieu 1981). This may be expressed in different ways. For example, ad hoc terms invented for ad hoc arrangements might acquire some generality once such ad hoc arrangements become a type. On the other hand, terms which might have reflected real types might take a while to make an exit, for once established they would need to be made completely unnecessary to disappear altogether. These processes operate on the margins of what is doxa, the fit between the modes of perception and appreciation of the world, and the constitution of the social world.

I should stress that I am not arguing that all historical changes proceed in this way, that is, from practice to terminology. Especially within stratified societies and at the crossroads of global systems, impositions from alien centres of power can bring about change in a more abrupt manner, which will move from the structured view of society to its structure of daily practice. The elimination of sibling marriages in Roman Egypt by the imposition of the Roman civil code is an example of a radical social transformation in the structure of the world – siblings ceased to be marriageable – as a result of an imposition of a different worldview, namely the worldview encoded in the Roman civil code (Hopkins 1980). Foucault advanced a similar argument for the process of the imposition of bourgeois sexuality on the dominated classes of society in Victorian times (Foucault 1980). But other than instances of imposition from external sources of power, the general trend is for practice to change first, and only then for explicit linguistic and cultural encoding of practice to follow.

For the most part, internalized dispositions and social structure mirror one another to the point that they are indistinguishable. It is important to stress that the terminology under consideration here is the 'universal' default one. It is 'universal' in the sense that it is assumed to be clearly understood by other members of society with whom one interacts, including those individuals with whom one is not acquainted. In the ad hoc use of kinship terms social agents are able to adapt the official terminology to their own needs, to correspond with their social structure. But even at the practical level one cannot accord total analytical supremacy to the realm of ad hoc behaviour in the face of terminology.

The standard terminology and the structures it implies are taken as the default basis of interaction. These structures may be deliberately modified, as happens in the numerous heterodoxies I discussed in chapter 5. But unless such modifications to this 'universal' worldview occur, its structure materializes. This default standard is part of the mechanisms which privilege the status quo. So much so, that for lack of a large-scale, systematic practical variation from the standards it implies, the default terminology and its structure act as the collective conceptual meeting place for social agents. They also create, to a large extent, that very collective by its function of determining the meeting place. Those who do not arrive at the meeting place, as it were, those whose default terminologies are different, would be conspicuously excluded from the collective. In other words, the use of the default terminology defines the group members because it is the 'universal' terminology which is used by all members of the group. Such tautologies are essential aspects of the operation of practical logic.

The universal terminology contains a specific worldview. The distinction along gender lines holds across the kinship universe. Except for cousins, kinship terms are never gender-neutral. Indeed, there are gender-neutral English terms for different roles which are associated with particular positions, terms like parent, sibling or offspring. Because of their gender neutrality, these terms found some currency as kinship terms in the State bureaucracy and in those areas of social space where gender-blind individualism is valued. These terms class together persons of the different gender who otherwise share a similar position for the purpose of emphasizing this very position. However, my informants' basic level categories were invariably gendered; for example, the terms father and mother, brother and sister, son and daughter. These distinctions were mirrored in the terms of address, e.g. mum and dad, which conformed to the same structure as the terms of reference. Even when addressing or referring to cousins, their gender would become explicit because when identifying a specific cousin the name of the cousin is normally attached to the term, thus indicating the cousin's gender through the genderedness of the cousin's given name. (Gender-ambiguous given names were uncommon among my informants. Mismatching gendered names, i.e. calling a boy by a girl's name and vice versa, never happened.[6]) In other words, the structure

---

[6] Perhaps one might cite as an exception some nicknames of girls, constructed by the shortening of female names to male-sounding names, such as 'Sam' for Samantha. This was

which produces, and which is produced by, the kinship terminology, includes a vision of social division in which the gender division is a basic-level distinction.

Generations are distinguished in the relative usage of kinship terms. This applies to both lineal as well as collateral relatives. Among the latter the exact genealogical level (e.g. +1 as opposed to +2) is not important in itself. Rather, it is the relative position to ego as ascendant co-generational or descendant. Etiquette requires that one should refer to, and address one's ascendants by epithet – the epithet alone in the case of lineals (e.g. Grandma) or with a given name in the case of collaterals (e.g. Uncle Ralph) – and to relatives of the same generation or descendants by name alone. This means that when one addresses a member of a descending generation one will use the given name only, but would be addressed in return by epithet, thereby underscoring the inequality in social position. This generational distinction is somewhat contingent upon age differences. Where collateral relatives who are members of adjacent generations are very close in age they might well resort to the use of given names alone. By the same token, the use of given names could be a way of signalling a certain egalitarian familiarity between such relatives which transcends the generational difference.

But gender and generational distinctions do not inhere in terminology alone. Traditionally, anthropologists have bracketed off terminology from practice, and analysed the semantics of kin terms in isolation from the total social relation which kin terms denoted and in which they were embedded. It would be beneficial, though, to include those ritualized conventions which are part of the kinship terminology system. Indeed, each of the distinctions which my informants' kinship terminology established was accompanied by a whole set of matching ritualized behaviours. Regarding gender, for example, when family members met and greeted one another, regardless of their genealogical or geographical distance, females would normally embrace and kiss females, females and males would also embrace and kiss, but males would shake hands with, or occasionally hug other males, but not kiss one another. Similarly, relationships among co-generationals are modelled most closely after friendship relationships in that they are freer of obligations and include people who are structurally equivalent, that is, who have no authority over one another. This is reflected in the choice of subject matter for conversation and in the manner of interaction. It is through such rituals that the distinctions of the kinship system are reiterated and reinforced in daily practice to the point of becoming part of the nature of things.

Not all divisions which are organized by the web of kin and family relations are equally fundamental. The most fundamental aspect of kinship designation is the individual as designated by name and specific parentage. The person is constituted as a holistic unit, an atom of society, with an essence which endures through time,

---

not very common among my informants either, and in any event, the full name was still gender-specific. Nonetheless, for reasons I will explore below in chapter 7, just like with unisex clothes, when names were appropriated across gender lines by shortening or by nicknaming it was always females who adopted male-tagged names and not vice versa.

and is embodied in one's body, in one's memory and in others' memories of oneself. Probably other than the designation of the human organism as an individual, gender is experienced as the most immutable and fundamental aspect of a social agent's being. Among my informants, current medical technology notwithstanding, everybody was assigned a sex at birth – either male or female – a condition which was significant and permanent. In fact, the separation of gender and individuality is completely artificial, as there is no neuter individuality among my informants. In other words, the basic level categories for individual persons, categories which structure my informants' world, are all gendered. The first bit of information people sought about a newborn baby was its gender. (The question was normally 'is it a boy or a girl?', rather than 'what sex/gender is it?', reflecting the highly gendered nature of basic level categories of personhood.) The gender of the baby has profound immediate practical implications, ranging from the proper pronoun to apply to it (it being a de-humanizing pronoun generally reserved for objects and non-human organisms) to the type of gift that should be bought for it and its mother.

Age was less fundamental. It combined consideration of both biological age – a socially significant trait – and the relative position a person occupies within a genealogy. The practical correlation between the two means, for example, that one's uncles and aunts would usually be clustered in age around one's parents' age, and would not normally be closer in age to oneself than to one's parents. The paucity of instances in which genealogical generation and biological age conflict is due to the limited number of children per family, to the close spacing of births, and to a limited extension of effective genealogy.

Biological age is important in two ways. The first is in enabling some and eliminating other types of relationships between any two or more persons. An adult and a child would form a different kind of relationship from that between a couple of adults or a couple of children. Age is also important in that it correlates in the practical scheme of things with life stage. Childbearing, for example, is not randomly distributed across the fertile years of women. The usual period to have a first child is late twenties or early thirties. Having a first child at 15 or at 50 is extremely uncommon, and may well invite the intervention of State agencies or other individuals and agencies in ways which would not be appropriate if that particular event, childbearing, had occurred at the 'normal' age of maternity.

Both age distinctions and gender distinctions are rooted in family life and the kinship structure. In fact, the relationship between offspring and parent – the epitome of generational difference – is the prototype for symbolic domination par excellence. I will argue that this relationship acts as a practical metaphor for gender relations in the family. The familial experience of maternity and wifehood or paternity and husbandhood are, in their turn, the prototype for gender distinctions throughout society. When my informants accounted for the structural distinctions between generations and between genders, they invariably resorted to generalizations from familial structure to social structure, and from the particular gendered/aged familial functions to social structure in general. The two structural distinctions, of age and of gender, are thus intimately linked.

The issue of age is considered in the remainder of the chapter. The following chapter takes up gender, and argues for the essential link between the gender order and kinship and family.

Age Distinctions and the Differences in Age-Grade Experiences of Family

My informants had an overview of the progression of human life which involves passage through various stages in three trajectories. The content of these trajectories is essentially linked to the transition through stages in the idealized trajectory of the nuclear family, and to sexual and reproductive functions.

The first trajectory is that from infancy, through to toddlerhood, childhood, adolescence, to young adulthood. This trajectory is closely associated with chronological age and based on anatomical and physiological markers of developmental age. Then a second trajectory takes over, a trajectory which is more closely linked to the family: living at home, moving out as an 'un-attached' single, employment, becoming part of a couple, 'having a family' (parenthood), then moving back from nuclear family to a couple as the children move to their families of procreation, followed by retirement. At this point the third trajectory – growing old – is in full swing, leading eventually to senility, death/widowhood, death. The second trajectory does, in fact, overlap with the first and third ones, although it characterizes that plateau period in which the social significance of physiological development is experienced as attenuated or frozen. That period of adulthood is the one which characterizes most of my informants' paid-labour and/or homemaking life in which the process of becoming is finished, the individual is who s/he is, but the process of decline (during which a person becomes a 'has been' – that is, a person is who s/he used to be) has not yet set in.

The prime position in this age structure is that of the young adult, who is in the middle, between childhood and old age. This stands in stark contrast with other social arrangements in which old age implies higher status and the process of maturing is a unidirectional, continuous trajectory (e.g. among Bedouins, see Abou-Zeid 1991). Unlike this latter instance, which is experienced as a unidirectional progression, the schema which organizes adulthood among my informants resembles a stereotypical mountain. Adulthood is the peak or summit of one's life trajectory. It is also the middle-of-the-road position, the position which shuns the extreme, which is superior to either extremes. A person who is growing old is, thus, 'over the hill'. The physical progress from adulthood to senility seems to reverse the processes of adulthood. A common complaint among the elderly is that they are treated like children. Very often, the social life trajectory was discussed by my informants as if it were an ascent from dependency (childhood) to independence (adulthood) culminating in a relapse into dependency (old age).

The first and third trajectories use the metaphor of development applied to some physical markers. The second trajectory is static, and therefore does not rely on physiological markers of change. The very physiological markers which produce – at the same time that they are produced by – the processes of growing up and growing old, are similarly implicated in gender differentiation, an issue to which I will return below.

The most important idiom for the process of moving from infancy to adulthood is increasing in size and moving upwards. Babies 'grow up' and ultimately become adults. They are 'little' when they are young (the word 'little' was often used interchangeably with 'young', especially when conversing with children), and they grow 'bigger' as they grow older ('big' was used also to denote age seniority in childspeak). Once an adult, a person stops growing up or becoming 'big'. Instead a person starts growing old, and the shift in stature is subsequently reversed as a person is said to shrink with age. It is common knowledge among my informants that younger adults are taller than the elderly. The stereotypical old person is shrivelled and hunched over.

There are specific physical markers which punctuate the process of growing up: the appearance of bodily and facial hair, puberty and sexual maturation, the deepening of voice in men, as well as being better able to control one's emotions, bodily processes and so forth. These are all reversed in the process of growing old, which is associated with weakening, loss of hair, loss of sexual stamina and of fertility (when menopause is the reversal of menarche), shrinkage of stature and so forth.

Furthermore, it is as if the process of moving from sexlessness to sexedness which is attributed to the progress from childhood to adulthood is also reversed. The physical markers which are used to distinguished male from female among young adults are attenuated in older people. Older people among my informants also seemed to be spending less time in nurturing those markers and accentuating the differences between the genders. In fact, the very sexual nature of the person becomes less significant in old age. Various gestures which would be totally unacceptable if made by a young adult male to a woman would be seen as 'cute' and 'tongue-in-cheek' when made by an elderly man to a young woman. An elderly man is no longer deemed 'dangerous'. 'Dirty old man' can be used tongue-in-cheek to convey a positive image of an older person as a vivacious character.

Ultimately, just as the process of ageing becomes the undoing of the process of growth, a retreat from adulthood, so does death become linked, in a mirror image, to birth.

Summary and Conclusions

From the discussion above, reproduction emerges as the idiom which organizes kinship and relatedness among my informants. Filiation similarly emerged as a critical principle in the kinship system. The ego-centred kindred forms a social category that may be mobilized on ad hoc bases, but does not operate as a corporate body. This is in contrast with the nuclear family which may well operate as a corporate unit (see chapters 4 and 5).

Kinship terminology and related etiquette embody a worldview which structures the world in particular ways. In this study I am most interested in the division into individual persons, divisions by age and by gender, all of which are intimately linked to one another and are predicated upon the conception of reproduction which was at the core of my informants' kinship system. Having discussed the person (in chapter 4 above) and age distinctions, I turn to gender distinctions that form an essential aspect of personhood and self (i.e. there is no immediate sense in which agents are un-gendered) and are metaphorically structured by the juxtaposition of adult to infant, and other aspects of maturation and ageing.

Chapter 7

Internalized Gender Structures

The previous chapter described some of the fundamental distinctions that are built into the kinship system of Novocastrians. One of them was gender. In fact, gender and kinship cannot be properly separated into distinct cultural domains – at least not in European societies (e.g. Yanagisako and Collier 1987; Yeatman 1983).

This chapter explores the ways the gender order is incorporated into the subjectivities and worldviews of the people I studied in particular, and others like them in Australasia, anglophone America and the UK. I show how genderedness in general derives its meaning from the prototypical familial roles played by men and women; and furthermore, that the form and content of the gender order are themselves cognitively structured by the generational structure of the prototypical family. This highlights the critical role the family plays in producing and orchestrating the dispositions that make up genderedness and the gender order. This cognitive contribution of the family to the gender order is confounded with – yet remains distinct from – the material effects of the division of labour and the organization of the family household.

Masculine Domination as 'Symbolic Violence'

Gender is a relational category. It makes little sense to analyse masculinity or femininity apart from one another, because in societies like my informants', those two categories are both mutually constitutive and mutually exclusive. In order to avoid an essentialist analysis of either masculinity or femininity, I will use Bourdieu's relational analysis of masculine domination as the point of departure for the discussion that follows.

Bourdieu approached masculine domination as an instance of what he called 'symbolic violence', that is, symbolic domination par excellence (Bourdieu 1990b; Bourdieu 1994; Bourdieu 1996–7; Bourdieu 1998). It is rooted in doxa, giving the social order of genderedness the quality of self-evidence, that is, the appearance of the natural order of things. More specifically, the social agent comes to incorporate the structures of male domination through a dual process. One is the internalization of the male point of view by both men and women, constituting the male as a subject and the female as an object. The second process is the acquisition of gender-specific bodily hexes and (psychosomatic) dispositions (tastes, modes of action and so forth) which result in women adopting feminine styles, and men masculine styles. These two processes naturalize the gendered differences in style, and their consequences. At an immediate level, these differences appear to derive from peculiar life choices of particular individuals. At a systemic level, the cumulative gendered patterning of practice – the gender order – is experienced as the outcome of spontaneous, innate and pre-social tendencies which distinguish females from males.

In other words, there is a circular process at work here. The gendered quality of the practices of social agents is embedded in their tastes, preferences, commonsense and the like. Therefore, women seem to spontaneously act as women, and men to spontaneously act as men. These internalized generative structures – habitus – conform to the ideological structures of masculine domination. This conformity, in turn, serves to justify this very ideology, in that the differences between the genders appear natural and self-evident, inscribed as they are into the very being of human beings. As a result, the consequences of these gender differences are naturalized: they appear to derive from peculiar life choices of particular individuals. The nature of things, in its turn, imposes itself on agents and structures their agency (i.e. their habitus).

Below, I describe several examples to render concrete the general domination of the male point of view. I demonstrate the domination of the masculine perspective in the habitus of both men and women. In the course of the analysis I demonstrate that the internalized gender order is more complex than simply a universal manifestation of masculine domination. I present one major exception to the domination of the masculine perspective, namely the domain of reproduction and parenthood, where it is the feminine perspective that predominates.

I will show that both the feminization of the domestic domain and masculinization of the marketplace are incorporated into both male and female habituses. This incorporation underpins the material basis of masculine domination – the distinction between the marketplace and the domestic domain, and the domination of the latter by the former.

I will further demonstrate that prototypical conjugal relations form a cognitive anchor for gender relations at large, including masculine domination. Moreover, masculine domination itself is commonly incorporated into the habitus of Australians in a specific way – femininity is juxtaposed with masculinity in a homologous way to the juxtaposition of infancy with adulthood. In other words, the idiom of reproduction, embodied by the prototypical family and incorporated into the realized category of the family (see chapter 6), is critical in structuring the internalized dispositions which make up the gender order.

Methodologically, I have departed from Bourdieu's mode of structural decomposition. For the purposes of elaborating the structures of habitus, I have borrowed and adapted the structural method of analysis as developed by Lakoff and Johnson in their exploration of the cognitive basis of meaning (Lakoff 1987; Johnson 1987; Lakoff and Johnson 1980), and of Eleanor Rosch's studies of the structures of categorization (Rosch 1978). There were several reasons for this analytical shift. Mostly, departing from the deductive formalism of traditional structuralism allows for a closer approximation of the fractured and fuzzy logic of the lived world (for more details on the shifts that are involved, and their significance, see Uhlmann 2000, 142–143).

Related to this is my adoption of the concept of motivation to tackle the issue of causality. Following Lakoff and Johnson I mean by motivation a relationship which is not fully causal, but is more than arbitrary. Specifically, I will argue that the structure of the *adult:infant* dichotomy provides a paradigm which habitus subsequently applies to structure the dichotomy of *man:woman*. Because the relationship is not deterministic, one cannot predict from the infant–adult relationship what the gender relationship will look like. But, due to the motivation, it is possible to relate aspects of the construction of gender back to the structure of the *adult:infant* dichotomy. This principle of motivation – a central phenomenon in cognition (Lakoff 1987, 96, 346) – is the basis of what Bourdieu has identified as the economy of practical logic, whereby the structure of experience in one context may be transferred to a new context, and structure it (Bourdieu 1977).

The Prototypical Family as a Cognitive Paradigm for Gender Practice

The prototypical family provides a concrete experiential paradigm for genderedness, a paradigm that helps organize behaviour in other contexts too. Specifically, it is the prototypical reproductive and productive functioning of women and men within the prototypical domestic sphere that becomes the concrete anchor for conceptualizing gendered behaviour, and accounting for the gendered nature of social action in other spheres. Or, put differently, within the universe of gendered practice, the prototype of the conjugal division of reproductive, emotional and domestic labour stands in a synecdochic relation to other instances of gendered relations.[1] Genderedness in general may be thought of as an epiphenomenon of the gendered structure of reproduction. This appears to hold true across European metropolitan and settler societies (cf. Yanagisako and Collier 1987; Errington 1990).

Accordingly, among Novocastrians, the substantive content of the two gender categories was made concrete by the domestic division of labour, rather than the substantive content of the conjugal role being derived from generalized notions of masculinity and femininity. This was most apparent when people were called upon to explain the differences between the roles played by men and women in different social contexts. The rationale they used to account for these differences was almost always brought back to the prototypical gendered division of familial labour, especially emotional labour and reproduction. Most often, the differences between men and women were naturalized and attributed to some maternal

---

[1] Synecdoche is very common in the cognitive organization of the world, when a concrete and well-structured aspect of something serves to cognitively organize the whole thing (Lakoff 1987, 77).

instinct or similar predisposition of females and males to fulfil their usual reproductive and familial roles. Typical career choices made by women, such as secretarial or receptionist work, nursing and teaching, were explained in focus groups by women's natural proclivity to communicate with others and their greater communication skills, the very reason they are 'better with children' and in 'running the family'. Such deterministic explanations complemented voluntaristic ones proffered by Novocastrians, such as the preference of women for jobs which are part-time or which conflict least with their family responsibilities.

Significantly, while women's interrupted participation in the labour market was explained by the more significant role women played in the domestic domain, never did my interlocutors account for women's greater involvement in the domestic domain by reference to women's limited opportunities in the workforce. This generalization holds both for general observations my discussants made, and to their explanation of their own life choices. In short, when Novocastrians thought about gender differences, they very often envisaged males and females in their prototypical reproductive, emotional and domestic roles. These roles were immediately accessible, and mediated the way gender in other contexts, and gender in general, was experienced and discussed. In other words, prototypical domestic gender roles provide rich images – political myths, as it were – that lend themselves to the construction of gender in other contexts. The explanatory/causal direction was not symmetrical, though, as patterns of labour-market participation were not used to account for the domestic gender order.

Interestingly, while the prototypical family at the heart of gender construction appears rather uniform, the actual configuration of relations between spouses was much more fluid. For example, in two of the families with young children I came to know the woman acted as main breadwinner. In several others both spouses were engaged in full-time employment in the labour market. This, however, did not indicate that conceptions of gender are different among those who organize the division of labour along non-'traditional' lines. Rather, people experienced their peculiar arrangements as idiosyncratic, or as variations on a well-structured prototypical theme. This is yet another manifestation of the functioning of the nuclear family as a realized category (see chapter 4).

In the two families where the wife was the main breadwinner, the wives had a substantially better earning capacity than their husbands. In one instance the wife, Catherine, was an occupational therapist. Her husband, Raymond, had been made redundant several years before, and was working casually as a taxi driver. In another instance the wife, Esther, was employed as a mid-level trainer in the public service, while her husband, Jack, who had worked in a series of dead-end blue-collar and service jobs, was at the time working at weekends as a sales assistant in a hardware store.

In both instances the discrepancy between the common practice and the standard division of labour was explained to me by recourse to the economic rationality of the choice made. Neither instance was explained as simply the outcome of the desires of the couple – a typical explanation for prototypical arrangements. Both women tended to discuss their full-time paid work as an external compulsion, and lamented the lack of time to spend with their children. Further, in their personal relationships neither couple broke with the common gendered division of disposition and responsibilities. While their practice might have been heterodox, the internalized dispositions of the members of such heterodox couples led them to adopt strategies which reproduced the dominant forms of gender, organized as they are around a prototypical division of productive, reproductive and social labour.

In fact, both women took great care to continue breastfeeding their children as long as possible, much longer than most other breastfeeding mothers I encountered. For example, Catherine regularly met Raymond for lunch at a coffee shop near her office so that she could breastfeed their toddler. It was their third child. She said she would breastfeed him for as long as she could. She breastfed each of her previous two children for about three years. Esther extended her maternity leave for as long as she could and when she resumed full-time paid employment she continued to breastfeed. She would express milk in the evening so that the baby could be bottle-fed with her milk during the day. Gradually the baby started being fed solids and other foods during the day, but was still breastfed at night. Strategically, breastfeeding reinforced the primacy of maternity over paternity in access to the child. The women cherished the experience which enabled them to bond with their children in a very unique way, and men acknowledged that part of the interaction with the child made the maternal bond with the child that much stronger and exclusive. It was a kind of relationship that could not be shared with or communicated to men, a kind of primordial, elementary and unmediated contact which is direct and unbreakable. This is very much in line with the construction of relatedness and reproduction that was explored in chapter 6. It is the unmediated contact between mother and child in the (culturally constructed) process of reproduction which structures the supremacy of maternity over paternity.

Breastfeeding is thus not only a physiological necessity for the well-being of the child, but at one and the same time, a potentially powerful assertion of the primacy of maternity over paternity. It was on the basis of their primary roles as mothers that women I encountered exercised greater authority in matters pertaining to childcare. When, in my presence, the full-time working mothers would meet their partners for lunch or after a day's work, the husbands would report on how the baby behaved, and receive further instructions if necessary. Never was there any doubt as to who was the final authority in making decisions such as whether the child should be allowed to have sweets or not, when the child would be put to bed and so forth. This was squarely the maternal domain of authority, which may or may not be delegated to the father, but was ultimately the mother's sphere. Thus, in one instance, Jack sheepishly reported that the child was out of order and he smacked him. This annoyed Esther who was opposed to corporal punishment. She reproached him, clarified to him that this was unacceptable, and that they would discuss it later. Never was her final authority in relation to the child questioned.

Not only among these non-'traditional' couples, but also among the other couples I studied, feminine strategies led to a maximization of women's social capital in the domestic domain, while men spent more effort strengthening their access to economic capital. First and foremost, when it came to decisions regarding major expenditure, men tended to be dominant, making the major decisions, even, it seems, where the wife was the main breadwinner. Further, in the two cases in which the males were not in full-time employment, they still sought part-time or casual paid employment. They participated on a casual basis in the labour market in what one of them described as a 'shit job'. Both hoped to find a better job, neither considered dropping out of the labour force altogether, and neither was committed to remaining secondary breadwinner. During my stay in Newcastle, I did not encounter, nor heard of a full-time househusband. Nor did the men who were primary caregivers get involved in social networks like those of full-time women caregivers, who visited each other during the day for a 'cuppa' (a cup of tea, a chat, and an exchange of information. This is probably mostly the result of the paucity of other full-time, male homemakers, and the inappropriateness of men exchanging regular visits with women while their husbands are at work.

The internalized dispositions which link women to the domestic domain, and men to the marketplace, are expressed more clearly in families where the man is employed on a full-time basis. When both partners were involved in full-time paid work it was the man who was the main breadwinner. The salary differential between men and women would be maintained by the men working extra hours. Further, following childbirth, the men's increase in hours of work was seen by both men and women as the former's equivalent familial contribution to the latter's decreased participation in the labour market and greater expenditure of time at home.

The feminization of the domestic domain is not experienced as an external imposition upon women. It is an important stake in quotidian feminine politics and an important object of political negotiations and struggles among women – paradigmatically the structural conflict between a mother-in-law and a daughter-in-law. This situation was confirmed to me both in private interviews and in focus groups with both men and women. In one of the all-women focus groups, when I inquired about the tension between mother-in-law and daughter-in-law, one of the women explained that 'two bosses can't share the same nest [...] as a home manager', an answer which met with nods of approval from the other participants in the group.

Faced with the apparent complicity of women in the reproduction of the gender order, some class-sensitive research on gender has sought to resurrect the rationality of the choices made by working-class women by pointing out that involvement in the labour market is not necessarily liberating or empowering at the lower ranks of the socio-economic order, and that gravitating towards the domestic domain may not be a strategy of disempowerment (e.g. Bryson 1985; Donaldson 1991). As Barbara Ehrenreich and Deidre English put it,

> From a permanent position on the assembly line or in a typing pool, it does not look so terribly degraded to bake cookies for spoiled children or to fake orgasms for an uninspiring husband. At home you can be 'yourself', a person with intimate significance for others. In the Market you are abstractly interchangeable with any other quantum of human energy which can be had for the same price. (Ehrenreich and English 1979, 286–287)

While the poor alternatives to specialization in caregiving might reward women's attachment to the domestic domain, it does not account for the actual process which leads women to the domestic domain and men to the marketplace. Ehrenreich and English's typification of some labour-market experiences applies no less to male participants, and therefore cannot explain the gender differences in preference and propensity to engage in paid labour. Moreover, Novocastrian women's attachment to the domestic domain was not immediately motivated by a rational appraisal of alternatives offered by the labour market, but by dispositions strongly incorporated into their habitus. Such dispositions include, for example, difference in standards of cleanliness and orderliness which predispose women to deal with household chores (Uhlmann 2004, 89–90).

In one couple with a 'traditional' division of labour, the wife worked on a casual basis in social services. She loved her job, but said she preferred to stay home with the children even though she could spend more time at work. Her husband worked as a quality inspector in industry, and hated his job. He said that had he not had a family, he would have left a long time ago, and that every Sunday he perused the job advertisements in the newspaper. I got the impression that the question of whether he should be the main breadwinner, and she the main caregiver, never came up spontaneously. When I raised it, I was told that she preferred to stay home with the kids, and that at any rate, he was probably able to earn more money at his job than she at hers. They had two children, a son of hers from a previous marriage and a baby daughter. The wife was the one who had wanted the second child. The deal the couple had struck before their daughter was born was that they would have a child, the mother would take a break from paid employment, and then when the child was old enough she would go back to work so that her husband could leave his job or move to part-time employment, and retrain in a different field. Only then would they have another child. However, she unexpectedly fell pregnant again very shortly before she was supposed to resume her paid labour, and decided to stay home and go ahead with the pregnancy. Informed sources doubted the accidental nature of the pregnancy. As one of her close friends told me, she wanted another child, she liked being home with the kids – it was a very convenient accident on her part.[2] The child was born in the year after I left Newcastle. In this domestic drama, the two main protagonists followed rather common gender strategies. Had there been a close adjustment of gender strategies to the quality of labour-market choices, we might expect a different division of labour. She, who liked her job, might be the main breadwinner, and he the main caregiver.

It appears, then, that the default attachment of women to the domestic domain, and men to the marketplace, is doxic, and is not challenged even in families with heterodox patterns of labour-market participation. Moreover, the gendered structure of the prototypical family and reproduction motivates gendered strategies in other spheres of practice, such as labour-market participation.

This doxa is part of a broad gestalt – the prototypical nuclear family. This gestalt serves as a practical paradigm that habitus employs to organize the world in many different contexts. This division of productive, reproductive and social labour is organized around the ideology of reproduction which forms the very basis of the cognitive structuring of gender. It is experienced as life choices of individuals, and is expressed in dispositions, preferences and an aesthetic which spontaneously reproduces the dominant structures, those very structures that had impressed these very dispositions, preferences and aesthetics into the very habitus of social agents.

This doxic association of women with the domestic domain, and men with the marketplace, was further reinforced in the way Novocastrians thought of the labour market. For example, in women's focus-group discussions of the gendered structure of the labour market, even those advocating equal opportunity for women were reinforcing the dominant view of gender. The discussion revolved invariably around whether women could operate equally to men in prized positions in the labour market. Discussants failed to question the legitimacy or necessity of such masculinist standards as emotional stability, cool-headedness, primary commitment to the job over and above familial duties, and the accompanying *a priori* presumption that men do live up to these standards. The whole scope for debate and action was limited to whether and how women can live up to such demands, and whether women who could, should or should not be treated equally with men. In other words, the association of sources of economic capital – high-powered economic positions, for instance – with characteristics that are normally identified with masculine style, was fully accepted without question. The scope for debate was the extent to which women can adapt to that style.

This is an instructive instance of internalized symbolic domination. The *a priori* adoption of masculinist standards necessarily excludes those agents whose habitus conforms to feminine style. The presumption that males fulfil these

---

[2] In her interviews in Melbourne in 1976, Richards, too, encountered a couple of instances in which women who wanted to get pregnant suffered a suspiciously fortunate contraceptive failure (Richards 1985, 74).

standards exempts males from needing to demonstrate their fulfilment of such standards, and gives males an added advantage even when there are no objective differences between the genders. Further, the desirability of such standards is never in itself questioned.

In its turn, the presumption of male conformity to these standards, coupled with the open question of female conformity to them, probably affects the socialization of agents in an unequal way. The taken-for-grantedness of male conformity leaves little scope for legitimate alternative masculinities. As a youth worker pointed out: 'Women in a lot of ways have more options, at some level, 'cos it's quite acceptable for females to take on leadership roles; it's socially admirable for them to be working. You know, I don't think that has happened for men, in childcare, in being a houseparent'. A different counsellor lamented the lack of alternative role models for men, and added,

> I feel really concerned for what it means to be male in this society ... This really, I mean, they have nothing to draw on ... Their fathers were like this, and their fathers' fathers were like this, 'I get up in the morning, I go to work, and I come home and I don't need to go out and socialize, I might go to the pub'.

Masculinity is defined and measured by masculinist standards. Those agents who embark on a lifelong project of being male are left little choice but to incorporate these standards to varying degrees of success, because there are very few other ways to be male. On the other hand, the explicit question surrounding female conformity means that those social agents who embark on the project of becoming female may or may not find themselves conforming to such standards. Alternative ways of being female are legitimately available. In other words, the presumption of male conformity to masculine standards acts as a self-fulfilling prophecy by supporting the very differentiation of styles that it implies, and by reproducing it.

The next section of this chapter explores the depth and immediacy of the incorporation of the gender order. This is done by taking up the two main themes Bourdieu has identified for masculine domination, namely the internalization of the male point of view, and the internalization of gender-specific dispositions. The major focus is on behaviours whose genderedness is neither reflexive nor wilfully deliberative – in other words, behaviours which betray the gendered doxa at its most immediate and unmediated nature – such as common patterns of speech and techniques of the body.

I follow with considerations of the actual metaphoric organization of the gender order. I argue that masculine domination is modelled after the dichotomy of adult vs. infant.

Unlike Bourdieu, by analysing concrete practices in various areas of practice, I argue that in some contexts femininity predominates. The logic of which contexts are masculine-dominated, and which are feminine-dominated, goes back to the prototypical productive and reproductive functions which organize the experience of family and gender among Novocastrians.

The Internalization of the Gender Order

The attachment of femininity to the domestic domain, and its subordination to masculinity in general contexts, is internalized into the very habitus of both male and female agents. Bourdieu argues that a fundamental aspect of the persistence of male domination is the ubiquitous domination of the masculine perspective. This is so in Australia, too.

One fundamental demonstration of the domination of the masculine perspective is the fact that gender forms a crucial aspect of accounting for women's behaviour, whereas the genderedness of men comes to the fore only when compared with women. For example, when in conversations I raised the issue of gender, Novocastrians used notions of gender to account for why women were not involved in the labour market to the same extent that men were, and why women were overly involved in homemaking. The explanation focused on that which is special about women. The parallel phenomena, namely men's relative under-involvement in homemaking, and over-involvement in the labour market, were not directly accounted for by gender. Nor, for that matter, did normal accounts of gendered behaviours focus on the peculiarities of masculinities, unless I brought it up myself. It is as if gender (normally referred to as sex by interlocutors) was a concept interchangeable with femininity, which functioned so as to account for a feminine handicap. At the risk of overstating my case, I would say that usually when Australians talk about gender they think female-ness. This is akin to the observation which has emerged in feminist research, according to which masculinity is the unmarked category, and femininity the marked one.

These instances of the domination of the masculine perspective are still at the level of explicit discussion in rather artificial contexts – mostly ethnographic interviews. In what follows I will try to go deeper, as it were. I will first discuss non-conscious speech practices which clearly demonstrate the internalization, by both men and women, of the domination of the masculine perspective. I will then consider some non-discursive practices which demonstrate how the domination of the masculine perspective is incorporated into the different orientations men and women develop towards their own bodies.

Habituated Speech Practices

The domination of the male point of view inheres in some non-conscious, habitual speech practices common throughout the English-speaking world. I will explore now one such example. Where English syntax does not impose a particular order among words, some words seem to be ordered in a rather fixed manner. William E. Cooper and John Robert Ross (Cooper and Ross 1975) set out to analyse what determines the order of such conjuncts as listed in Table 7.1:

Table 7.1 Usual and unusual conjuncts

Usual	Unusual
up and down	down and up
front and back	back and front
active and passive	passive and active
good and bad	bad and good
here and there	there and here
now and then	then and now

Cooper and Ross identified both phonological and semantic factors involved in ordering these words. The semantic factors are relevant to the current discussion. The researchers developed an essentially cognitive explanation of the semantic constraint on conjunct ordering: 'First conjuncts refer to those factors which describe the prototypical speaker (whom we sometimes refer to as "me")' (Cooper and Ross 1975, 67).[3]

Keeping in mind Cooper and Ross's findings, Table 7.2 (overleaf) provides a short list of some habitual patterns of ordering words in Australian English usage. This list, which accords with Cooper and Ross's US data (Cooper and Ross 1975, 65), suggests that men are more prototypical than women, and women more so than children. This seems to be a general pattern across many different contexts of speech acts. The agreement between Cooper and Ross's findings on the one hand, and mine on the other, further supports their claim that the emergent linguistic picture they discovered is typical of the English language, and its native speakers, as a whole.

---

[3] There are two particular exceptions to this 'me first' principle, namely, when speaking of the divine (e.g. God and man) and of plants (e.g. flora and fauna), but these are of little consequence for the current discussion (Cooper and Ross 1975, 67). Also worth mentioning is the fact that these findings do not seem to hold in other languages (Cooper and Ross 1975, 100).

Table 7.2 Gendered conjuncts in general

Usual	Unusual
male and female	female and male
man and woman	woman and man
men and women	women and men
boys and girls	girls and boys
brothers and sisters	sisters and brothers
husband and wife	wife and husband
husbands and wives	wives and husbands
father and son	son and father
mother and son	son and mother
father and daughter	daughter and father
mother and daughter	daughter and mother
women and children	children and women

However, Cooper and Ross's findings need some conceptual refinement. The existence of a concrete, rich image, which is more a man than a woman and more a woman than a child is impossible in a universe like my informants', where man and woman are qualitatively different and mutually exclusive categories. Since Cooper and Ross published their paper, the theory of cognitive prototypes has developed in a way that makes it possible to resolve this difficulty and incorporate their findings into the general framework I am developing here. Prototypes are no longer thought to be concrete, rich images, but rather abstract concepts or scales of sorts: a prototype *effect* which describes the product of cognitive processes rather than their actual structure (Rosch 1978; Lakoff 1987, 136 ff.). In the matter at hand one can say that men rank higher than women, and women rank higher than children on a scale of prototypicality, regardless of the physical way this scale might, in fact, be embedded in agents' consciousness or cognitive apparatus.

Rather than relating the scale to a prototypical person or speaker, I will refer to a prototypical perspective. This would be a more accurate appraisal of the cognitive processes at work. Women use the same habitual word orders as men do, but do not usually have a sense of themselves, as speakers, which is male in any meaningful way. They do, nonetheless, adopt a specific perspective on things, including themselves, which is reflected in these habitual word orders. This perspective incorporates the scale of prototypicality in which men rank higher than women, and implies the domination of the male point of view over its female counterpart, in line with Bourdieu's argument, and the domination of the adult point of view over the infant point of view.

There are exceptions to this, though, which, unless accounted for, threaten to undermine the entire analysis. Table 7.3 shows terms typical of Australian discourse:

Table 7.3 Parental gendered conjuncts

Usual	Unusual
mum and dad	dad and mum
mother and father	father and mother
mothers and fathers	fathers and mothers
grandma and grandpa	grandpa and grandma
nanna and pop	pop and nanna

Contrary to the previously quoted examples, normal speech places female ahead of male in these couplets. This does not disprove the practical logic which Cooper and Ross uncovered, but rather complicates it. This series of conjuncts – all of which highlight the parental functions of the persons denoted – is a sociologically meaningful expression of structural relations. There is a division between areas of the domination of the masculine perspective and areas of a domination of the feminine perspective. When thinking about people as parents, the centrality of the feminine seems to be asserted in habitual speech practices, just as the domination of the male point of view seems to be reflected in more general contexts. Women, in other words, rank higher as prototypical parents than men do – a structural situation which is reflected in these linguistic patterns. (Cooper and Ross themselves were aware of the fact that there are a few conjuncts in which there was a clear bias towards placing the feminine ahead of the masculine. However, they failed to explore the extent of the phenomenon and its systemic logic.)

Incidentally, I found no clear gender bias in conjunct ordering in one related context, namely that of aunts–uncles or uncles–aunts. This probably reflects the ambiguity of these collateral relatives. On the one hand, they can be conceived of as essentially equivalent to parents. On the other hand, their main cause for inclusion in the family is their being siblings of ascendants.

Apart from this ambiguity, these habituated, non-intentional speech constructions clearly delineate the gendering of dominance in different contexts. The male perspective is dominant in general, non-familial contexts, while the female perspective is dominant in the contexts of parenthood and reproduction. These patterns of linguistic practice conform to the general configurations of the division of power and the genderedness of social practice.

Put more generally, there emerges a correlation between social structure on the one hand and regularities in linguistic practice on the other. This correlation is a manifestation of the doxic relationships; that is, the fit between, on the one hand, the internalized structures (expressed, among other things, in speech practices) and on the other hand, social structure (as emerges from sociological surveys, field notes and other social-scientific products). I will now move to adduce more evidence from non-discursive practice to further demonstrate and substantiate this doxic fit. But before I do that, I should review some earlier analyses of corporeality.

Orientation to the Body

Echoing two decades of feminist work, Bourdieu observed that one crucial component of the domination of the masculine perspective is a profound difference in the orientations of males and females towards their own bodies. Women's bodies are experienced as objects, while men's are experienced as subjects. As Bourdieu points out, there are exceptions to this. For example, female athletes learn in the process of their training to become more attuned to their bodies' needs, and experience their bodies as subjects rather than as objects (Bourdieu 1994, 103–104; cf. Young 1990c, footnote 10). In order to account for Novocastrian experiences I will elaborate upon the process of the objectification of bodies both male and female. The overall picture that emerges supports Bourdieu's analysis of masculine domination, although here, too, parenthood forms a sociologically significant context which reverses these relations of domination.

The analysis of concrete bodily comportment and motility, and their relation to the gender order had been carried out before. Philosopher Iris Marion Young's seminal discussion of the embodiment of gender, especially the act of throwing (Young 1990c) is critical. Young uses the typical way girls throw as a basis for the analysis of the embodiment of femininity in comportment and motility. She links this feminine style of motion to the embodiment of restrictions that are placed on the female body in modern societies. Briefly, she sees in the distinct feminine throwing style an expression of a distinct tripartite modality of feminine motility. Feminine motility exhibits, in her words, ambiguous transcendence, an inhibited intentionality, and a discontinuous unity with its surroundings (Young 1990c, 147). Ambiguous transcendence means that women's bodies do not give women the same capacity to negotiate the world that men's bodies give men, but rather limit and inhibit their scope of action. Thus a woman typically refrains from throwing her whole body into a motion, and rather concentrates motion in one part of the body alone. Inhibited intentionality reflects the fact that women do not perceive their environment as potentialities for their action, but rather as potentialities for action which someone, but not they, can carry out. Discontinuous unity reflects again the concentration of motion in one isolated part of the body, which thereby becomes discontinuous with the rest of the body, which remains immobile. All three elements are self-contradictory, reflecting the fact that woman experiences her body not only as subject, but also as object. It is the latter, the product of the sexist social regime, which posits woman's social existence as the object of the gaze of others (Young 1990c).

Young draws her inspiration from the work of Simone de Beauvoir and Maurice Merleau-Ponty (de Beauvoir 1972; Merleau-Ponty 1962), to create a blend of existential phenomenology which she brings to bear on the subject of her analysis. I am taking a more sociological approach here, which leads me to a somewhat different interpretation of findings like Young's. I will return to Young's conclusions shortly.

In Newcastle, male bodies were no less objectified than were female bodies. There were definite images of what male bodies should be like. Over-developed breasts in boys or high-pitched voices in late-teenagers might be a source of great anxiety and social difficulty. Still, there was a qualitative difference in the types of standards which were used to objectify male and female bodies, in line with Bourdieu's analysis. The criteria used to objectify and judge male bodies had to do with action and an active orientation towards the world, indicators of strength and power being the most obvious. On the other hand, the criteria used to evaluate the female body stressed passive attraction: they focused on the aesthetic value of the female body and suppressed its functioning. Thus, the odour of sweat might be conceived of as masculine and, up to a point, attractive on a male body, but would normally be experienced as unacceptably repellent on a female body. Women were much more likely to buy and use scented shampoos, perfumes, anti-perspirants and deodorants than their male counterparts.

This gender differentiation is part of a broader gender differentiation in the construction of desire in modern consumerist society. Ann Game and Rosemary Pringle observe that desire is articulated differently for men and women, and that 'masculinity builds on aggressiveness, activity, a desire to control; while femininity builds on passivity, narcissism, and receptiveness' (Game and Pringle 1983, 94). This is more than a description of the construction of gender in mass media. Woman's objectification as object, and man's objectification as subject, are both internalized. Thus a woman who had cosmetic surgery to her breasts explained to me that she did not do it for men, but so that *she* could feel good about herself and that, following the surgery, she did. Other women gave a similar rationale for various other behaviours which might have appeared as conformity to an externally imposed regime of objectification. Sexy attire, provocative make-up and various other elements of their appearance were explained in similar terms. Being attractive was first and foremost about 'feeling good about yourself'.

In Newcastle, then, both male and female bodies were objectified, males as subjects and females as objects. The intensity of such differences between males and females was age-related. (In this, too, Novocastrians are not unique.) These differences were most pronounced in adolescents and in young adults who were actively involved in the 'trade' on the 'first-marriage market'. Older people seem to have undergone an attenuation in the urgency of these differences in orientation towards the body. Once settled in a long-lasting conjugal relationship, both men and women tended to spend less effort on managing their physical appearance. This seems to be part and parcel of the general process of ageing, in which the relative value of physical capital diminishes.[4]

Moreover, Novocastrians felt that the physiological markers of ageing detracted from the physical attraction of women. One young woman I spoke with expressed

---

[4]   Mike Donaldson pointed out that as blue-collar workers grow older, their skills and experience become more important than their diminishing physical strength (Donaldson 1991).

concern about breastfeeding because she feared it might make her breasts sag earlier than would otherwise happen, and she was anxious to keep them as firm as possible for as long as possible.

Significantly, there were contexts in which it was the female body which was objectified as subject. A major change in bodily orientation among women – equivalent to that among women athletes under the influence of training and competition – would occur during pregnancy and childbirth. It is at these times that the needs of the female body would come to the fore. Cravings in particular and 'capricious' behaviour in general were pandered to and acceptable among pregnant women, and were commonly attributed to the pregnancy. In interviews and conversations women construed pregnancies as times when they could take leave from normal requirements of societal bodily control – they could eat what they liked when they liked. (These women are not unique in experiencing in pregnancy a sense of power, cf. Young 1990b, especially 166–167.) Many, in fact, experienced pregnancy as the demise of the waistline and liberation from many bodily restrictions. In focus groups, some took delight in recounting how they 'terrorized' (as one woman facetiously put it) their male partners, for example by repeatedly sending them at ungodly hours to buy some peculiar, craved-after foods (e.g. mustard and pickles), or by being physically and emotionally very demanding and volatile. The functions of the female body would remain in the fore following the birth, too, breastfeeding and its constraints being a case in point. Whereas normally women would be reluctant to expose their breasts in public, women I spoke with professed no shame or embarrassment about breastfeeding in public. Rather, breastfeeding was commonly sought after by Novocastrian mothers as personally rewarding. In fact, to such women breastfeeding in public constituted an essential right, an all-but-won political battle against those who consider it inappropriate.

The politics involved in the presentation of breasts in everyday life were considered by Young (Young 1990a). Young argues that breasts – a critical physical manifestation of the self – are a scandal in modern patriarchal society. They combine two aspects which should not be combined, that of maternity and that of sexuality. The former, she argues, requires selfless giving. The latter involves selfish demands. The two are therefore incompatible (Young 1990a, 198–199). In Australia, though, as seen through the Novocastrian experience, the scandalous elements are inverted. The domain of maternity is that in which woman is dominant, that is, she is a subject. The domain of sexuality is that in which she is objectified. Reconstituting Young's argument this way makes sense of the very intricacies of the two different modalities of the presentation of breasts, both among Australians, and in Young's own US-based analysis.

Young points out that there are very clear norms governing the presentation of non-lactating (and hence sexual) breasts. They should be firm, round, upright, and the presence of the nipples should be repressed (Young 1990a, 190–192). This mode prevailed in Newcastle, too. I mentioned earlier the woman who was concerned that breastfeeding might make her breasts sag. The counter-argument that women put forward to such a position was that breastfeeding was important, that it was a worthwhile sacrifice, part of the act of giving which defines maternity. Whatever their position on breastfeeding, though, women informants concurred that sagging breasts were less attractive than firm breasts.

Young herself interprets this mode of presentation as an objectification of the breasts, an interpretation which agrees with my argument regarding the suppression of the functioning of the woman's body when she is treated as object. 'To be understood as sexual, the feeding function of the breasts must be suppressed, and when the breasts are nursing they are desexualized' (Young 1990a, 199). By contrast, there are no equivalent specific norms to govern the presentation of lactating breasts. In other words, by Young's own account, sexual breasts are objectified the same way the sexualized feminine body is – as an object. Once the functions of the female body parts are highlighted, they cease to be sexual objects.

Novocastrians, too, did not explicitly regard the exposed breast of a breastfeeding woman as erotic. Breastfeeding altogether was generally construed as non-sexual. In the very least, breastfeeding was construed as an illegitimate source of sexual titillation to the observer. In one instance when discussing some objection to breastfeeding in public, a group of women expressed disgust at 'sick' men who might be turned on by such practices. While women were quite open about breastfeeding being rewarding, they stopped short of elaborating on the physically gratifying erotic aspect of breastfeeding (cf. Young 1990a, 199–200). This may be, at least in part, a result of a reluctance on the part of women to acknowledge erotic sensations in an activity which is construed as non-sexual, 'pure' and maternal. Another factor which may be involved in de-sexualizing breastfeeding is the incest taboo – construing breastfeeding as an erotic act on the mother's part might challenge one of the most fundamental aspects of familial relationships.[5]

In short, contrary to her own interpretation, I would interpret Young's description of breasted experience and the double modality of the presentation of

---

[5] An example of the possible strength of the anxiety over the erotic aspect of breastfeeding can be gleaned from some recent court cases in the US. In the early 1990s a panicking woman phoned a local hotline in Syracuse to report she had sensed some arousal while lactating her baby daughter. She was immediately located and apprehended by the police, interrogated, and briefly detained. In mid-2000 a babysitter reported to authorities that a five-year-old boy she looked after said that he was still being breastfed, and wanted to be weaned, but that his mother wanted it to continue. The mother admitted to still breastfeeding the child, and said she intended to wean him whenever he wanted to stop, and that he had not expressed such a wish. A (female) judge had the child immediately removed from his mother because extended breastfeeding had 'enormous potential for emotional harm' to the child (obviously greater than an immediate separation from his mother). Seven months later, custody over the child was returned to the mother on the proviso that she should take counselling and parenting classes. The anxiety even afflicts some who support mothers' breastfeeding rights who feel compelled to stress that the arousal caused by breastfeeding is essentially different from erotic arousal (Lewin 2001).

breasts among Novocastrians in line with the division between, on the one hand, spheres of bodily orientation which objectify the female body as a subject – maternity in this instance – and, on the other hand, spheres in which the female body is objectified as an object, as in the instance of the sexual objectification of women's breasts.

This is not to say that in the course of everyday symbolic struggle, women do not construe their maternal efforts as selfless giving. At least in Newcastle, they often did. But adopting such a position must be seen within its strategic context in the symbolic struggle of everyday life – being the martyr carries with it a high symbolic premium. Women are not unique in this regard. Quite often men construed their own involvement in the labour market as selfless giving to the family, in a similar symbolic strategy. While both men and women may genuinely experience their contributions as selfless, it would be wrong to mistake these constructions for expressions of direct structural subordination of women to men in maternity, and of men to women in labour-market involvement.

The domination of the feminine point of view in reproduction is further underscored by the fact that the policing and disciplining of women's behaviour in this area, and the domestic sphere more generally, is itself primarily a domain of women's action (with the notable exception of the professional-intellectual elites, such as medical practitioners). In Newcastle, women reported that when they felt external pressure to conform to standards of maternal and domestic behaviour, it was not normally from men but rather from women. Bones of contention could range from the levels of cleanliness inside the home (major pressures coming from mothers and mothers-in-law), through the way they handle their babies in public, down to their very bodily techniques and appearance. Similarly, women cited other women, rather than men, as obstacles to their breastfeeding in public. Of particular notoriety was a woman who owned a cinema in town who had banned breastfeeding in her theatre. The fact that the protagonists in these clashes were primarily women reflects the gender segregation of issues relating to breastfeeding. Men did not express strong opinions one way or the other on the issue of breastfeeding in public. It was women's business. All this further demonstrates the assertion, by women, of their exclusive authority in feminine spheres.

I would like to return now briefly to Young's tripartite modality of self-contradictory feminine motility (see above). It seems to me that she indeed describes a specific modality of motility, but that feminine is the wrong term for it. Rather, it should be considered subordinate motility to distinguish it from dominant motility. This motility is typified by a measure of self-consciousness and lack of confidence, and typically occurs when agents operate in spheres where they are not dominant, that is, when people are 'out of their depth' or are like 'fish out of water'. In fact, this modality appears to be feminine because of Young's focus on the act of throwing. Throwing a ball is an activity which is quintessentially masculine in the prevailing gender order both in the US and in Australia. Indeed, in distinctly masculine spheres women's bodily orientation may well exhibit the quality of self-awareness and lack of confidence. However, were Young to write a sequel to her paper along the lines of 'holding a baby like a man', 'changing nappies like a man' or 'feeding a doll like a boy' she might have been able to reverse her analyses of masculine and feminine modalities of motility.[6]

This, at least, was the situation among Novocastrians. When it came to balancing a baby on a hip, when it came to changing nappies, when it came to holding a baby and bottle-feeding it, there seemed to be a difference in the approach of both men and women to the task. This difference is general, and a great variation occurs within the groups of men and women. Still, gendered patterns did emerge. It was women who took to such tasks with great ease, naturalness and expertise – using all their bodies in an integrated, unreflective fashion to perform the task – while men tended to perform such tasks in a clumsy, cumbersome and stilted manner. Ironically, by choosing a masculine sphere to focus on women's action, and by problematizing women's motility only, Young falls into the trap of gendering feminine practice while naturalizing masculine practice, thereby reproducing the general doxic domination of the masculine perspective, just as Novocastrians regularly did.

It emerges from the foregoing that Young's findings can be incorporated into a broader framework. The different orientations to the body are distributed across society in a clearly gendered pattern. Part and parcel of the gender order is a general situation in which male bodies are objectified as subjects, while female bodies are objectified as objects. This is reversed in the context of parenthood. This fundamental aspect of the internalized structures of habitus parallels the total division of labour and authority which accords women primacy in the domestic domain, and men in the more general spheres of social practice. Agents' gendered orientation to their own bodies, as well as their speech practices which I analysed earlier, assume a masculine perspective as the prototypical perspective in general spheres of practice, while the feminine perspective becomes dominant in the restricted context of parenthood.

The Metaphoric Organization of Internalized Masculine Domination

As I pointed out above, the material structure of masculine domination – the subordination of the domestic domain to the marketplace – is paralleled by internalized structures of masculine domination. Here I will argue that it is the adult–infant juxtaposition which acts as a practical metaphor for male domination and plays a role in structuring that domination. I will begin by demonstrating that

---

[6] If my analysis is correct, and Young has identified a subordinate rather than a strictly feminine modality of motility, her analysis might be generalized and extended to other contexts of social domination. For example, in bourgeois contexts we might expect working-class agents to exhibit a subordinate modality of motility, and similarly in working-class contexts we might expect bourgeois agents to exhibit such a modality.

some of the very markers which constitute the feminine in contrast with the masculine are, in fact, those which constitute infancy in opposition to adulthood.

The homology between male–female differentiation and adult–infant differentiation is not wholly unconscious. The tradition of identifying femininity with childhood is well entrenched. For instance, 'patriarchal' notions of war, politics and economics place both women and children in a dependent status, dependency thus typifying both femininity and infancy, and juxtaposing both with masculinity and adulthood. Further, the cognitive models that Novocastrians invoked in assessing the physique of women and young children tended to converge. 'Cute' and 'beautiful' were adjectives they normally applied to women and babies, not men. These adjectives, when applied to men, carried with them a diminutive and effeminate connotation. In fact, the very co-occurrence of diminution and effeminacy – a normal conceptual event – itself obeys and reinforces the logic which equates femininity with infancy. Also, the standards that were used to appreciate and evaluate techniques of the body incorporated an isomorphism between the infantile and the feminine. For example, when a young boy would cry, he might be told to stop because he was no longer a baby, or he might be told not to cry like a girl. In this instance, through their identification with crying, the underlying homology between femininity and infancy was expressed and reinforced.

The same isomorphism prevails in the socio-somatic construction of gender. What distinguishes a man from a woman is, in fact, the very thing which distinguishes adults from infants. To demonstrate this I will approximate the structure of my informants' lived world by using dichotomies and postulating a cognitive relationship between them.

I should stress that unlike some structuralist and post-structuralist analyses, these dichotomies are intended as approximations – that is, as a projection from the realm of practice to the realm of formal logic and presentation. I am not arguing that these dichotomies *are* the way my informants' world is structured. Gender constructions (and adult–infant constructions) can be approximated by the use of dichotomies because among my informants, those gender constructions are largely organized as discrete, mutually exclusive and mutually constitutive. The existence of borderline situations, like transvestites, does not disturb this practical dual categorization. This is so because practical logic is fuzzy, and because the categories of male and female, like those of adult and infant, are themselves internally structured around prototypes. In other words, the prototype metonymically signifies all other non-prototypical practices. Instances which are more borderline are perceived as precisely such – borderline cases – which do not in themselves undermine the existence of a borderline between masculinity and femininity. The dichotomies I use to approximate internalized Novocastrian gender structures tend to reify the prototype and downplay the variation within the categories – a necessary heuristic step in accounting for the underlying logic of the system. This should be borne in mind when considering these dichotomies.

man:woman::hirsute:smooth skin::adult:infant. Male bodies are hairier. Women's skin is smooth. Smoothness of skin also marks the infant body in opposition to its adult counterpart (cf. Fergie 1988). Of course, this distinction and the ones that follow are both culturally encoded and wilfully accentuated by social agents through their techniques of the body (see below).

man:woman::muscle:flesh::adult:infant. Men are more muscular. This very same distinction also differentiates the infant body from the adult body.

man:woman::strength:flexibility::adult:infant. Men are stronger than women while women are more flexible than men. This statement describes primarily physical reality, but also extends to a prevalent Australian ethno-psychology. Infants, too, are flexible and weak when compared with adults. Ethno-psychology also has them as more malleable, and not fully formed emotionally.

man:woman::hard:soft::adult:infant. This dichotomy, too, could describe the perceived differences in the physique of men and women, as well as that between adults and infants. This distinction of hard and soft further corresponds to the division of social and emotional labour along gender lines. For example, when one interviewee argued that gender relations were changing, she commented that women were doing many things that men had used to do. She said she thought that things were 'starting to change for men, too' and that they were now 'taking soft options'. These 'soft options' included spending more time in the education system, studying humanities and arts at university, and spending more time with children.

In some of the families I studied, the division of disciplinary labour followed this very paradigm: the mother, more compassionate and understanding, would mete out lesser punishments for ordinary violations, but would refer the children at times of exceptional misconduct to their father for exceptional, harsh punishment. In one such family, for example, the mother, Kathleen, ran the home and dealt with the children on a regular basis. At times, however, the father, Victor, would make his forays into the mundane familial arena. Kathleen did not normally like Victor's intervention. She described him as lacking subtlety when dealing with the children. For him there was right and wrong, and when a child misbehaved, punishment followed hard and fast. This, she said, created great tension between the father and children. Often she found herself acting as the go-between, trying to massage egos and keep relationships going. If one of her children got in trouble at school, she might advise the child on how to bring up the topic with Victor to avoid excessive conflict. On the other hand, when she felt like her children needed a particularly stern reproach she would enlist Victor to punish them and 'do the dirty work'. We can see here two styles at work: the masculine, direct, 'no-nonsense' approach; and the calculated, socially aware feminine approach. The structure of interaction between the family members resembles a star, or a wheel with spokes, in which the mother is at the hub, and controls the flow of information and interaction between other members of the nuclear family. By various practices, like leaving the 'dirty work' of harsh discipline to her husband, she helps maintain the structural tensions in the relationships between other members of the family, father and sons for example. In their turn, these tensions strengthen her own position as the mediator and as the hub of communications. The structure of relationships in this family reflects the structuring structures – habitus – which were incorporated into the family members and which organize both their corporeal existence, as well as their social existence, in a gendered way.

   man:woman::straight:curved::adult:infant. While the physical postures that males adopt stress muscular control and straightness, the postures women adopt are more often curved. Genderedness is also incorporated into the way people walk and other aspects of motility. Women's movement seems to be more 'ornamental' as compared with the more 'functional' and 'purposeful' mode of male movement. These are the types of values that Novocastrians themselves used in response to my questions to assess and describe the typical gender differences in motility. Functionality, uprightness and purpose also distinguish the comportment of adults from that of infants.

   There is one instance which seems, on the face of it, to counter this argument. When sitting, it was usually women who adopted a straight, controlled, sometimes even stilted, posture, whereas men were more likely to relax control and 'spread out'. This difference in posture was not, though, motivated by an inversion of the relations of *straight:curved*. Rather, it was a direct result of the different orientations of men and women to their own bodies. Their bodies being objectified as objects of sexual desire, women must take great care in managing the way their bodies are presented and exposed, often treading a fine line between the limit permitted by legitimate seductiveness on the one hand and 'cheap' indecency on the other (cf. Young 1990c, 151–153). Women resort to their controlled sitting so that they do not subvert the strategy of their appearance, for example by accidentally exposing the parts of their bodies which should remain hidden, or by conveying in their comportment some lack of self-control. Consequently, women were more likely to take care to keep their knees together (especially when wearing shorts or skirts), of not leaning forward too much so as not to expose their breasts (especially when wearing tops designed to expose the cleavage – which can legitimately be displayed in public as opposed to areolae and nipples – cf. Young 1990a), and so forth. Further, whereas men's limbs could be spread quite freely over a larger space, those of women were kept closer to their bodies. All this notwithstanding, other than sitting styles, the observed differences in motility supported the homology *man:woman::straight:curved*.

   This physical imagery of straight vs. curved also typifies some basic, internalized strategies of social interaction. As far as Novocastrians were concerned, men were those to take the direct route to their target. They would say what they thought and what they wanted without mincing words. In one of the focus groups the women explained that men had no patience for 'babble', that you generally could not simply talk to them but had to talk to them *about something*, and that you could not be emotionally open with them. In an interview, another woman accounted for the fact that women speak 'better' (referring to their linguistic proficiency) by the fact that women communicate better than men.

Related to this difference in communication styles was a very common complaint among the numerous counsellors and service providers I interviewed, to the effect that men might find it harder to deal with difficulties in relationships, but are much less likely to come and seek advice or help.[7] Further, the way men access services is also different from women. One family counsellor said they tended to come at the very last moment and seek 'instrumental advice', an approach that clashed with the preference of counsellors to raise and discuss 'issues'. She added: 'I believe we could get more men if we offered advice on what women really do want out of sex, for example, rather than to get men to come in for counselling'. (She did note, though, a generational shift in men in their mid-twenties to mid-forties being more likely to talk about things, and easier to get to participate effectively in counselling.) Later in the interview she referred to women's superiority in using emotions, and added: 'My experience is that men don't often complain outright about it, but we see lots of examples where women do have the power by being more verbally articulate or emotionally articulate and I think that men are caught on the back foot'.

According to both males and females, women were adept at personal politics and would more readily use roundabout, manipulative tactics to have their way. As one woman explained in a focus group, 'the natural make-up of the gender is that the man is more dominant, and the woman manipulative'. This reflects two basic internalized aspects of gender: one is the mode of social negotiation, the other is the type of resources which are typically available to social agents. The masculine mode of social interaction involves the deployment of power resources in a straightforward way. Intrigue and manipulation are the domain of women, whose power is often insufficient for a direct course of action (Bourdieu 1977). In focus groups both men and women assumed in their discourse that girls are more manipulative than boys. For example, when discussing discipline in the family, one woman said she had a young daughter, which made her role more complex than her interlocutors who had boys, because, being a girl, her daughter was particularly adept at 'pushing buttons', especially with her husband. She found it very hard to set ground rules, because her four-year-old daughter 'manipulated' [*sic*] her husband. She said that mothers of boys had a much easier task, in that way. None of the other participants queried that statement.

Women's control of social capital, the dominated form of capital, was based precisely on persuasion and manipulation, as it were, rather than straightforward coercion. Such strategies as the use of guilt and emotional blackmail were mentioned and described, primarily in interviews with women, as particularly feminine. They were said to be used in various intra-gendered conflicts, such as between mothers-in-law and daughters-in-law, as well as by women in inter-gendered negotiations. Thus, women often complained how their mothers-in-law might (ab)use their position by emotionally manipulating the son/husband, or

---

[7] Youth counsellors also commented on the lesser likelihood of boys, as compared with girls, coming to counselling or staying in counselling.

might cast doubt on the adequacy of the daughter-in-law. This might take subtle forms such as passing a critical gaze on the cleanliness of the household of the daughter-in-law, questioning some of the child-rearing priorities of the younger couple and so forth. At times, the conflict might be more explicit.

In any event, power relations shift firmly towards the daughter-in-law once she has children. Her children form a new stake in the political game of the family. Daughters-in-law often exercised their control of access to their own offspring to assert their position against their mothers-in-law (and in a few cases, even against their own mothers). I did not encounter first-hand cases in which a woman stopped access between her children and her in-laws. However, by being able to do so, and by actively regulating such contact, mothers came to hold a formidable amount of social capital. Commenting on her relationship with her ex-husband's parents, Lucy admitted 'his parents hate me ... they put up with me because if they get cranky with me, get nasty with me, obviously I'm gonna say, well, you have Buckley's[8] of seeing Max [i.e. her son, their grandson] then'.

The gender differences in the mode of social negotiation and in the distribution of capital are linked. Their mastery of social capital is what constitutes women as the lynchpin of the family and of informal social networks in general. Their habitus, which predisposes women to use this capital, is what directs them towards investments in and accumulation of social capital. It is that seemingly miraculous aspect of doxa whereby women seem to spontaneously possess greater social skills, which makes women superior candidates for the role of social and familial organizer, the role which social structure has allotted to them anyway. Men's dispositions are similarly attuned to their roles.

To recapitulate briefly, by and large my informants' practice tends to reproduce the following homologous dichotomies: *man:woman::hirsute:smooth skin:: ::muscle:flesh::strength:flexibility::hard:soft::straight:curved*. These, in their turn, are homologous to the *adult:infant* dichotomy.

There are, however, people who do not or, better yet, refuse to conform to these general dichotomies. The status of their practice is different. Such individuals are making 'statements', whether they like it or not, as for example when a woman does not shave her legs or her bikini line or, even more so, when a man shaves his. For a man not to shave his legs or his bikini line, and for a woman to shave hers, is a different order of action – it is making no statement. It is being normal.

Furthermore, when Novocastrians violated norms of gendered practice, it was almost always women who adopted a masculine style, and not vice versa. During my fieldwork in Newcastle I did not encounter men who wore skirts or dresses, or who were heavily made up. Similarly, some women were comfortable in describing themselves in un-feminine terms, but men never voluntarily undermined their own masculinity in an equivalent fashion. One woman, for example, referred to herself as a 'tomboy' and said that as a child she had always preferred to play with boys and do 'boys' stuff'. She also said that as an adult she tended to get on

---

[8] 'Buckley's chance' means no chance.

better with men than with other women. Similar sentiments were echoed by other women. By contrast, never did men describe themselves as 'sissies', nor did they ever profess to having preferred to play with girls when they were young, or to do 'girls' stuff'. Further, none of the men confessed to getting on better with women than with men. Presenting oneself in such terms would have been an extreme embarrassment. The consequences to a woman's social standing of rejecting standards of femininity in favour of masculine standards are much more benign compared with the consequences to a male of rejecting standards of masculinity in favour of feminine standards. There is some kudos to be gained by women by adopting masculine style, and only losses to be made by men by gratuitously adopting feminine style. This greater tendency of females to adopt male characteristics reflects the very domination of the masculine perspective, which privileges that which is male over that which is female.

Another manifestation of this is the area of unisex – choice of clothing and other modes of self-presentation which are said to be non-gendered. In fact, they are extremely gender-specific. They rely solely on masculine standards. Unisex is licence for females to adopt masculine style. Unisex does not include the adoption by males of feminine styles.

Embodied differences between men and women are normally experienced as objective reality. However, contrary to Australian ethno-science, many of the markers which they use to distinguish males from females are not instances of socially independent, congenitally predetermined, physiological traits. Often, these markers are produced or, in the very least, greatly accentuated by socially specific techniques of the body. In other words, the social agents themselves reinforce the differentiation of these careers through their bodily techniques which are motivated by the structures of their habitus. A case in point is bodily hair: depilation contributes to the situation that the existence of bodily hair distinguishes adult men from women. By suppressing the markers of adulthood, such practices, in fact, deny the maturation of the female body. By the same token one may account for some of the gender differences in muscularity, strength and flexibility by reference to the difference in frequency and intensity of physical activity among boys and girls.

Moreover, even though the mean muscularity, hairiness and strength for women is lower than for men, there is an obvious overlap between the distribution of these traits in men and women, so that there still are many women who are more muscular, hairy and strong than many men. This overlap is negated in the common Australian cosmology, as both cultural construction and bodily techniques serve to accentuate the differences between the genders (cf. Matthews 1984, chapter 2; Connell 1987).[9] This turns the two genders into distinct categories, separated, in this case, by physiological traits.

---

[9] While Connell reduces cultural construction to negation (Connell 1987), I prefer to discuss accentuation. The differences that lend themselves to distinguish between men and women are, more often than not, rooted in some way in that real world which is independent

Deane Fergie has reached a similar conclusion in her analysis of visage management in Australia. She analysed the logic of the public presentation of face in Australia in the early 1980s, and the underlying logic of beauty in its masculine and feminine forms. When femininity was accentuated – e.g. by making the eyes and mouth appear bigger – the underlying logic of feminine beautification turned out to be a negation of mature sexuality and the pursuit of baby-like features. Fergie concludes that:

> Femininity is a determined denial of the evidence of signs of maturity (for example, pimples) in women and fear of the signs of ageing (for example, wrinkles). It is, however, made more forceful by recognizing that those aspects of the face which this analysis has identified as the nexus of femininity have critical parallels with the faces of pre-pubescent children and particularly of babies. The faces of infants are dominated by their eyes and mouth and set in contoured but untextured context [...] By their construction of conventional femininity in their faces, women produce themselves on the one hand as visually more child-like than they would otherwise be. They reinforce visually their political and personal dependency, powerlessness and lack of responsibility. They reproduce the message that they require a 'strong' other to protect and care for them. But at the same time they must also overcome the apparent contradiction between this child-like appearance and their sexual availability to those 'strong' others. They do so by being the active constructors of their faces. (Fergie 1988, 43–45)

However, this practical homology between the *male:female* and *adult:infant* dichotomies is more acutely expressed in two physical aspects of spouse selection, namely in stature and age biases.

man:woman::tall:short::adult:infant. Novocastrians commonly explained that women are naturally shorter than men. That is how they accounted for the rarity of couples in which women were taller than men. This reasoning is wrong, though. The great overlap in stature between men and women means that if mate selection were random as far as stature is concerned, a very large minority of couples would comprise a shorter man and a taller woman. This was not so among the Novocastrians that I studied. Couples in which the woman was taller than the man were conspicuous, and rarer than would be expected if mate choice were random as far as stature is concerned. Moreover, such couples needed to overcome the stature incompatibility (whereas execution of the default gender stature differential requires no such overcoming); and that the peculiarity of such couples would be noticeable to native social agents.

---

of social construction. For instance, while the mental image which associates hairiness with masculinity in opposition to femininity suppresses much of the physical reality it refers to, it does not in this instance negate it. Negation would imply that hairiness would have an equal chance of being associated with femaleness as it does with being associated with maleness. Such a postulation of negation would fail to account for the clear way that the material, physical world does, in fact, motivate its own cultural construction.

The common recourse to the 'natural' stature differences between men and women in order to account for the paucity of couples in which the female is taller than the male, is, indeed, erroneous, but nevertheless socially significant. It is, in fact, an expression of an aesthetic preference that within a couple the woman should not be taller than the man. It conforms to the standards discussed above, according to which women are constituted in relation to men in a homologous way to the constitution of infants to adults. Consequently, the value of stature on the marriage market, as it were, depends on gender. It is commonsense in Australia tall women and short men have a great handicap in the 'marriage market', much greater than similarly tall men and short women.

man:woman::old:young::adult:infant. Couples tend to be composed of older men and younger women. This situation is even more 'scandalous' than the bias in stature, as it does not even conform to any folk-scientific observation regarding age difference. Women's mean age is higher than men's. Women enjoy a greater life expectancy. If mate selection were age-neutral, we would expect a small majority of couples to be composed of younger men and older women.

When pressed in interviews, the explanation most commonly proffered by Novocastrians was related to folk-developmental psychology, namely that women mature faster. This is an expression of the fact that women enter the 'marriage market' at an earlier stage than men do. However, even if the mean age of women on the 'marriage market' were a bit lower than men's, we would still expect a very large proportion of couples where the woman was older than the man if 'marital trade' were age-neutral. The paucity of such couples indicates a process similar to that which happens in relation to stature, namely that habitus incorporates structures of assessment which structure behaviour in a particular way, predisposing men to be more readily attracted to younger women, and women to be more readily attracted to older men. Here, too, a homology emerges between the socio-somatic constitution of the genders on the one hand, and the constitution of infancy as against adulthood on the other.[10]

---

[10] The active role social agents play in reproducing objective structures, for example in their mate-selection strategies, should serve as a reminder that social structures are productive, not only constraining. Marital choices are experienced as free expressions of individual aesthetic, and not as some conformity to external 'rules'. All too often theorists slide into the mistake of thinking of social structure as a set of constraints (e.g. Connell 1987, 92, 97). This assumes that the socialized human being is preceded by a non-socialized human being with a great many potentialities, and that social structure chips away at these potentialities to mould the human being to its role. This view is too restrictive. Social structure not only constrains – it creates. It is what produces the potentialities in the first place. It creates the subjectivity, not merely constrains it. It creates the wants, the needs, the interests (including aesthetics) and the desires of social agents. It motivates agents at the very same time as it inhibits them. It plays a no-less-productive role in the making of outrage and subversion, than it does in inhibiting social agents and securing the consent of the oppressed. It is equally true, of course, that social agents' interests and strategies are the building blocks of social structure, and that the interaction of social agents is what in fact

One objection that might be raised at this point is that the very folk-psychological tenet that women mature earlier than men contradicts my claim that the dichotomy *man:woman* is homologous in practice with *adult:infant*. This would appear to be a contradiction because the notion of women maturing faster than men would suggest, on the face of it, a prevailing association of femininity with adulthood, and the juxtaposition of both with masculinity. The solution to this seeming contradiction lies in the folk-psychological construction of the two trajectories of maturation. Feminine maturation is simple. It is, as it were, a continuous process of subtle quantitative change from infancy. Because the target of feminine maturity is placed closer to infancy, the road to its achievement is shorter and easier. Masculine maturation is more complex and fraught with difficulty and danger precisely because it entails a series of decisive, qualitative breaks with that which is infantile and feminine. Socially, it is a transition from being dominated and dependent to dominance and independence. Physically, it is the development of a set of characteristics which qualitatively break with infant style. In other words, the reason women achieve adulthood faster than men is that feminine adulthood is more infantile than masculine adulthood. Such an infantilization of femininity appears quite common in the European cultural sphere (e.g. Stardardt 1995; Gorsuch 1996; Fergie 1988).

This, of course, is not a reflection of extra-cultural reality, as it were, but of a cultural construction of biology and difference. The juxtaposition of some physiological markers of adult masculinity with their feminine/infantile counterparts is enabled by the social reworking of physiological difference. There is no inherent biological reason why menarche should be any less significant a qualitative break with infancy, than any of the markers of male adulthood, such as deep voice, facial hair or a reluctance to cry. It is rather those incorporated structures of assessment and judgement that evaluate males and females differently, which distinguish between the significance of the physiological careers of men and women.

I would therefore interpret this gender-differentiated maturation processes as further support for the homology *man:woman::adult:infant*. This homology may be motivated by the structural similarity between the dependence of women on men, and the dependence of infants on adults. Moreover, the contiguity between mothers and infants would further support this identity: women and infants are concretely connected through the processes – both cultural and biological – of gestation, birth, lactation and infant care.

---

produces this structure. The opposite fallacy, of seeing culture as active and the physical body as merely offering resistance and limits (e.g. Grosz 1994, 187–192), should also be avoided. If culture was the sole active producer of habitus, there could probably be no sexual heterodoxy in the strongly heterosexually centred European world.

The *adult:infant* dichotomy is cognitively more basic than *man:woman*, and generates the image schema which is symbolic violence par excellence.[11] Image schemata are not concrete rich images or mental pictures. Rather they are abstract patterns that can be manifest in rich images, perceptions and events (Johnson 1987, 2). The dependency of the human young is pre-conceptual and universal. This makes it an ideal concrete rich image to anchor the image schema of symbolic violence, and motivates its extension to gender, as well as to other instances of symbolic violence, like slavery, colonial relations, or class domination in the welfare state. This extension does not exclude the use of less-symbolic violence in these situations, as in the instances where women are battered or striking workers are shot. Nor does it exclude the use of non-symbolic violence in parent–child relationships as happens in some instances of child abuse.

Because of the nature of practical logic the homology between the dichotomies of *adult:infant* and *man:woman* need not be symmetrical. The former structures the latter, while the reverse need not occur. In other words, whereas the dichotomy of *man:woman* is homologous with that of *adult:infant*, and can therefore be modelled upon it, the dichotomy of *adult:infant* may or may not be modelled on that of *man:woman*. This might seem outrageous to formal logicians, but operates quite well in practical logic.

Domination Inverted: The Domestic Domain

As I pointed out above in relation to orientation to the body and patterns of linguistic structuring, the domestic domain, including parenthood, is one in which masculine domination is inverted. It is an area where female ranks higher than male on the prototypicality scale, and where the female body is objectified as subject. Likewise, the structural infantilization of woman is inverted in contexts in which the feminine perspective dominates – namely the domestic sphere. In these limited areas in which women exercise authority, they might relate to their male partners very much the way they would relate to children. This is an integral element of the strategies used in the symbolic struggles of everyday life.

Thus in one instance a woman compared men to children in relation to doing housework. She pointed out that like their children, her partner was often oblivious to mess and would take longer to recognize it and do something about it. The secret of managing men was training them well. Otherwise, she said, men might try to wiggle their way out of doing things, leaving the responsibility for getting things done to the women, at times underperforming, whingeing, etc.

An example of an actual process of negotiations emerged in one of the focus groups. A woman recounted the story of how she trained her partner to perform some parental duties following the birth of their first child. She said he was finding

---

[11] In this I differ with Bourdieu, who considered masculine domination per se to be symbolic violence par excellence (Bourdieu 1998).

it hard to handle nappy-changing and thought he would get away with very little participation in such dirty chores. On the first few times she sent him to change nappies, he took a long time, operating clumsily, waiting for her to step in and take over. She admitted it had taken great dedication to avoid taking over and doing the job herself. But as she explained to her fellow women participants in the group, 'you just can't let them get away with it'. If he knew he could get away without doing it, she would end up doing all the work. And so she insisted that he should do his share, and refused to interfere in his nappy work. Then she smiled at her sympathetic listeners and claimed that that was how she trained him.

This inversion of the adult–infant metaphor to construct femininity in oppositions to masculinity is motivated by the dominance of women in the domestic domain. It is, however, restricted to this domain, and is ephemeral. As my analysis of the embodiment of gender in previous sections shows, it is femininity which is generally constructed in relation to masculinity in a homologous way to infancy in relation to adulthood.

Conclusion

This chapter considered some aspects of the internalization of masculine domination by both men and women. It argued that the internalized attachment of women to the domestic domain runs deeper than calculated, deliberate choices, as does the attachment of men to the marketplace. The domination of the male point of view was demonstrated in non-conscious patterns of habitual speech practices, and Novocastrians' orientations to their own bodies. There emerged, though, a sociologically meaningful and remarkably consistent exception – namely the domain of parenthood and reproduction, where the feminine perspective dominated. The prototypical family, which includes a prototypical model of reproduction, forms the cognitive basis upon which gender and its practice are constructed. It metonymically motivates the structures of gender in general. The embodiment of gender in Newcastle, and more broadly throughout Australia and the anglophone world, includes aspects which generally constitute the feminine to the masculine along lines homologous to the juxtaposition of infancy to adulthood. Many of the expressions of these differences are motivated by pre-conceptual differences which are culturally accentuated. In a restricted context – namely, the domestic domain, where women are dominant – masculinity might be constituted in relation to femininity in a homologous way to the constitution of infancy to adulthood. These homologies attest to the fact that the dependence of infants on adults is a powerful cognitive anchor for domination. This is so because the dependence of infants on adults (or, more precisely, that which is denoted by the culturally mediated notion of the dependency of infants on adults) is pre-conceptual, concrete and universal.

It is an integral aspect of the gender order that the spheres in which the female perspective dominates are subordinate to those in which the male perspective dominates. This is clearly expressed in the power relationship between the home and the marketplace, a relationship which is fundamental to capitalism. The association of women with the domestic domain is a sociological truism. That women derive power from their dominance in this circumscribed area has also been acknowledged in the literature (e.g. Bryson 1985; Rapp 1992). The overlap between these areas and the spheres in which the feminine perspective dominates, demonstrates the extent to which the division into male and female spheres, and the subordination of the latter to the former, have been incorporated into the habitus of contemporary Australians. This hierarchical division is equally internalized by both men and women, and is largely doxic – it does not depend on any conscious decision of social agents and is embedded into the nature of things both at the systemic level (in the form of the overall gendered structure of the political economy) and at the localized level (in the form of particular preferences and characteristics of particular social agents).

An interesting point that emerges from the foregoing is the conservatism of the internalized structures of gender. Gender is but one of many factors that influence the way relationships between social agents are negotiated and reproduced. Economic compulsion is another such factor which motivates heterodox gender practices. Thereby heterodox conjugal relationships do not necessarily reflect a radical transformation in the way gender is experienced.

Thus, when people choose to highlight their genderedness, they normally adopt in practice personas that are based on the gendered logic of the idiom of reproduction and the prototypical family. The stability of gender is intimately linked to the stability of the nuclear family as the realized category of the family, even at times when transformations in demography and the political economy force some shifts in the way family households are practically organized. This is not to say that gender will not eventually transform in a radical way under the mounting pressure of heterodoxy. This is to suggest that, as embodied among the Novocastrians I studied, the embodiment of masculine domination by both men and women is doxic and exerts a conservative influence on social relationships.

Chapter 8

Family and Gender, and Society at Large

Social theorists and anthropologists used to imagine that 'primitive' societies were organized by kinship, and that this distinguished them from modern society which was organized by other principles, most notably the rationalist regime of the market and bureaucracy. It is currently accepted among anthropologists that such views misconstrue 'primitive' societies, and the term itself has been discarded. Yet the commonsensical understanding of European modernity seems more enduring. In this chapter I argue that the juxtaposition of the primitive to the modern also misconstrues modern societies. In fact, upon close examination, the field of kinship and family emerges as a crucial foundation of social structure at large.

Chapter 2 began with a historical narrative of the evolution of the Australian family. This evolution was situated within broader social and political economic contexts. The chapters that followed focused on the field of kinship and family in relative analytical isolation from other spheres of practice. This chapter reintegrates the field back into its broader social context. It highlights the critical role that the field of kinship and family plays in shaping society at large, and particularly the structure of the market economy and the class structure.

The first section considers some of the less obvious interactions between the field of kinship and family on the one hand, and the class structure on the other. The section focuses on gender style, and shows how it interacts with the prevailing class structure. Significantly, gender style and class location are shown to be mutually constitutive rather than one being an epiphenomenon of the other. The second section of this chapter considers the family within the broader political economy, only this time focusing on the role of the field of kinship and family in structuring Australia's political economy.

The Interplay between the Field of Kinship Practice and Class

This section demonstrates the significance of the field of kinship practice to social structure at large by focusing on the way gender style – a set of internalized structures of the field of kinship practice – is implicated in the embodiment of class. In what follows, I situate my informants' embodied structures within the broader social structure in essentially two interdependent ways. One is by identifying the social logic of specific forms of working-class masculinity and femininity; the other is by demonstrating how masculine domination is mapped onto class relations by constituting – from a working-class perspective – the elite as feminine, and working class as masculine.

Chapter 1 theorized the internal structure of the working class, and the contradictions among its fractions as they appear among my informants. This division was linked to the segmented labour market. The dominant fraction of the working class is rooted in the primary segments, while those relegated to the secondary segments of the labour market form the dominated fractions. This section further elaborates on this association. It relates different gender styles within the working class to the fractured structure of the working class. Masculine style and class-fraction location emerge as mutually constitutive – so much so that the two cannot be posited in a definitive causal relation, in which one is always the cause, and the other always its effect.

Gender Style and the Internal Conflict in the Working Class

One thing the working class and the employing class do have in common is the domination of the masculine perspective. This basic parameter, however, is confounded by class location. Working-class gendered consciousness is intimately linked with the genderedness of the labour market. Notwithstanding substantial exceptions, the Australian labour market has been masculinized in a process that reached its peak in the early years of the twentieth century, being institutionalized, among others, in the family wage (see chapter 2). The labouring male and his body – the repository of his labour power – have emerged as the essence and symbol of working class-ness to members of both the elite and the working class. For instance, in a study of working-class culture in Wollongong, Leanne Blackley demonstrated that the iconography of the labour movement from the 1920s through at least the 1970s celebrated the body of the male manual labourer (Blackley 1996; cf. Hobsbawm 1978; Rose 1992).

The traditional iconography of the labour movement is an instance of the more general cross-class predomination of the masculine perspective. In fact, in symbolic class struggles the masculinity of the different classes becomes the image schema that embodies those classes, and acts as a synecdoche for the class as a whole. When thinking of the 'working class', 'working Australians', 'workers', 'blue/white-collar workers', it was primarily an image of the male of the class that my working-class informants – both male and female – had in mind. Similarly, when referring to the elite, the males of that class were what my interlocutors would normally imagine.

Working-class gender practice is, of course, no more uniform than the working class itself. Chapter 1 distinguished between the dominant and dominated fractions among my working-class informants. The structural cleavage across the working class is reflected in various ways in the field of gender styles, most crucially in masculinity. Researchers have long observed that working-class masculinity was not uniform. Andrew Metcalfe, following E.P. Thompson, distinguished between two kinds of Australian working-class masculinity, larrikin and respectable. He associated the respectable with mature, settled, breadwinning males; and the larrikin with young, rough-around-the-edges, unruly males.

Metcalfe uses the term larrikin as an Australian gloss for Thompson's 'rough' masculinity. The Australian term connotes good humour and innocence to a greater extent than the English term. The distinction between larrikin and respectable masculinity seems to parallel Stivens's distinction between 'real man' and 'family man' in her study of kinship in Sydney (Stivens 1985, 17 ff.), although she does not investigate the social bases for these different styles of masculinity.

Interestingly, Metcalfe comments that these categories do not necessarily distinguish between two different groups of individuals. The two ideal types he identified often typify different stages of single life trajectories, rather than different male careers altogether: the same male can conform to the larrikin type as a young, unmarried male, and subsequently adhere to the respectable type as a mature, settled male who is typically 'saddled' with a family (Metcalfe 1988).

Metcalfe's observation regarding the transformation of masculinity style with age agrees with my informants' experience. Quite a few of the men I interviewed would reminisce about their wild youthful days. One typical example was Meyer, in his thirties, who recounted how, as an adolescent, he had very little interest in school, performed badly there, and often got into trouble with teachers. He left after year ten, shifting among employers for a while, quitting whenever he got bored. All this changed when he moved in with his partner and became a father. He had to settle down. He stuck it out with a heavy-industry corporation, participating in numerous technical training courses, and ultimately gaining substantial promotions. By the time of my fieldwork he had become a salaried staff member. Having his current familial responsibilities meant that he lost his flexibility in moving in and out of jobs. He resented that loss of flexibility and he hated his job. He also disliked being separated from waged workers (staff had their own toilets, were discouraged from joining unions, and stuck together). Still, he had to grit his teeth and persevere. He also adapted other aspects of respectable masculinity. He cut down on his drinking (although he was no teetotaller by any stretch of the imagination), tried in vain several times to give up smoking, and limited his consumption of marijuana to special social occasions. While I was in Newcastle, he was also involved in politics in the labour movement.

Although this instance shows the transformations that occur with ageing, one must approach this and similar life stories with caution. Ageing is not the only process at play here. Up until the 1970s, work in heavy industries was pretty abundant and apprenticeships were easy to come by. The subsequent squeeze on the labour market in the 1980s and 1990s means that, regardless of ageing, the capacity to change employers has diminished, as has the quality of the labour experience. Further, general awareness about the harmful effects of smoking and excessive drinking has also become more widespread. In other words, that which my informants like Meyer might experience as a personal change in style may be partially a reflection of a broader social change around them, rather than life-cyclical change in dispositions. Still, the fact that my informants identify the process of ageing with transformations in gender style, and the fact that similar findings have been made in other periods of different cultural and economic dynamics (e.g. Metcalfe's study of the Hunter Valley in the decades leading up to the 1960s), underscore the link between the change in style and the process of ageing.

This process of mellowing with age and responsibility is not independent from the material conditions in which it is embedded. The association of masculinity type with life-stage difference parallels some age-related changes in the involvement of males in the production process. Donaldson (1991) pointed out that for blue-collar workers ageing often entails a reduction in physical capital as a result of the toll of the labour process on the body of the worker. This reduction is offset by an increase in skill level and experience.

In other words, in the lives of specific working-class males there are often two processes which occur at the same time. One is a shift in the composition of capital, as the relative significance of physical capital diminishes while that of cultural capital increases. The other is a shift from larrikin style to respectable style of masculinity. Metcalfe observed the transition in masculinity style over individual life spans. Donaldson related such a process to the material conditions of the working-class life trajectory. I have recast Donaldson's explanations in terms of the relative weight of the different species of capital. This makes it possible to generalize the association of the relative weight of cultural capital with respectable masculinity. I am arguing that this is a general link – it can be seen not only over the life course of individuals, as Metcalfe observed, but also by comparing different class fractions. A comparison of the two fractions of the working class reveals that both a higher relative weight of cultural capital, and respectable masculinity, are more common in the dominant fraction as compared with the dominated fraction.

Protest masculinity – an extreme variant of the larrikin type – is a case in point. In his ongoing investigation of masculinities Connell argues that protest masculinity stems from social powerlessness and expresses itself in exaggerated and destructive displays of masculine prowess, androcentry and unruliness. Connell associates protest masculinity with the most disempowered segment of the working class (Connell 1995, 109 ff.) – the dominated fraction which engages with the margins of the secondary labour market.

A group of youngsters who lived next door to me in the 'rough' inner-city suburb of Islington, also exemplified protest masculinity in the dominated fraction. Nominally, the flat had two tenants – two teenage women. In practice, up to nine young men and women might have resided there at any one time. These youths, some White and some Aboriginal, were well on their way towards permanent marginalization in the labour market. Most of them had quit school but had no permanent jobs. The young men in the group were given to those very kinds of destructive displays that Connell ascribed to protest masculinity. For instance, one day a fight erupted between the inebriated males over a hamburger. The women who were present at the time tried to calm the guys down, but to no avail. The brawl continued off and on throughout the day, with the police turning up several times at the call of neighbouring residents and shopkeepers. (Whenever the police arrived the young men dispersed temporarily, only to return after the police left and continue where they had left off.) Extensive damage was caused to the flat that day.

Napoleon, one of the central protagonists in the fight, was the brother of one of the two nominal tenants and a regular inhabitant of that flat. His sister frequently complained that he never contributed his share of the rent. When his sister or other people got him 'pissed off' he would fly into fits of fury, at times smashing windows, doors and furniture. On a couple of occasions, while seemingly under the influence of intoxicating substances, he could not be bothered going to the dunny[1] outside and urinated from the window onto the driveway. He and his friends also broke into the video shop around the corner (a feat which landed Napoleon in gaol for a short period of time), broke into the second-hand store across the road, and engaged in petty theft within the neighbourhood. It was the conduct of Napoleon and his male comrades which ultimately brought about the eviction of the whole group.

Another example from Islington was Marshall, then in his late sixties, who throughout his life stuck to larrikin style, bordering on protest masculinity; to the dominated fraction of the working class; and to a low level of objectified cultural capital such as formal training and qualifications. Marshall was born into a poor working-class family in 1927. He grew up in a shantytown on the outskirts of Sydney during the Great Depression, where he and his family were, in his words, 'living like hillbillies'. His parents were 'virtually illiterate'. His father had worked most of his life in casual manual jobs. He himself became a seaman in his teens, joining the Communist Party as a young man. He subsequently left the sea, and for years moved among manual jobs. Marshall's biography is a long litany of conflicts with authority. He said he had been a rebel long before he knew of the Communist Party. Throughout his working life he would invariably fall out with employers, with union officials, and with CP leaders. He put his problems with the CP leadership down to the latter's contempt for 'us fuckin' prolies'. His last job was a ten-month stint as a cleaner at the Workers' Club. He was sacked after falling out with the officials of the Trades and Labour Council. His interrupted involvement in the labour market (including a long spell of unemployment) and his related labour activism were also partly responsible for the collapse of his two marriages. At least the first marriage was doomed from the start. His mother-in-law ('I detested the fuckin' bitch') was, by his account, a 'man hater' and set his wife against him. His wife herself was extremely selfish and 'made a cunt of me in front of me mates'. Marshall, both in his biography and in his self-presentation, exemplifies the association of class fraction and larrikin masculine style.

---

[1] The dunny (outhouse toilet) was shared by the residents of a few of the flats and one of the shops downstairs.

Marshall, along with Napoleon and his friends, can be opposed to Meyer who exemplifies the respectable style of the dominant fraction, and its reliance on cultural capital (Meyer's training) to secure its position (in this instance – Meyer's position as salaried staff).

As Meyer's biography shows, working-class male subjects often incorporate both larrikin and respectable styles of masculinity. Social agents are directed towards one style or the other in different contexts. Different agents incorporate these styles to varying degrees of success. Because respectable style seems a necessary (although not a sufficient) condition for the successful accumulation of cultural capital such as trade qualifications, agents who do not sufficiently incorporate the respectable style, or who are not able to properly affect it in the right context, are much less likely to accumulate cultural capital. Further, the processes of accumulation of cultural capital further reinforce the respectable style – for example, to complete a training course at a technical college many aspects of respectable masculinity need to be honed, such as successful acceptance of subjection to authority and tolerance of pedagogic rituals. Finally, the cultural capital, once accumulated, attracts social agents towards further situations which are associated with respectable masculinity, for example, supervisory positions or positions of technical authority, both of which were obnoxious to the egalitarian sensibilities of dominated-fraction male informants. (Moreover, some of the men in such supervisory positions also felt uncomfortable about their position of authority.) In other words, respectable masculinity and higher levels of cultural capital are mutually constitutive, rather than one of them causing the other.

Significantly, within the working class, membership in a particular fraction is not predetermined. Young males – at least the ethnically mainstream – occupy a liminal space, and are yet to develop both a clear masculine style and the cultural capital which will determine to a large extent their ultimate attachment to a particular class fraction. The high-school years and the early years in the labour market are critical for the acquisition of both gender style and cultural capital (cf. Connell et al. 1982; Willis 1977).

Because of this fluidity and uncertainty in social reproduction, dominant-fraction informants took great pains to ensure to the greatest extent possible the access of their children to the primary labour market, by attempting to instil various skills and (respectable-masculine) dispositions in their sons. One such skill was work ethic. In a few dominant-fraction families, for example, the payment of a son's pocket money was directly linked to performance of tasks such as cleaning his own bedroom and feeding the family pets. Another important skill was literacy: it was common among dominant-fraction parents of babies and toddlers to acquire baby books, brag about their children's rapid acquisition of reading skills and, if they could afford to, seek commercial childcare providers who taught literacy and numeracy skills. The demand for placement with 'good' childcare providers far outstripped supply. Some of my informants had to rush to enrol their offspring with their preferred providers before these offspring were actually born. All of this was done with the express intention of giving their children a competitive edge in life, and ensuring they would not be disadvantaged in their competition with others.

These complications of social reproduction and the broader daily conflict between the two class fractions (discussed in chapter 1) expressed themselves in various practical ways, not least of which was the obsession with youth discipline that characterized quite a few dominant-fraction parents, especially mothers. This obsession was very much a symbolic clash between the fractions of the working class. Dominant-fraction parents feared that larrikinism would interfere with their children's education, might land their children in trouble with the law and consequently threaten their children's future. Put differently, these parents were concerned about the risks posed to their children's capacity to reach the dominant fraction of the working class. A decent secondary education and work ethic, and a clean record with the police, were seen by my informants as necessary conditions for a 'good job', that is, for attachment to the dominant fraction. My informants perceived the main threat to be posed primarily to boys by those among their peers who exhibited the protest style of masculinity, and it was this type of masculinity which the parents would combat in their attempts to protect their offspring. They commonly complained that schools were too soft on discipline and that there were too many children (especially males) who had a potentially bad influence on their children. One strategy adopted by some of my informants was to transfer their children to Catholic schools, which were perceived to be tougher on discipline. Another was an attempt to control the movement of children, especially their sons, in such areas as shopping malls, because other youths who hung around shopping malls were perceived as potentially corrupting. Even parents who regularly consumed alcoholic beverages and smoked both cigarettes and marijuana were extremely worried that their sons might be encouraged by friends to do the same.

Members of the dominant fractions of the working class, owing their dominance within their class to the same political-economic structure which nonetheless confines them to the working class, thus find themselves in a somewhat contradictory position. In their daily life, the conflict between the two fractions of the working class seems more prominent. Respectable masculinity, a compliant working-class style, thus shares with bourgeois, elite masculinity an antagonism towards larrikinism – a stylistic expression of the dominated fraction of the working class.

Both the clash of interests and the differences in masculinity style combined to produce in daily life a measure of social segregation along fraction lines within the working class. Among my informants, at least, primary labour-market workers tended to socialize outside work with other primary labour-market workers from both within and outside their industries, much more than they did with secondary labour-market workers within their own workplace. Such networks constituted an essential element of social capital: they formed an important tool for members of the dominant fraction to defend their position. Information about employment opportunities and advice about career paths circulated in such networks, as did details about investment opportunities, the merits of different educational institutions, and other significant information for social reproduction. This process might also help account for the fact that in the transition from blue-collar labour to white-collar labour there seems to have been a degree of fraction retention: information about good jobs and their requirements would be more readily available in dominant-fraction social networks.

Interestingly, it was women in their capacity as the main social organizers who contributed most to the maintenance of class-fraction segregation of social networks. The social networks of married men were almost invariably based on the network-maintenance work of their wives. When one partner had an independent social network, that partner was usually the woman. The much venerated Australian mateship and networks of mates were surprisingly foreign to my partnered informants' everyday experience, much though it persisted in folklore. In their lack of independent social networks, my male informants resemble working-class males from Britain (Allan 1979). The situation among my informants seems to agree very much with that among the Sydneysiders that Stivens studied in the late 1960s (Stivens 1978; Stivens 1985, and see chapter 4 above for a discussion of mateship).

In their own independent social networks, wives of primary labour-market workers and women who were themselves primary labour-market workers tended to socialize within their fraction rather than with women whose access, whether direct or indirect, was restricted to the secondary labour market. Immediate social networks did sometimes cut across class fractions, although judging from my informants' experience, this stems primarily from close relatives being in different fractions.

The close social network of Meyer and his partner, Lucy, was typical in that it was virtually restricted to the dominant fraction, although it was much larger than most couples' networks. Meyer was a salaried staff member of a heavy-industry corporation, Lucy was casually employed in social services, although at the time of my fieldwork she was on maternity leave. Their close social network included two other couples, who along with Meyer and Lucy were buying, improving and reselling or hiring out real estate. In one of these couples, the husband was also a salaried staff member in industry, and his wife a bureaucrat at a tertiary educational institution. The other couple was comprised of Esther, who was a training officer in the public service, and Jack who was employed in retail on a casual basis and otherwise worked on their real-estate investments and looked after their baby son. Other members of their social network included a woman who worked as a financial adviser to clients of the Department of Social Security, a union organizer, a fellow worker in heavy industries (who at the time was completing a postgraduate degree in cultural studies), Meyer's sister who was studying industrial design at the University of Newcastle, an erstwhile colleague in industry who moved to work for the public service at a mid-level managerial position and a few other persons who were attached directly or indirectly to the primary labour markets. These people might drop in for a beer (mostly the single men), a cuppa and chat (mostly women), or have dinner together (mostly couples).

One clear example of the symbolic struggle in gender style between class fractions occurred on New Year's Day 1995. Meyer and Lucy and their close friends (a group of between ten and fifteen people) had had a four-year tradition of meeting on New Year's Day for a day-long game of croquet and a barbecue at their place. They owned a large block of land with three dilapidated houses, which they had been slowly renovating over the years. They lived in one of the houses, and the other two were let. The combined backyard afforded enough space for the whole event. In 1995 there was one unusual feature to the event. The couple had been out drinking a week or so before at the bar of a local club. Meyer got a bit tipsy, and ended up inviting all the people at the pub to the event. The turnout was rather impressive – around 50 people (including children) turned up during the day. The social distinctions were clearly visible in the way people spontaneously congregated. The couple and their close friends tended to sit in one area. The respectable types tended to gravitate in that direction. Another area was occupied by a group of guests with a clearly more larrikin style, and who very much belonged to the dominated fraction. The groups included a few casual workers and their family, some unemployed people, a cleaner. The differences between the two groups were stark. The language used was rather different (more 'crude' in the second one), clothing style was different too (less trendy, and much cheaper clothes in the second group), as was appearance in general (heavier tattoos in the second group, more people with bad teeth, more of the men with the working-class goatee), and the interaction was generally more boisterous.

A third group was the students – Meyer's sister and her friends – who turned up as well. They were very close in style to the first, respectable group. However, they were generally younger, and remained apart from the general crowd of families.

In the middle, the croquet tournament continued lazily for the better part of the day. The children were mostly in and around the small backyard pool. Around lunch time Lucy and her female friends – all members of the dominant fraction – retreated into the kitchen to cut salad. When I followed them to find out what was happening, I happened upon a discussion carried out in low voices. The women were irate with one of the couples of the dominated fraction. The latter had turned up with their unruly adolescent son. The women in the kitchen were livid that this couple allowed their son to smoke and drink, that he backchatted, and that he was visibly out of his parents' control. Lucy, who from the start did not like the idea of inviting the mass of people to the barbecue, was lamenting how hard she needs to work to keep her own adolescent son disciplined, and that all her hard work might come undone under the influence of this unruly boy, and others like him. Her interlocutors agreed wholeheartedly.

By contrast with the clash over masculinity, conflicts between styles of femininity are neither as explicit nor as direct as those between larrikin and respectable masculinities. In fact, my dominant-fraction female informants primarily opposed dominated-fraction masculinity rather than femininity, perhaps because also within the working class, it is the male of the fraction who is the prototype of his fraction. As the example just cited illustrates, a major criticism which flowed from dominant-fraction women towards their dominated-fraction counterparts centred on the latter's 'failure' to properly rear and control their children, especially their sons.

On the whole, the divergence in feminine style across the fractions of the working class seems less clear-cut than that of masculine style. The domestic division of labour itself inhibits the emergence of larrikin or protest femininity. Among my Novocastrian informants it was generally women who were primarily charged with childcare and with running the domestic economy like paying bills and making ends meet – they could ill afford the 'irresponsibility' of larrikinism. Moreover, once a woman had dependent children she assumed primary responsibility for them. This greater burden of responsibility was matched by the internalized dispositions and postures of a caregiver. This internalized structure both adapted women to their social role as major caregivers, and underlay some of their strategies in the daily symbolic struggles, as when a woman would assume the high moral ground by virtue of her sacrifices, in an attempt to make as much virtue as possible out of necessity. The moral dividends of martyrdom were a major stake in many symbolic struggles between parents and offspring, and between partners, struggles which took the form of the imposition and manipulation of a mix of guilt and gratitude. There was a cross-gender consensus among my informants that women were superior to men in this kind of struggle. Moreover, the fact that in the dominated-fraction married mothers generally depended on men's participation in the labour market for their own living put them in opposition to the larrikin tendencies of their male partners, tendencies which might spell disaster to the household's income. All this made something resembling 'larrikin' or protest femininity rare among my informants. Rather, 'respectable' femininity was common in the dominated fraction as well as in the dominant fraction of the working class.

Furthermore, at least among my informants, women's mobility between the fractions seemed even greater than men's, inhibiting the solidification of fraction-specific styles of femininity. In the period immediately following marriage breakdown or separation, women were more likely to find themselves in the dominated fractions than men were, especially if they had custody over dependent children (cf. Wolcott et al. 1997; and see above, chapter 2). By the same token, women had a greater opportunity of upward mobility through marriage, compared with men. This was so partly because due to the 'patriarchal' logic of nuptial 'trade', women's 'value' was weighted more heavily by 'assets' such as physical attractiveness and charm, which are comparatively independent of class, whereas men's 'value' was weighted more heavily by 'assets' such as earning capacity, which very much define class. This allowed some women of the dominated fraction to acquire a greater 'return' on their 'assets' than their male counterparts.

Put differently, the type of job of the main breadwinner is the single most important determinant of the class-fraction location of the household. To the extent that men are generally the main breadwinners, so would they be fixed in their class-fraction position. To the same extent women have a chance at mobility through marriage. But these regularities of practice should not be mistaken for destiny. In previous chapters I discussed two families where the wife assumed the mantle of main breadwinner. In both families, marriage afforded the men, rather, a chance at upward mobility.

The crowd of next-door adolescents are a good example of the difference between masculine and feminine styles in the dominated fraction. Above I mentioned the escapades of some of the young men. The young women had a different style of conduct. They were the mainstay of social networks in that flat, trying to mediate between the young men and solve problems whenever tensions reached the surface. While both women and men would binge-drink and use narcotics, the inebriated women might get giggly or 'stupid', while the boys were more likely to get violent. Employment was another factor which distinguished the genders. The two women and their female friends were either working, in training or looking seriously for work. The men in that group did not actively participate in the labour market or in training, and often scoffed at the women's attempts to integrate into the labour market or improve their qualifications. It was the women alone who paid the rent and looked after the apartment.

Within the working class, then, differences in gender style, especially masculinity, are implicated in the very class structure. A respectable style of masculinity is virtually obligatory for a continuous attachment to the primary labour market, and is itself in many ways a product of such an attachment. Larrikin masculinity is similarly linked to the secondary-labour market. Masculine style is a project which places the two fractions in opposition to one another. This is so especially for the members of the dominant fraction whose privilege is closely contingent upon respectable masculinity, and who have a lot more to lose than their chains.

Gender Style and the Conflict between Classes

The difference in gender styles within the working class should not be over-emphasized. The material basis for the distinction between the fractions and their gender styles is rather tenuous. Mobility across the fractions is sufficient to undermine any sense of security my dominant-fraction informants had in their position. And of course, both fractions share a common position in the broad political economy. Thus, while foremen and staff might be in daily conflict – explicit or implicit (see chapter 1) – with ordinary workers, they all share a similar position and fate in the total scheme of things, because of their common total dependence on the labour market. When Newcastle's erstwhile largest employer, BHP, wound down its operations there, workers of all fractions were laid off. Moreover, the children of salaried workers run a realistic risk of not maintaining their positions in their fathers' fraction, especially as the traditional basis of this fraction in Newcastle – skilled, manufacturing labour – can no longer sustain this class fraction.

In addition, the manifestations of gender style might often be camouflaged by the requirement not to appear condescending or conceited, an imperative which unites the different fractions of the working class. Normally it was men of the dominant fraction who would resort to a larrikin style of self-presentation in mixed-fraction contexts. I was quite amazed the first time I went out with a local union organizer to a meeting with workers. The man who in private discussions with me adopted a respectable style of self-presentation and could eloquently reiterate the Australian Council of Trade Unions' firm policy on gender equity, resorted to a totally different style when meeting with male workers at a steel plant. His accent broadened, he would slap people on their back in larrikin fashion, and peppered his speech with 'vulgar' expressions and references which were highly androcentric or misogynist. Another man explained that when he talked to mechanics and similar tradesmen he always reverted to broader accents, and mimicked their behaviour because he did not want to appear pretentious, and be consequently 'screwed' by being over-charged or having his car mischievously damaged.

Most importantly, the different variants of working-class masculinity, and femininity for that matter, share elements which distinguish them from elite styles. Among my informants, it was invariably the women who were the more articulate, who were given to abstract, non-instrumental conversation, and who had wider social networks. The style of the 'respectable' men in speech and in social interaction was still rather close to that of the 'larrikin' men I encountered, much more than the style commonly found among working-class women or among the elite.

There is a systemic logic to these differences between the elite and the working class – that is, the dominant and dominated classes. Working-class masculinity is constructed in opposition to elite, bourgeois masculinity, and in juxtaposition with working-class femininity.[2] Consequently, a homology exists between bourgeois masculinity and working-class femininity – namely an opposition to working-class masculinity. (An equivalent situation in the elite may create a homology between bourgeois femininity and working-class masculinity.) This structural homology motivates some gender constructions. Consequently, bourgeois and working-class gender constructions become at times inversions of one another. In other words, that which distinguishes male from female in the elite might actually have the opposite effect of distinguishing female from male in the working class (in addition to distinguishing elite males from working-class males).

Researchers often have an intuitive notion of an aristocratic Freudian/Victorian construction of classed genderedness, where masculinity is contrasted with femininity as the rational, disembodied and 'culture' element of the dichotomy (e.g. Connell 1995, 164 ff.). Although expressions of this kind of gender logic can still be found, it may no longer be the dominant form among the contemporary

---

[2] Sonya Rose identified a similar structure for respectable working-class masculinity in nineteenth-century England – Rose 1992, chapter 6.

elite. Furthermore, the gender order in the ruling class is not uniform. It may greatly vary by age and generation, for example. It does, in fact, vary among the different fractions of the elite (cf. Connell 1995, 165). The references to bourgeois or elite style in the following text should therefore be taken as merely suggestive or illustrative.

The following juxtapositions approximate the gender construction among my working-class informants. They appear to be the reversal of some gendered experiences and constructions which originate in some fractions of the dominant class.

man:woman::wild:tame[3] (as opposed to *man:woman::tame:wild* in some elite constructions). To my informants, it is the men who are wild. They have the capacity to be volatile, hot-headed, physical and brutal. Boys play rough, are more likely to binge drink, get in trouble with the law, or get involved in violence or rape. Women, on the other hand, are better socialized, as it were, and more responsible. To this we can add *man:woman::dangerous:safe* (in contrast with some elite constructions of *man:woman::safe:dangerous*). Working-class men are more dangerous and more threatening to the bourgeoisie, to women, to their fellow men, and to themselves – protest masculinity and larrikin working-class youths being a case in point.

man:woman::nature:culture (in contrast with the elite notion of *man:woman::culture:nature*). Among my informants women exhibited a greater linguistic proficiency, were more likely to be interested in reading in their spare time or in other 'cultural' or 'elevated' pursuits. Among the youngsters I spoke with, girls reacted more positively to school, did better academically, and were less likely to have disciplinary problems. Men's demeanour and favourite pastimes tended to be more physical, more 'violent', less 'refined'. The linguistic proficiency exhibited by men was much less 'developed' than women's, and they were more likely to use 'vulgar', 'dirty' or 'crude' language. Modes of cultural expression like poetry and literature were deemed feminine. So was talking 'too much', especially about issues of no immediate practical consequence, such as emotions or abstractions. We can therefore add here the couplet of *man:woman::crudity:refinement* (in contrast with some elite constructions of *man:woman::refinement:crudity*). In her analysis of visage management, Fergie reaches similar conclusions. Men's proper presentation of self should show little effort to modify one's appearance, whereas women's self-presentation is based on an intensive process of modification, management and improvement (Fergie 1988).[4]

---

[3] As I pointed out in chapter 7 – the dichotomies in this analysis are employed as mere formal approximations of the non-formal logic of practice.

[4] Fergie's work was not concerned specifically with particular class, but reflects popular culture in general. I would suggest that the proliferation of the dichotomy *man:woman::nature:culture* reflects the influence of working-class culture on Australian popular culture in general.

The *nature:culture* dichotomy further accords with men's greater interest in sex as opposed to women's greater interest in romance, as does men's hairier and more muscular physique (see chapter 7). This 'man-the-animal' masculinity fits in with a bourgeois pejorative construction of the male physical labourer – the prototypical member of the working class. In fact, in the rebellious, uncontrollable, protest masculinity this construction is accepted by males of the working class, but given a positive spin. In other words, in this context dominant-class notions (that is, notions of the elite) construct the working class. It is within these ideas of the dominant class that members of the working class (that is, the dominated class) find the symbolic space to construct an opposition of sorts.

From the perspective of the elite other dichotomies might assume greater importance. Power or grandeur, rather than physical strength, might become significant. For example, Bourdieu discusses a character in Virginia Woolf's *To the Lighthouse*, to expose the innermost workings of genderedness in modern society (Bourdieu 1990b). Mr Ramsay is a specimen of bourgeois masculinity. At one point, he fantasizes about himself standing in command of troops and dying heroically, as befits a man of his status. By contrast, the mythic person of the ANZAC digger – an honest, unassuming, hard-working soldier who is loyal to his mates above all else – is a working-class manifestation of the fantasies of military glory. While both masculine fantasies share much in the way of obsession with power, heroic Mr Ramsay's and the ANZAC digger also differ in a socially meaningful way.

Similarly, elite perspectives might reconstitute the *crudity:refinement* dichotomy into some version of the *simple:sophisticated*. Altogether different dichotomies might also be invoked, such as *traditional:advanced* or *savage:civilized*, to celebrate the inferiority – temporal and developmental in this instance – of the working class. My brief here, however, does not extend to the elite, so I will not pursue this issue further.

Because of the oppositional nature of some aspects of the masculinities of the working class and the elite – that is, the dominated and dominant classes – and because of the structural homology between gender domination and class domination, some parallels emerge between the embodied constructions of gender and class. In fact, the inverted construction of gender which I described above could be used to map out the class relations among males from a working-class perspective as follows:

worker:boss::wild:tame::dangerous:safe::nature:culture::crudity:refinement ::strength:weakness::manliness:effeminacy(::man:woman).

It should be noted in passing that the constitution of the working class as effeminate and infantile is not recent, and falls within the broader tendency of effeminizing and infantilizing exploited and dominated groups in general, be they slaves, colonized people, peasants and so forth – a cognitive practice made possible by the logic of the domination of the masculine perspective and the economy of practical logic which extends it to other situations of domination.

This convergence of class and gender structure is not far from the daily consciousness of my informants. As part of their daily symbolic struggles, men often highlight the disagreeable nature of their paid work. This happens across the fractions of the working class, sometimes resulting in a somewhat perverse homology. Men work for their families. They also work for their bosses. This homology between the 'missus' and the 'boss' emerged in some conversations I had with a few disgruntled husbands. In other situations it emerged more implicitly, as when a dominant-fraction worker told me that although he hated his employer and his job, and although he had been trying for a couple of years to find a way out of his position, he had no alternative but work because he had to support his wife and kids. Another dominant-fraction worker explained that his job was indeed boring, but that was the reason his wife and kids had food on their table.

Even in consumption, the mapping of the gender divide onto the socio-economic divide has the consequence that the masculinity of the elite is, at times, equated by members of the working class with femininity (cf., *inter alia*, Mennell et al. 1992; Morgan 1996). To many of my informants, practices and preferences of male members of the elite were effeminate. Similarly, the way men were juxtaposed to women in their consumption style tended to replicate the way working-class men were juxtaposed to elite men. For example, drinking beer rather than wine was identified and presented as masculine in a gendered context and working-class in a classed context. Wine connoted elegance, subtlety, refinement and delicacy which were tagged as feminine in a gender context, and elite in a class context. In my experience, the actual consumption practices varied strongly in both these ways. The situation was similar with regard to salad vs. steak, vegetarianism vs. meat-eating and other such dietary preferences. Here, too, the symbolic association reflected actual preferences among my informants. Preference for vegetable salads and a vegetarian lifestyle (including partial vegetarianism, such as avoidance of red meat) were not very widespread among my working-class informants, but when they were found they were almost invariably among women. Otherwise they were more commonly found in the elite.

Such homologies as *man:woman::beer:wine::working class:bourgeoisie*, and *man:woman::steak:salad::working class:bourgeoisie* seem to reflect the preferences and prejudices of virtually all my working-class informants, whether larrikin or respectable, male or female, blue-collar or white-collar, homemaker or paid worker. Such constructions were not confined to food, and could be found in many other aspects of lifestyle, such as preferred pastimes, sports and clothing style.

A counsellor working in the low-income suburb of Boolaroo put down much of these trends to attitudes to health and the body:

Health is also a commodity, and it's a commodity that the working class really can't afford. It's something that they accept as a necessity, but they don't have an idea of their health being their own. I think that's a very middle-class thinking, the idea of looking after yourself […] and eating well. I don't meet very many working-class kids who are vegetarian: I met lots of middle-class kids who study and become vegetarian, you know. I don't know what's going on there [...] I do not meet, it's very rare for me to meet a working-class family that has kids who've made a real conscious decision to become vegetarian.

She proceeded to comment about other aspects of health consciousness like jogging, which she described as essentially middle-class.

The genderedness of the salad vs. steak has reached near-mythical proportions in the institution of the 'Aussie barbie', an important Australian icon which is very much alive and well. At the barbecues which I attended it indeed was usually men who attended to the steaks and sausages around the fire outdoors, while women would often colonize the kitchen, cutting the salad.

To sum up, even though gender style is profoundly implicated in the division of the working class into two antagonistic fractions, the gender order forms an integral aspect of the structure of the contradiction between the elite and working classes. The different working-class masculine styles share some basic components which set them apart from elite masculinities. Opposition in masculinity style thus becomes one acute manifestation of this class conflict. This motivates the structure of gender construction which becomes, in the working class, a reversal of elite constructions. Eventually, gender distinctions become mapped onto class distinctions, and can be extended to many and varied aspects of lifestyle. Up to a point, then, gender and class are mutually constitutive. The differentiation of gender style motivates the differentiation of class, and class differences motivate the differentiation of gender style, thus creating an overlap between distinctions of class and distinctions of gender style. In no way can gender style be mechanically collapsed into the class structure, as if it were a mere epiphenomenon of the latter. It is the challenge of social analysis to elucidate the logic which connects those two structures – the gender order and class. The juxtaposition of the style of the elite with that of the working class must remain suggestive and provisional, though, because my substantive analysis is centred primarily on the symbolic aspects of working-class gender style.[5]

This, of course, in no way exhausts the connection of kinship practices with class. A full account of the linkage between class structure and the field of kinship and family is yet to be formulated. Here I chose an angle which is not commonly used in order to contribute some new ideas on this linkage, and to demonstrate that the gender order – rooted as it is in the field of kinship and family – and the class structure are not independent of one another. But the field of kinship and gender affects the political economy not only through its effect on class. The very structure of capitalist production has been greatly conditioned by this field.

---

[5] Karen Pyke (Pyke 1996) has made a very similar theoretical argument for the US.

The Field of Kinship Practice and the Structure of Capitalist Production

Social researchers often treat the economic structure as originary, as that which conditions – in some final analysis – the rest of the social structure. This view has given way in recent years to a more interactive perspective in which decisions about family and decisions about the economy interact with one another and shape each other, so that neither sphere can be seen as primary (Creed 2000). This section seeks to further develop such an interactive view by focusing on some Australian practices. I am arguing here that Australian capitalism is predicated on the specific structure and function of the field of kinship and family.

The following inevitably sketchy discussion does not attempt a comprehensive analysis of this multifaceted link between spheres of practice. Rather, by focusing on specific themes it seeks to belie both the pervasive view of the independence of the market economy from its historical and cultural contexts, and the image of the originary nature of the political economic structure within the broad social structure.

In fact, the very structure of the economy, that is, of Australian capitalism, is conditioned by kinship and family structures and practices. Ideologically, the field of kinship and family is the essential site of the production and articulation of such ideological tenets as the distinction between private and public, the embodied individual, and other idioms which construct both the market as a whole, and specific institutions such as the corporation (see above, especially chapter 6).

Moreover, at the cultural level at least, the family and the market are mutually constitutive opposites. They often define each other negatively; that is, that which is personal is not public nor political, while that which is political or public is not personal. (Radical attempts to confound the personal and the political have had some effect, albeit limited, for instance in the environmental movement – see Connell 1995, chapter 5.) Market relationships are conceived of as antagonistic, motivated by self-interest and driven by rationalist strategies of individual utility maximization. As such they are diametrically opposed to family relationships, where *homo oeconomicus* loses his egotistical edge and cooperates.

This opposition is an inherent part of the ideological construction of the two spheres. For example, to extract surplus value from the toil of kith and kin is often deemed illegitimate (definitely among most of my informants). Similarly, the introduction of family considerations into various aspects of market relationships is considered wrong, and is often illegal. Nepotism, cronyism and so forth are all terms which describe precisely this kind of crossover from the sphere of the personal to that of the impersonal. The distinction between the types of social action which prevail within the family and those which prevail in the marketplace structures much social practice.

The extent to which this abstract ideological distinction between the two spheres is reflected in practice is a moot point, which will be avoided here. Rather, in what follows, I would like to emphasize the significance of the field of kinship and family for the direction of economic evolution. Specifically, I argue that fundamental economic processes such as the direction of technological development and the dynamics of economic development are critically shaped by the dynamics and structure of the field of kinship and family.

I first reinterpret the link between Australian kinship and the Australian economy from the perspective of the household, and then from the perspective of the total economy.

From the Household Perspective: The Household Mode of Consumption

Writing about peasant societies, Aleksandr Vasilevich Chayanov famously defined the household mode of production (Chayanov et al. 1986), whereby household needs – determined by such factors as the number of persons living within the household – determine the household's productive output. In this mode of production household needs are independent of the household's productive capacity, and once these needs are satisfied, the household does not engage in further production. In sum, the consumption needs of the household determine its level of production.

One of the consequences of the specific organization of the contemporary capitalist political economy is what can be termed, with apologies to Aleksandr Vasilevich, the household mode of consumption. It is, in a sense, a reversal of the household mode of production. In urban Australia, at least, consumption is very elastic upwards, but very inelastic downwards. The level of consumption is largely determined by the level of income of the household, with the needs rising quickly to match any increase in earning capacity. Related to this is the phenomenon observed by scholars such as John Kenneth Galbraith, that contrary to neo-classical dogma, preferences and demand are not independent of supply in modern consumerist political economies. Rather, corporations expend much effort on arousing needs for their products – hence the great investment in industries like advertising whose sole purpose is to drum up demand for supplied goods and services (Galbraith 1969). In other words, there is a seemingly unlimited potential for consumption. The level of household consumption quickly rises when the level of income rises. Readjustment of consumption downwards in case of a drop in income is not so easy.

The upward pressure on household expenditure among Novocastrians (as elsewhere in Australia) was not only for the purposes of 'mindless' or 'irresponsible' consumption. Part of the reason for this tendency of needs to rise was the general inflation in cultural and material capital, an inflation which increases the cost of social reproduction. The parental desire to protect and enhance the social standing of offspring – an integral aspect of the field of kinship and family – pushes towards increased expenditure on education, for example. This causes an inflation which can be gauged, among others, by ever increasing high-school retention rates, and mushrooming enrolments in academic institutions. The Australia-wide retention rate to year twelve rose from 34 per cent in 1980 to 77 per cent in 1992, coupled with a substantial increase in the rate of those pursuing tertiary education. Similarly, the proportion of 15–19-year-old full-time students had risen between 1961 and 1992 from 28 per cent for men and 24 per cent for women to 62 per cent for men and 69 per cent for women. In the age bracket of 20–24 the ratio of full-time students rose from 4 per cent for men and 1 per cent for women in 1961 to 14 per cent for men and 16 per cent for women in 1992 (McDonald 1995, 27).

The very inflation in cultural capital is fuelled by the structure of the household mode of consumption. Because family units operate in an uncoordinated fashion – an essential structural aspect of the field of kinship and family – they are thrust into a continuous competition for social reproduction. This competition becomes particularly fierce at times when the structural shift in the economy results in a shrinkage of the traditional basis of the dominant fraction of the working class. (In Newcastle this basis was essentially skilled blue-collar jobs in heavy industries.) This competition over shrinking stakes is a major driving force for the further commodification of social reproduction, as exemplified by the increasing rate of inflation in educational qualifications.

The inflation in the value of educational and vocational qualifications in the last few decades means that more and more investment is required in the education of offspring merely to maintain their relative position within the social structure. In addition, beyond the investment which is required by the children, the reduction in child labour-market participation, coupled with recent cuts in youth wages, increase the children's dependency on their parents' access to the labour market and thereby increase their parents' dependency on the labour market (Hartley and de Vaus 1997).

In other words, households operating individually need to spend resources on social reproduction. The opportunities to spend on social reproduction, in fact, outstrip the spending capacity of working-class households. Due to the competitive nature of social reproduction these opportunities quickly impose themselves as necessities on households, with an urgency that is particularly amplified at times of increasing disparity such as the 1990s were in urban industrial Australia. Thus, both consideration of social reproduction and the increased cost of living – considerations whose logic derives from the structure and functioning of family households – create the need for maximization of income, thereby securely fastening household units to the labour market.

Of course, to these considerations of social reproduction and household maintenance must also be added the weight of the internalized imperatives of consumerism, those insatiable demands for narcissistic gratification (cf. Lasch 1978). All this explains the ease with which consumption rises and the difficulty with which it declines.

Accordingly, Novocastrians observed that when they increased their earnings, they did not normally increase their savings. An exception to this was when the worker increases his/her earnings (e.g. by taking extra work) for a specific and well-defined purpose (e.g. buying a car). Further, my informants claimed that taking on extra work for more pay was not easily reversible. Higher levels of consumption proved habit-forming. I should stress that among the dominant fraction of the working class the levels of consumption go well beyond the bare necessities of life. In one particular factory, for example, workers could significantly increase their income by working overtime. Many workers earned between fifty and sixty thousand dollars in 1994, whereas one young worker who worked quite a few extra shifts on a regular basis earned in excess of A$90,000 that year.

In any event, familial levels of income may dramatically drop for reasons outside of householders' control, as when the breadwinner is made redundant. The difficulties faced by families in readjusting consumption downwards may be overwhelming for any number of reasons. For instance, a great degree of the economic activity of families is based on credit. Indebtedness compels the household to maintain an increased level of income. Households may also face other long-term commitments, especially in the ongoing purchase of services, like private school/childcare and private medical insurance, which are based on a forecast of continued high levels of earnings. These, like credit, oblige householders to maintain a steady level of income. Furthermore, property ownership may involve financial commitments (e.g. rates on housing, high maintenance costs) which may be very hard to minimize, at least in the short run. To such hard economic reasons must be added some emotional reasons too. There is generally an ongoing direct and pervasive pressure towards consumption, especially to the extent that self-realization is based on purchases of goods and services. A conspicuous cut in consumption may thus cause householders to lose prestige and self-worth – symbolic capital, that is. Also within the household the value of some householders, especially breadwinners, may be correlated with their continuous and consistent earning capacity.

In the prevailing household mode of consumption the level of consumption is sensitive to the developmental stage of the household, although this point may be overstressed. Pressure increases dramatically with the birth of children. Among Novocastrians, a common reaction of a couple to the birth of children was for the mother to reduce her participation in the paid workforce, and for the father to increase his. As children become adolescents their financial needs increase, and the pressure they bring to bear towards increased consumption is very great. When offspring move out and find a job, consumption may drop in the short run, although transfer of funds from parents to now-mature offspring may continue, and may actually intensify as the offspring start having their own children. This continued transfer of economic capital down the generations might be a source of continued power of the parents over their adult children. However, another consideration to keep in mind is that children normally establish their own family households close to the time at which their employed parents may be required to increase their saving rate in preparation for retirement (cf. Millward 1993).

The maximization of consumption is ironic in two ways. One is the result of the competition among households. The more an individual household increases its expenditure on social reproduction, the better it would be able to maintain and improve the social standing of its offspring in the next generation and the better it will be able to enjoy the cheaper cost of living which accrues to the more affluent. On the other hand, once all households do so, none of the households will accrue any benefits, and all will have to increase their earnings and expenditure only to retain the same position they had occupied before. The second irony is that each household experiences itself as dependent upon the labour market, even though in total, it is the labour market and the political economy at large which is dependent upon the product of working-class households, namely labour power and the absorption of production through consumption. As Graeme D. Snooks points out, 'the household can exist without the market, but the market cannot exist without the household' (Snooks 1994, 125).

Both ironies are due to the fact that households operate as independent units which cannot wilfully and deliberately coordinate their activities. Ultimately, therefore, households do make the political economy, but not as householders please.

From the Total Economic Perspective

The monopolization by the working-class household of the reproduction of labour is itself a result of long historical processes. In colonial Australia, labour was originally supplied through additional means such as indentured labour (including convicts whose labour was sold by the government, and the Kanaka) and an immigration policy tied, among other things, to labour-market needs, although since the mass migration of the 1950s, the reproduction, maintenance and supply of labour was left largely to working-class households (Grimshaw et al. 1994, chapter 4; Rapp 1992; Snooks 1994; cf. Zaretsky 1982).

But not only the workers are reproduced by households. Capitalists also reproduce primarily through households. The integrity of private ownership and of capitalist estates down the generations is also predicated on family lines. The Murdoch and Packer family empires are high-profile examples of how the integrity of capitalist relations is maintained by family connections, as the owners, as well as the workers, are reproduced by family households. As was shown in chapter 6, inheritance is an integral element of the regime of kinship and family. People acquire their identity from their forebears. With it, along homologous lines, they acquire property. Ownership is passed down the generations primarily on the basis of kinship and family. This is how the integrity of class is maintained. If the death of a person meant the dissolution of his/her estate, Australia's political economy would be vastly different from what it is. *Ipso facto*, the non-ownership of the means of production – a lack which essentially defines the working class – is equally inherited. The inheritability of social, cultural and material capital makes the field of kinship and family the arena where social structure is maintained and reproduced through time.

But the significance of the field of kinship practice goes beyond class reproduction and the maintenance of the integrity of capitalist estates down the generations. The household produces goods and services whose significance is easily overlooked because they are not normally included in national accounts. There is probably not a single activity which regularly takes place within households which could not, under some conditions, be commodified and supplied through the market. Some goods and services, especially those which are labour-intensive and are not given to mechanization, like childcare, would be very expensive if left to the market to produce. By producing these goods and services outside the market, working-class households – whose main contribution to production is the maintenance and supply of labour power – end up subsidizing the employers. They do so by reducing the cost of reproduction of labour which would have been much higher had the entire process of labour maintenance and supply been achieved through the market (cf. Middleton 1974). The reason that household production of such services can come at a lower price than market production is that households do not extract surplus value from the production of goods and services for their own immediate consumption.

The structural competition between workers on the labour market further drives working-class households towards the absorption of an increasing share of the costs of the maintenance and the reproduction of labour. This situation is regularly glossed over in 'sciences' like economics by failing to define the production at home as work, and shrouding it in the feminized mystique of familism and selflessness – that is, as labour of love.

A more positive spin can be put on the household subsidy of production when considering the households as consumers. Making the employers pay more for labour would increase the cost of production, and with it the price of consumer goods and services, an increase that would be borne by the households. Other factors will determine how far these benefits to the household as consumer make up for the cost to the working-class household as producer, although it is unlikely the benefits will ever make up for the entire cost. This is so because the subsidy for production is extracted from working-class households alone, while its benefits are distributed across society to all households, making the working-class households' share of the benefits less than their share of the cost.

Thus, the working-class subsidy to industry plays a complex role in the dynamics of capitalism. By reproducing and maintaining labour it supports the production of goods and services. The more it subsidizes the costs of labour reproduction and maintenance, the cheaper production becomes and the greater the output of industry and the pressure towards the further commodification of everything. At the very same time, by providing such services outside the market, the household provides a check on the expansion of the market into such areas. In any event, the volume of goods and services produced by households continues to be large.

From a broad structural perspective, the aggregate of households forms a critical sector within the economy which consumes much labour and produces a substantial output (Reiger 1991, 5–8, 56–57). In his analysis of the Australian total economy, Snooks distinguishes between three sectors: the public and private sectors – which together make up the market economy – and the household sector which is outside the formal economy and tends to be ignored by economists. In the period 1860–1990, the household sector has been slightly bigger in size than either the public or the private sectors: the household sector accounted for 35.8 per cent of Australia's gross community income (GCI = market + household income), the private sector for 32.4 per cent, and the public sector for 31.8 per cent (Snooks 1994, chapter 2). At different times different sectors led the growth of the Australian economy.[6]

The different sectors function within the economy in different ways. The household sector largely determines the rate of expansion of the market. While in the past immigration played an overwhelming role in this expansion, ever since the end of the wave of immigration following WWII it was largely the local households which determined the rate of expansion through reproduction. On the other hand, economic growth is the preserve of the market sector where the economies of scale and the legitimacy of extracting surplus value[7] motivate and enable an increase in productive efficiency (Snooks 1994). During periods of rapid growth – that is, increase in GDP or GCI per household (Snooks 1994, 266) – the market sectors have shown a slight ascendancy in growth over the household sector. The latter, by contrast, has shown a significant ascendancy during periods of sluggish growth or stagnation (Snooks 1994, 30).

The household sector systematically affects the dynamics of the market sectors. In the short run, it has a dampening effect on trade cycles, which counterbalances the fluctuations of the market sector. But while the cyclical process played by the household sector is reactive, in the secular process the household sector falls in line with the market sector. Thus in periods of rapid growth, the household sector plays a positive, if secondary, role. It grows as well, though not at the same rate, as the market (Snooks 1994, 30–32). Intuitively, the countercyclical role of the household in periods of market downturns makes sense. My informants who were old enough to remember the Great Depression years recounted stories of improvisation and cooperation, when households exchanged more goods and services outside the

---

[6] The growth in the household sector during the nineteenth century was fuelled by massive immigration, which in its turn required a rapid expansion in the public sector (Snooks 1994, 40). In the period 1788–1850 the household sector grew fastest, and the two market sectors were very slowly emerging; between the 1850s and 1890s the core of the political economy was an interaction of the household sector and the public sector; even in the period of early industrialization, from the 1890s to the 1940s, a period of global economic uncertainty, the public sector dominated economic growth, and only after WWII did the private sector push ahead to become dominant, still not without massive support from government through protectionist trade policies and supportive immigration policies (Snooks 1994, 136–148).

[7] The point about the surplus value is my own rendition of Snooks's argument that in firms people forego family and personal relationships in favour of market relationships. Snooks seems to take on board, without critical reflection, the ideological dichotomy between the two types of personal relationships.

formal market. Hard times like the Depression are times when people 'make do' and resort to mutual aid (that is, household production and provision of services) and to improvisation.

But the significance of the interaction between the sectors of the economy goes beyond the dynamics of growth and expansion. The two market sectors and the household sector condition and structure one another. Curiously even economists like Snooks who seek to highlight the significance of households remain oblivious to the profundity of this mutual constitution. The shifts in technology of production and the gender segmentation of the labour market are cases in point.

The gender segmentation of the labour market goes to the heart of the issue of the gendered division of labour. The gendered division of domestic labour accounts for much of the gendered segmentation of the formal labour market. It is rooted in the different dispositions – habitus – of both men and women as expressed, for example, in career aspirations and life choices (cf. Uhlmann 2004). The truism that service-industry work suits women more than men is based precisely on the division of labour within the household. It is those jobs which apparently most resemble what women prototypically do in the household which become feminine. Women tend to gravitate towards caring professions like nursing, or jobs that have to do with children, like schoolteaching (Boreham and Hall 1993; Game and Pringle 1983, 91 ff.). Women were also more prone to interrupted involvement in the workforce, and generally preferred to participate on a part-time basis in the labour market because of their household responsibilities. Furthermore, being usually the second income earner, women's wages could be more easily pushed down, so that the feminization of professions also entailed a deterioration of remuneration. So much so, in fact, that even with the added cost of relying on a larger pool of part-time, casual workers, employers still find it profitable to employ the cheaper labour, commonly women, in many such low-skill jobs (Game and Pringle 1983, 91 ff.). This way, the 'casual-ness' of jobs becomes one major means of gender segmentation of the labour market. Married women mostly prefer part-time employment and are willing to settle for lower wages. Hence feminization and deterioration of working conditions become linked. The gender segregation of the market thus continues, with women being overrepresented in causal and part-time employment, based on the division of labour within the household. In other words, the gender structure of the household motivated the kinds of technological changes that occurred in manufacturing, which in turn brought about the increase in participation of married women in the labour market. It is also responsible for the fact that the total number of hours that households sell to the labour market has increased.

The gendered division of labour, rooted as it is in the division of domestic labour, is an important element in shaping the manufacture processes and technological development. Snooks is persuasive in his demonstration that the increase in the participation rates of married women in the labour market following WWII was precipitated by technological change and structural shifts in industry (Snooks 1994). He is incorrect, though, in assuming that this proximate relationship exhausts the causal linkage between the changes in industry and the manufacturing process on the one hand, and the gender order on the other. The family-wage system as it emerged in the first half of the century was the direct result of the gendered structure of the family household. Manufacturing industry had to rely primarily on a masculine workforce, which was rather expensive. The cost of labour was a major driving force for technological development. Capital was created to replace the masculine skilled and heavy labour.

This demonstrates how the household structure influenced the very manufacturing process in Australia. Married women formed a residual source of cheap labour. As conditions ripened, with the increase in consumer spending following WWII and the creation of many new unskilled, light-duty jobs, the demand for female labour grew and women moved into the labour market, while households imported more technological processes. It was the particular division of labour which made women's labour cheaper, especially the fact that women were predominantly secondary wage earners who supplemented their husbands' income. The availability of cheaper female labour created the economic incentive for industry to develop its technology in the particular direction that it did, namely to replace skilled and heavy labour.

Recounting the dynamics in brief, then, the economy of scale and the availability of wage labour have enabled industrial capitalism to emerge. It was the division of labour within the family household that brought about the family-wage system (see chapter 2). The system was centred around a male breadwinner who supported a dependent nuclear family. This situation made it inevitable that male labour would be more expensive than female labour. Moreover, the gendered specialization in homemaking and breadwinning produced gendered differences in involvement in the labour market. This situation created initially an incentive for firms to replace male labour with machinery and to mechanize masculine labour processes. This also created a subsequent incentive to feminize much of the labour process in order to tap the pool of cheaper labour in the form of married women. In its turn, this greater involvement of married women created the further incentive for increased mechanization of household tasks, and the deskilling of homemaking. We thus see that the direction of the manufacturing process and the structure of production cannot be understood independently of kinship and family.

Conclusion

This chapter outlined a few ways in which kinship and family condition the Australian political economy in the broadest sense. The first section addressed the complicity of kinship and family in producing the gender/class order in Australian society. The following section confronted the very structures of the market – allegedly the privileged independent site of rational action – to highlight the critical structuring role of the field of kinship practice.

The argument here is significant well beyond the narrow concerns over the role of kinship and family. In much current ideological production, capitalism and 'the markets' are presented as forces of nature which are essentially independent of the cultures in which they are embedded. Demonstrating the cultural and historical specificity of capitalism in particular, and through it modernity in general, is a critical point that is yet to be driven home in the public arena.

Chapter 9

Some Theoretical and Methodological Elaborations

The practices that are described in this book, although specific and occasionally idiosyncratic, are consistent with those described by scholars of kinship and gender in comparable societies both in Australia (e.g. Richards 1985; Stivens 1974; Stivens 1985; Stivens 1981; Stivens 1978) and elsewhere in the White anglophone world (e.g. Schneider 1980; Schneider and Smith 1973; Rosenberg and Anspach 1973; Firth et al. 1969; Young and Willmott 1962; Willmott and Young 1967; Rosser and Harris 1965; Strathern 1981).

But this study is intended as more than an exploration of kinship and gender narrowly conceived. Rather, I have used it as an opportunity to elaborate and demonstrate in practice an approach to the study of practice that is rooted in Bourdieu's heuristic economics of practice.

I do not propose in this chapter to synthesize the full theory of practice into a coherent and integrated statement. Rather, I begin with a brief outline of how I have developed and departed from Bourdieu's sociology of practice. (The interested reader will find a more detailed exposition of the heuristic economics of practice in Uhlmann 2001, chapters 7–9.) I then move to demonstrate the utility of the approach by confronting some theoretically intractable – if seemingly trivial – conundrums of practice, such as why people have children.

The Logic of Practice: An Analytical Recapitulation

Bourdieu's sociology of practice forms the theoretical launching pad, as it were, for the theorization that follows. Especially useful are his heuristic or metaphorical application of an economy of practice, and his concept of habitus which sidesteps the false dichotomy of structure versus agency.

His metaphorical application of an economy of practice allows Bourdieu to construct the regularities of practice *as if* they conformed to an economic model, rather than explore whether they do, or argue that they do. Thereby, regular, predictable results of practice can be studied in order to find out what it is that practice seeks to achieve, instead of assuming *a priori* that practice must be geared to achieve some utility maximization. Bourdieu's approach thus allows us to identify how different classes of social agents play for different stakes, as it were. A key example of this is gender. Women and men are often motivated by different interests whereupon they engage in different modes of practice with different predictable results. A failure, born of a rigid materialistic economics of practice, to recognize such differences has led numerous sociologists to misconstrue the gendered logic of family practices (Uhlmann 2004).

Of course, the way different classes of agents come to play for different stakes is part and parcel of the process of internalization of the social structure at large into the very subjectivity of social agents. Agents in different social positions come to internalize different dispositions in this process. It is through the concept of habitus that such a process can be easily theorized.

But Bourdieu's analysis of the structure of habitus seems hamstrung by the formalism of French structuralism. In order to understand the inherent structures of the lived world I have found it most useful to rely on cognitive sciences' modes of structural analysis, especially Lakoff and Johnson's studies of metaphors (Lakoff and Johnson 1980; Lakoff 1987; Johnson 1987) and Rosch's of categorization (Rosch 1978). These approaches, perhaps truer to Bourdieu's intention than Bourdieu's very own formulations, apprehend the logic of the lived world empirically, that is, without a preconceived notion of formal logic. They are thereby better able to incorporate the formally illogical aspects of the logic of practice.

The reason cognitive studies are able to do so is precisely because they empirically investigate the organization of the lived world. For instance, by explicitly interrogating cognitive basicness (rather than relying on commonsensical formal analyses) it is possible to show that the nuclear-family gestalt is more basic than its formally simpler constituent parts. Similarly, by being open to the connections between disparate structures of the lived world it is possible to explore these connections, like the way the *infant:adult* dichotomy anchors other, more abstract, contexts of domination. Their engagement with the variability of categorization and mental organization of the lived world in practice, makes cognitive sciences a particularly powerful tool in reconstructing the logic of practice.

Exploring the connections between disparate areas of practice has proved a useful way to integrate the body back into the analysis. It is precisely because some experiences are material and involve the body, that they become powerful sources to structure more abstract experiences (Johnson 1987). Hence the dependency of infants on adults becomes a powerful practical metaphor for domination and dependency.

But the body has also been integrated into habitus in this study in another important way. Following Iris Young's work, which relied in turn on Merleau-Ponty and de Beauvoir, I have endeavoured to reintroduce the corporeal experience into the discussion. Young was primarily interested in feminine modalities of motility and bodily experience. I have adapted her methodology and subjected her findings, as well as similar findings in my own fieldwork, to a sociological interpretation. I have therefore problematized both masculine as well as feminine modalities, and sought the social logic to account for these differences.

The application of cognitive sciences and Young's phenomenology of embodiment make habitus a broader concept. But even in its broader form, it still fulfils the basic role it fulfilled in much of Bourdieu's theorization, namely historicizing both subjectivity and social structures by seeing both as parallel, mutually constitutive aspects of the historical process (cf. Uhlmann 2005).

Notes towards a Heuristic Economics of Practice

The modifications I have introduced to Bourdieu's methodology are substantial, although they are intended to serve the purposes of a heuristic economics of practice. I cannot develop here this economics of practice in a detailed and systematic way. Rather, I highlight some distinct characteristics of this heuristic approach by applying it to a few specific regularities of kinship and family practice.

I begin by further exploring habitus, and the question of interest and motivation. I then describe one of the dynamics of symbolic struggle of quotidian politics, namely the struggle over different visions of social divisions.

The discussion then turns to a further elaboration of the concept of field. Previous chapters treated kinship and family as an autonomous field of practice. But this designation of the field is only analytical, and the boundaries are obviously porous in practice. Below I describe two flows of practice that cross boundaries to demonstrate that ultimately the designation of fields is an analytic imposition. Specifically, I focus on how structures in one field are transposed to another field, and how agents in equivalent positions in different fields collaborate with one another. These flows are part and parcel of what Bourdieu has conceived of as the economy of the logic of practice.

The Work of Habitus

Habitus is the principle by which the broad structures of the world come to be internalized by social agents and constitute their subjectivity. It is through the mediation of habitus that individuals' practices betray their specific social logics. Habitus, then, is a structured, socially and historically constituted subjectivity (Bourdieu 1984, especially the diagram on page 171).

Habitus is not a set of pre-programmed algorithms. Rather, the most powerful aspect of habitus is that it incorporates standards of judgement, aesthetics and modes of assessment. It is through these functions that habitus constructs for the agent the very social situation, complete with the range of alternative modes of action which are embedded in that situation.

Habitus is thus the generative principle by which social structure is incorporated into a set of dispositions, modes of perception, action, understandings and, more generally, modes of being in the world. These are expressed subjectively as interests in things, as tastes, preferences, aesthetics, likes and dislikes and so forth.

In general, people who live under similar conditions tend to undergo similar experiences, and internalize similar structures. This means that their habituses would be more similar to one another than to the habitus of agents who emerge from different social contexts.

The miracle of the spontaneous coordination of practice. That the similarity of experience produces a similarity of commonsense is what, in fact, accounts for the bulk of the seemingly trivial coordination of practice among social agents. Without some notion of shared habitus, it would be hard to explain how individuals who are not brought up together can still marry and spontaneously recreate marital relationships. My informants did not recall explicitly negotiating most of the aspects of their married life. The same holds for respondents in other Australian studies (e.g. Richards 1985, 82–85). Such constant spontaneous recreation and coordination of relationships is only miraculous if we ignore the workings of habitus, which in the case of newlyweds, for example, predisposes them to act and react in certain ways which are predictable and comprehensible to each other without having explicitly negotiated them in any way (Bourdieu 1990a, 71).

Motivation and Interest

Substantivist approaches to motivation assume that agents have interests which are independent of their social position or the field of practice in which they are engaged, and that these interests precede and motivate practice. They further assume that these interests are material, quantifiable and objectively observable.

The heuristic economics of practice, as it is developed here, departs from such assumptions. The analysis seeks to deduce the causes of practice from regular, predictable effects of practice. The rationale is that the predictable effects of practice feed into the judgements that habitus forms. This may be through the power of conscious observation on the part of social agents or through other means, such as a sense of pride or shame, which may reflect an implicit accumulation or loss of symbolic capital.

In order to demonstrate the heuristic approach to interest and motivation as it is developed here, I will discuss the question of why people have children.

The question of interest, or why have a family? When I asked my informants why they had children, their reactions, though kind and sympathetic, indicated to me that this was indeed a 'stupid question'.

The commonsensical approach that pervades much of the social sciences postulates that pre-existing, objective interests effect strategies aimed at pursuing those interests. First comes the interest, then comes its implementation. All too often, though, social agents do not relate to their interests in a straightforward way as rational choice theorists might suggest. While it is true that sometimes agents are aware of their interests as interests and proceed to rationally attain them, often the process unfolds in different ways. In many and varied contexts, in fact, the process seems reversed; that is, people do things and learn of their interests only through their action. This is what, to some extent, happens with parenting.[1]

Having children involves a great deal of sacrifice. Children constitute an immensely expensive and demanding commitment, that involves a great transformation of the lifestyle of those individuals and couples who have them.

So why do people have children?

One of the statements that was repeated by parents time and again was that one could not appreciate how much joy can be gained from having children before one actually had them. This common rationale merits a closer look. People could recount stories either about themselves, or about friends who had their first child, being a bit apprehensive, but finding the experience extremely edifying beyond any expectation. In my fieldnotes I very quickly explained away such statements as expressions of a cognitive dissonance in action: people decided to have children, the baby proved a greater hassle than they bargained for, and in order to protect their self-image they rationalized, post-fact, the choices they had made.

But cognitive-dissonance theory has emerged as problematic upon further consideration, most significantly because very often the first child is not the pre-planned result of an explicit choice. Disparate statements by informants regarding the fortuitous-cum-fortunate nature of their first child started accumulating. In one of my focus groups an admission by one man that his first child was an accident – a contraception failure – was reiterated by three other participants. The other two remained silent on the issue. (Among Richards's interviewees, too, first pregnancies were not often pre-meditated. See Richards 1985, chapters 5–6.)

It is important to bear in mind that much cognitive-dissonance theory explains distortions of reality as an attempt by social subjects to defend their own self-image. That is, a person takes initially some form of conscious action which later proves to be inadequate. The premeditated nature of this action would threaten the self-image of that social subject. In order to protect his/her ego, the social subject distorts reality in his/her mind and avoids the recognition of the inadequacy of his/her original action. But even those informants who acknowledged that their first offspring were unplanned expressed a similar attitude towards that bliss of having children, that could not be communicated to those who have not gone through a similar experience. This detracts from the cognitive-dissonance hypothesis of parental bliss, whereby the positive attitude of parents towards children is taken as the result of a mechanism to defend their egos from the realization of the inadequacy of their action. This is so because once the parents acknowledge that their child was unplanned and not the result of a deliberate choice, the consequences of having the child do not reflect on the parents' egos.

---

[1] The reality I discuss here is in no way unique to my informants. An identical ethnographic picture, for example, emerges from Richards's interviews with 120 Australian-born young married couples in Melbourne in 1976 (Richards 1985, especially chapters 5–6).

Further, in many cases the failure was deemed to be that of the contraceptive device, thereby minimizing the threat to my informants' egos and reducing the putative need to distort reality in order to defend the ego. In all such cases there need not occur a cognitive dissonance which requires resolution by rationalization and self-deception.

The cognitive-dissonance hypothesis might be somewhat resurrected by the suggestion that the parents might have terminated the pregnancy but did not, and this failure to terminate is the act that requires rationalization. The problem with this rationale, though, is that to many of my informants, termination would not be an option because of factors external to ego such as moral injunctions. In other words, even persons whose egos would not be threatened by the conception and the continuation of the pregnancy experienced the appearance of their children in a positive way.

Furthermore, to varying degrees social agents, especially women, who have not yet had children looked forward to parenthood as a positive aspect of future life. Cognitive-dissonance theory would predict that people who have not yet reproduced would not experience the dissonance, and would therefore have a realistic assessment of parenthood.

It is for these reasons that one cannot interpret as the resolution of a cognitive dissonance the fact that so many parents find parenthood a greater happiness than they had imagined, or that they cannot communicate this to non-parents. Rather, what is happening here is that, faced with the travails of parenthood, from financial expenditure to sleep deprivation, agents make a virtue out of necessity and commit themselves morally and emotionally to parenthood. Like the worker who finds satisfaction in particular tasks which are productive, parents find satisfaction in their parenthood. For parents to experience parenthood as positive is 'natural', that is, doxic. People who are not yet parents have a pretty good idea that parenthood is a great challenge, but that it is a part of life and has its own rewards. Parents know that parenthood is what they want because they invest of themselves in these tasks. Investment as such is, of course, no guarantee of a positive experience. But in the case of parenthood, the ideology of parenthood is there to assist the parents in the interpretation of their actions and their experience, and to shape their experience. It is precisely because the physical investment and the long sleepless nights are necessary to convey to the parent just how important children are to them, that people cannot communicate to the uninitiated the joys of parenthood.

In this case the posture agents adopt reflects the agreement of internalized structures and the external social structure. Parents tend to experience their parenthood in a stereotyped way. Mothers, for example, love their children. This is part of the objective world (as expressed, among others, in the taken-for-granted expectations of fellow social agents), and every mother is constantly made aware of it by the congratulations of people around her and by the whole conduct of the whole universe in which she is situated, which constantly reiterates in so many ways that mothers naturally love their children and that children are inherently loveable, especially to their mothers. This is also a reflection of the habitus of women who internalize structures that have been embodied since early childhood, through specific games girls play, specific issues of interest to girls and so forth. It is impossible to isolate any particular cause of the loving mother precisely because she embodies the agreement of internalized structure and social structure.[2]

But not always does habitus meet social structure. The non-loving mother is explained away either as a curious outcome of strange 'cultural norms' (e.g. Bourgois's description of young mothers from El Barrio, Bourgois 1995), or medicalized as a case of some disorder – post-partum depression, for example. Both these strategies treat the 'loving mother' as self-explanatory, as something above a cultural norm or a mental state; that is, as something natural.

To use the metaphor of interest, social agents invest in parenthood because they have an interest in it. But at one and the same time, their very investment in parenthood is what constructs their interests in it. Because it appears to be a natural part of the life cycle, there seems to be little consideration of reasons why to have children. In fact, nearly all my informants never decided *whether* to have children. They only decided *when* to have children, some by actively deciding to have a child and following the decision with action, some by default by not doing anything to stop the process once it was accidentally set in motion. The few high-school pupils I interviewed all presumed they would have children when they grew older. 'That's the way things are,' explained one of them. It was taken as natural as growing old, as partnering, and as dying. It is one of those things that happen to a person as part of his/her life. At least to some of my informants it made as much (non)sense to wonder about the advantages or otherwise of parenthood as it did to wonder whether one wanted to grow older as time passed by (cf. Richards 1985, 79–82, 87 ff.).

Once the project has commenced, there is no turning back. This means that there is usually no conjuncture or context in which parents can reconsider or re-evaluate their parenthood. In fact, at least among my informants, most parents would rarely if ever step back and wonder whether parenthood was indeed something they wanted or needed, nor would they commonly waste time on investigating why they experienced parenthood the way they did. As long as people's access to parenthood and its implications is subjective, and parenthood is not objectified in any way, the doxic elements of the parental postures remain invisible. In the case of new parents, it is not only a general lack of inclination to objectify one's social behaviour which prevents the objectification of parenthood, but also the immediate relentless demands on parents' time and resources. Sleep deprivation and the pressures of the radical change in lifestyle which the first-time parents among my informants typically underwent made it all the less likely they would bother to step out of the natural flow of time and action to examine their parenthood from the outside, as it were. The parents' habitus offers them the

---

[2] Richards, too, discusses in her study the 'difficulty of disentangling the reasons for having children. Parents themselves seem rarely to have sorted those things out' (Richards 1985, 90).

postures of the happy, fortunate and loving, albeit tired, parent to make sense of, and to benefit from, their current ongoing heavy investments (cf. Richards 1985, 92–97).

The doxic and highly orthodox nature of parenthood is exemplified in people's attitudes towards voluntary childlessness. Voluntary childlessness is more than an individual choice in specific circumstances. It is a personal affront to all those who do have children and invest in them. For a married couple to choose not to have children was construed in interviews as an expression of selfishness, because it was explained as people preferring not to spend the money or assume the responsibility for children. The same attitudes prevailed among Richards's informants (Richards 1985, 90 ff.; cf. Callan 1984; Callan 1983). My informants who had children interpreted voluntary childlessness as a strategy aimed at the accumulation of material capital. Denouncing these strategies was as much an act of justifying their own strategy. What they were in effect doing, from a practical perspective, was to negotiate the exchange rate between the symbolic capital accumulated by doing the right thing, namely parenting, and the economic capital lost in the process. In other words, they were trying to maximize the relative symbolic value of their capital.

One conclusion that follows from this discussion is that the model by which interests precede practice and inform the decision-making of social agents does not reflect the way social agents operate in this instance. Commonly agents learn of their interests in the process of practice and through their engagement with practice, occasionally even as a result of practice. To most parents children happen, as it were, and only then do they discover the benefits of having them.

But even the interests agents have, and the means they engage to pursue them, are never quite fixed and are constantly open to reinterpretation. This is part of the symbolic struggle of quotidian politics to which we now turn in a bit more detail.

Struggle over Visions of Social Division

At any moment the reality of a social situation – who is doing what, with whom and why – is open to definition and redefinition. This contestable interpretation of what is actually happening in a social situation is what I refer to as a vision of social division. (It is the local manifestation of the broader political struggle that Bourdieu would refer to as the different visions of social division.)

Never are relationships between family members reducible to their relative kinship positions, ages and genders. Every relationship between any number of individuals at any given time is open to a number of interpretations and reformulations as to who is doing what with/to whom and why. These visions of social division underlie practice by defining its context. True to their nature as part of practical logic, these visions need not be coherent in a way that would satisfy formal logicians. Social agents might, in fact, hold conflicting visions of social divisions which are formulated in different contexts. Further, any interpretation as to any particular event need not be fixed, and may be creatively reinterpreted during, as well as after, the event with every recounting, or with every attempt to expunge it from living memory.

Thus, the structures of the relationship between spouses and the postures they entail vary as a matter of course. For instance, gender relations tend to be constructed in hierarchical, in complementary, or in serial modes, a distinction which is often blurred and lends itself to political manipulation as part of the struggle to impose a particular vision of social division. Often the different structural positions – embodied, as they are, in postures – that a particular husband and wife adopt towards one another in different contexts may be contradictory. When conceived of as partners the metaphor implies seriality and interchangeability. On the other hand, when conceived of as father and mother the metaphor implies an element of complementarity, and possibly of hierarchy too. Which notion prevails at a given time and which is relegated to the background is one of the stakes of the symbolic negotiations and struggles between husbands and wives.

Jack and Esther are a case in point. They were one of the couples discussed in chapter 7, where she was the main breadwinner and he the main day-time caregiver. They explained the rationale for their division of labour in economic terms. She had a better-paying job with greater job security (she was employed in the public service) and better working conditions. It therefore made sense that she should be the main breadwinner. Here, in relating to each other, the two adopted postures that imply seriality. On the other hand, when it came to decisions regarding their newborn baby, such as when it should go to sleep, when it should see a physician, disciplinary policy and so forth, it was she who was the main decision-maker. She was, after all, the mother. In the context of parenting she adopted a certain maternal posture which relegated her partner to an auxiliary paternal posture which involved secondary, or mediated, involvement with the child. In this context the relationship between the spouses was complementary. Relegated to two different contexts of their relationship, one as spouses, the other as co-parents, no contradiction was ever felt between the two visions of social division.

The temptation that women felt to take over parenting tasks is part of a posture of maternal expertise which women often adopt. They are assuming the position of the sole competent operator in that domain, while relegating their partner to the status of the incompetent, dependent element.[3] Some men use similar strategies to enhance the symbolic capital they gain from performing mechanical tasks at home. This posture has the effect of denying others authority over specific skills, and the opportunity to rehearse them.

---

[3] In a similar vein, Fürst suggested that daily home cooking is very much an integral aspect of Norwegian women's identity, and reflects 'a rationality of the gift' which stands in contrast to 'a rationality of the commodity' (Fürst 1997). Although couched in different terms from the ones I use here, her notion of the two rationalities covers much the same theoretical grounds as some of the concepts I am developing here.

The limits on postural flexibility – the granny flat. It would be wrong to assume that everybody can adopt any posture at any given time. One example of the limit of postures which agents may adopt is the incompatibility of the parent–child postures with the posture of an equal adult. This is behind the difficulty which gives rise to the granny flat. Various reasons might lead to a situation in which parents and their adult, married children share a house. This might arise because the parents wish to transfer some of the property to their children who might not be able to afford their own home, or because the parents need intensive care and attention from their children. My suspicion is that at times when young adults were justifying such arrangements in terms of looking after their ageing parents, it was also a way for them to save some of their economic capital by either moving to their parents' home, or else by selling their parents' home, or letting it out and having the parents move in with them. This area of ambiguity lends itself to creative impositions of alternative visions of social divisions and different constructions of the motivations involved. In fact, all alternatives might be equally true at this serendipitous convergence of familial obligations and financial advantage.

Significantly, among my informants simple house-sharing between parents and adult, married children did not occur. The series of parent–child postures which my informants adopt still excludes the relationship which could incorporate the parents into the household of their married children. Adults said they were reluctant to share their homes on a permanent basis with their parents because the latter would impede their freedom, would not let them run their own affairs the way they themselves saw fit, and various other complaints which suggested that aspects of their adult independence would inevitably be compromised by the mere continuous presence of their parents. When not sharing a household these contradictions between the parent–child relationship and that between independent adults can be glossed over quite easily, but this ease dissipates in the face of having to share a single backstage.

The granny flat is thus a solution to the problem of the incompatibility of egalitarian relationships between adults, and the hierarchical nature of cross-generational family relationships. It enables families to reap the financial and symbolic benefits of shared living while retaining the independence of the adult children's nuclear family from those adult children's parents. It becomes a necessity because of the limit on postural flexibility. Parents/parents-in-law and children/children-in-law cannot easily adopt an egalitarian practical vision of the relationships between them.

A Field among Fields: Structural Homologies across Fields

Fields (Bourdieu 1985) are, of course, heuristic designations which are external to the natural flow of practice. To be useful, they should isolate for analysis a space of practice, as it were, which is relatively coherent and autonomous. The analysis in the preceding chapters was based on a designation of kinship, family and gender as a relatively coherent and autonomous field of practice.

But the occurrences in one field carry over in many ways to other fields. Chapter 8 discussed some ways in which the products of the field of kinship practice affect the political economy at large. Here I would rather offer some suggestive observations on how dynamics and structures of subjectivity that are shaped within one field affect and structure the dynamics of other fields.

Practical logic establishes structural homologies across fields that form the basis for different types of flow. One occurs when schemata of experience from one field are adopted for practice in other fields. More generally, the economy of practice predisposes habitus to apply homologous structures to analogous situations. This homology has two main effects. One is that it sets up different positions in different fields which are homologous and might therefore collaborate across fields. The other, is that it allows techniques and modes of social practice which emerge in one field to be generalized across other fields as agents operate in similar ways in homologous situations. In what follows I explore these dynamics in the field of kinship and family. I briefly discuss the transfer of schemata from the field of kinship and family, and then focus on structural homologies across fields.

The Extension of the Metaphor to Other Fields

Above I argued that the family is a powerful practical metaphor. It is a fundamental, concrete, cognitively rich experience. What makes the family an effective metaphor for structuring other social relations is its largely doxic nature and its perceived universality, as well as the emotional attachment and affective commitment that family orchestrates. The idiom of the family in its urban Australian manifestation is bundled with all the emotional investment of sex, intimacy, parenthood, personal security, propriety and so forth. It is highly evocative, and is therefore an essential political resource. It is commonly symbolically mobilized to justify and naturalize (or criticize and undermine) the arbitrary and historical nature of the configuration of power within society.

Two powerful identities that prevail throughout white Anglo-Celtic Australian society are ethnicity and nation, both couched to a great effect in the familial idiom. This is expressed, for instance, in the symbols used to construe and imagine the imagined community, as in the lyrics of the national anthem, or in images used by the Australian government in a 1990s campaign under the slogan of 'Welcome to the Family' to encourage permanent residents to naturalize.[4] But in contravention of formal logic, ideas of nation and ethnicity do not equally structure the family.

---

[4] The implication of kinship in the construction of more abstract social groupings has been discussed in the literature, especially in relation to nation, race and caste (e.g. Williams 1995; Delaney 1995; Das 1995; Heng and Devan 1992; Schneider 1969).

There are good reasons why such transfers occur in the directions they do across cognitive domains. The family is an elementary and concrete structure, which agents experience with a particularly high intensity. It is what sociologists would call a social group, as its members interact with one another in concrete ways. Social groups stand in contrast with social categories which are classifications of people based on a common trait they possess, but without these people acting as a group in any meaningful way. Social categories, such as race, country, nation and ethnicity are abstract terms which may be imagined as community (Anderson 1991), but are still very abstract in and of themselves. Agents tend to use familiar and concrete experiences from the social groups of which they are participants to structure more abstract categories (Lakoff and Johnson 1980; Johnson 1987; Lakoff 1987). This is not only an intellective extension, but also an emotional/affective one, which is part and parcel of the economy of practical logic.

Collaboration between Structurally Homologous Positions

The practical identification of homologies in the structure of everyday life does not normally happen completely unconsciously. In a previous chapter I discussed Michelle, Margaret and Ruth, and their non-typical family arrangement. When we discussed how Michelle coped with two households, Margaret and Ruth pointed out that Michelle knew that there were different sets of rules. At Margaret's there were Margaret's rules, at Ruth's there were Ruth's rules, just like at school there were 'school rules'. In fact, as they tell it, from a very young age Michelle learned that there are different rules at different places. At the store there were store rules, and she knew that she should ask the shop attendant for permission to do things. The equation of different sources of authority – parents, teachers and shop-owners – is pretty explicit here. In all instances they are persons who decide the rules that Michelle, being a child, must live by. Furthermore, it was the parents, Margaret and Ruth, who reminded Michelle of the fact that there were different rules at different locations, directing her to the shop attendant or being involved in her schooling to support the authority of her teachers. The latter, in their turn, reinforced parental authority by treating them as the ultimate authority over the child's destiny (see below).

Such homologies express the economy of practical logic, whereby the social agent experiences homologous situations in a similar way physically, emotionally and intellectually. Social agents do not operate in a historical vacuum. The homology of particular social relations may have already been established by previous generations and encoded in language, folklore and convention. When people wonder who the boss is at a particular home, the analogy between the workplace and class relations on the one hand and the family on the other is clearly drawn.

The structural homology between parent–child and teacher–pupil relationships is paradigmatic. Nobody is terribly surprised when a school child 'slips' and calls his teacher 'mum', something which commonly happens at pre-schools and primary schools. Obviously the homology is clear enough to affect children's behaviour. This homology is reinforced by the ceremonial aspects involved in the relationships. Parents and senior relatives are normally referred to by epithet with or without their name. The teacher is referred to by an epithet (Miss, Mrs, Mr, etc.) and a surname, and addressed by the epithet only (normally 'Miss' and 'Sir'). Teachers normally address pupils by given name.

Practical homologies need not be symmetrical. If A is motivated by B, B for its part need not be motivated by A. In cognitive categories, where B is more central than A, speakers might perceive A as resembling B, but would not similarly perceive B as resembling A. This is so in the instance of the homology between the parent–child and the pupil–teacher dyads. The parent–child dyad is the more basic dyad. Thus, while young children may slip and refer to their teachers as 'mum' or 'dad', these children do not slip in the familial context, and do not refer to their mothers in the forms of address that are appropriate for addressing teachers.

The homologies between the structural position of agents in different fields form the basis for systemic collaboration across those fields. The cooperation between parents and schoolteachers is a particularly clear instance because it is one of the least disguised. This cooperation was considered important by both parents and teachers, although both sides often complained about the other's perceived lack of commitment to the relationship.

A common complaint among schoolteachers I spoke with was that the parents of 'problem' children are all too often not available to cooperate with the teachers in the management of the 'problem' children's problems.

One of the main complaints Lucy had against the state school system was that the schoolteachers did not pass on information to her on Max's misbehaviour and truancy, and consequently he was able to avoid many hours of schooling, neglect his homework, and perform continuously poorly at school. Max was transferred to a Catholic school. Lucy noted with satisfaction that she gets more information about Max's conduct from the teachers in his new school. Quite a few other parents thought it was important to get involved in their children's education and share information with teachers.

Even parents who were not actively involved in the education of their children still tended to uphold the authority of the teacher. Many of those I spoke with lamented the fact that they could not help their children with their studies at all as they knew little or nothing about the subjects that are taught at school. The cultural capital that they had acquired was largely irrelevant to schooling, as was whatever social capital they hold. The only way they felt they could 'make a difference' for their children was by reinforcing the authority of the teachers.

In a way this cooperation across fields, as it were, serves to underscore the arbitrariness of the boundaries around fields. The exclusion of teachers from the field of the family is an analytic decision, not a reflection of reality. Perhaps a study of child development might identify a field of child management which includes both parents and teachers. Ultimately, the boundaries which frame a field are imposed by the analyst for the purpose of focusing the social analysis. These boundaries may, but need not, conform to institutional boundaries.

Conclusion

This discussion of fields joins the earlier discussions of interest and motivation, and of the struggles over visions of social division, to exemplify an alterative, heuristic economics of practice. This heuristic economics of practice stands in contrast with prevalent substantivist approaches. The latter begin from a certain understanding of what constitutes rational behaviour and then proceed to analyse behaviour to see if it is rational. Rationality and its standards are seen as substantive qualities that are independent of the particular context to which they are applied. In other words, there are certain *a priori* standards of rationality, and the analyst is required to see how particular practices measure up to these standards.

By contrast, the heuristic economics of practice proceeds in an opposite way. The economic/rationalist paradigm is heuristically imposed on practice. That is, practice is constituted as if it conformed to a certain logic, except that no *a priori* assumption is made about what this logic might be. The methodological assumption is that the substance of rationality is contextual, and the analyst needs to find the context-specific logic of contextualized practice, rather than compare a given practice against a decontextualized measure of rationality. In other words, the question is 'what is the logic of this practice?' rather than 'is this practice really logical?' In this approach, rationality and the logic of practice remain subject to systemic variation across society, and as such must be subject to an empirical sociological investigation, along with habitus and everything else which varies across society.

Bibliography

Abou-Zeid, A. (1991), *Al-Mujtama'aatu (l)-ssahrawiyya fi masr: al-bahthu l-'awwal – shamaal siinaa' [Desert Societies in Egypt: First study – North Sinai (Arabic)]*. Cairo: The National Centre for Social Research and Criminology, the Section for Research of Rural and Desert Societies.

Allan, G.A. (1979), *A Sociology of Friendship and Kinship*. London: George Allen & Unwin.

Anderson, B.R. (1991), *Imagined Communities: Reflections on the Origin and Spread of Nationalism*, rev. ext. edn. London: Verso.

Aspin, L.J. (1994), *The Family: An Australian Focus*, 3rd edn. Melbourne: Longman.

Baxter, J. (1993), *Work at Home: The Domestic Division of Labour*. St Lucia, QLD: University of Queensland Press.

——— (2000), 'The Joys and Justice of Housework'. *Sociology: The Journal of the British Sociological Association*, **34**(4): 609–631.

Baxter, J., M. Lynch-Blosse and J. Western (1996), 'Gender Differences in Work Satisfaction'. *Australian Journal of Social Issues*, **31**(3): 291–309.

Baxter, J. and M. Western (1998), 'Satisfaction with Housework: Examining the Paradox'. *Sociology: The Journal of the British Sociological Association*, **32**(1): 101–120.

Bittman, M. (1993), 'The Nuclear Family and Its Future'. In *A Sociology of Australian Society: Introductory Readings*, 2nd edn, eds J.M. Najman and J.S. Western. Melbourne: Macmillan Education Australia.

——— (1995), *Recent Changes in Unpaid Work*. Australian Bureau of Statistics.

Bittman, M., G. Matheson and G. Meagher (1999), 'The Changing Boundary between Home and Market: Australian Trends in Outsourcing Domestic Labour'. *Work, Employment & Society*, **13**(2): 249–273.

Bittman, M. and J. Pixley (1997), *The Double Life of the Family: Myth, Hope and Experience*. St Leonards: Allen & Unwin.

Blackley, L. (1996), '"Demonstrating – Not Celebrating?": Working Class Wollongong, the Politics of Gender, the Social and the Cultural, 1920s–1970s'. Paper Presented at the Department of History Seminar, Australian National University, Canberra, 13 September.

Boreham, P. and R. Hall (1993), 'Work, Employment and Labour in Australian Society'. In *A Sociology of Australian Society: Introductory Readings*, 2nd edn, eds J.M. Najman and J.S. Western. Melbourne: Macmillan Education Australia.

Bouquet, M. (1996), 'Family Trees and Their Affinities: The Visual Imperative of the Genealogical Diagram'. *Journal of the Royal Anthropological Institute*, **2**(1): 43–66.

Bourdieu, P. (1962), *The Algerians*. Boston: Beacon Press.

—— (1977), *Outline of a Theory of Practice*, trans. R. Nice. Cambridge: Cambridge University Press.

—— (1981), 'Men and Machines'. In *Advances in Social Theory and Methodology: Toward an Integration of Micro- and Macro-Sociologies*, eds K. Knorr-Cetina and A.V. Cicourel. London & Boston: Routledge & Kegan Paul.

—— (1984), *Distinction: A Social Critique of the Judgement of Taste*, trans. R. Nice. Cambridge, Mass.: Harvard University Press.

—— (1985), 'The Genesis of the Concept of Habitus and Field'. *Sociocriticism*, (ii): 11–24.

—— (1986), 'The Forms of Capital'. In *Handbook of Theory and Research for the Sociology of Education*, ed. J.G. Richardson. New York: Greenwood Press.

—— (1990a), 'From Rules to Strategies'. In *In Other Words: Essays toward a Reflexive Sociology*. Cambridge: Polity Press.

—— (1990b), 'La Domination Masculine'. *Actes de la recherche en sciences sociales*, **84**: 2–31.

—— (1990c), *The Logic of Practice*, trans. R. Nice. Cambridge: Polity Press.

—— (1994), 'Division du travail : rapports sociaux de sexe et de pouvoir'. *Cahiers du GEDISST*, **11**: 91–104.

—— (1996), 'On the Family as a Realized Category'. *Theory, Culture & Society*, **13**(3): 19–26.

—— (1996–7), 'Masculine Domination Revisited'. *Berkeley Journal of Sociology*, **41**: 189–203.

—— (1998), *La domination masculine*: Edition du Seuil.

Bourdieu, P. and L. Boltanski (1981) [1975], 'The Educational System and the Economy: Titles and Jobs', trans. R. Nice. In *French Sociology: Rupture and Renewal since 1968*, ed. C.C. Lemert. New York: Columbia University Press.

Bourgois, P.I. (1995), *In Search of Respect: Selling Crack in El Barrio*. Cambridge: Cambridge University Press.

Bryson, L. (1985), 'Gender Divisions and Power Relationships in the Australian Family'. In *Family and Economy in Modern Society*, eds P. Close and R. Collins. Houndmills: The Macmillan Press.

—— (1995), 'Family, State, Market and Citizenship'. In *Issues Facing Australian Families: Human Services Respond*, 2nd edn, eds W. Weeks and J. Wilson. South Melbourne: Longman Cheshire.

Burbidge, A. and I. Winter (1995), *Urban Housing Report: The Australian Living Standards Study. Report to Commonwealth Department of Human Services and Health*. Australian Institute of Family Studies.

Burns, A. (1983), 'Population Structure and the Family'. In *The Family in the Modern World*, eds A. Burns, G. Bottomley and P. Jools. Sydney: George Allen & Unwin.

Burns, A. and J. Goodnow (1985), *Children and Families in Australia*, 2nd edn. North Sydney: Allen & Unwin.

185

Bibliography

Callan, V.J. (1983), 'Voluntarily Childless and Their Perception of Parenthood and Childlessness'. *Journal of Comparative Family Studies*, **14**(1): 87–96.

——— (1984), 'Voluntary Childlessness: Early Articulator and Postponing Couples'. *Journal of Biosocial Science*, **16**(4): 501–509.

Carmichael, G.A. (1988), *With This Ring: First Marriage Patterns, Trends and Prospects in Australia*. Canberra: Department of Demography, Australian National University, and the Australian Institute of Family Studies.

Chayanov, A.V., D. Thorner, B.H. Kerblay and R.E.F. Smith (1986), *A.V. Chayanov on the Theory of Peasant Economy*. Madison, Wis.: The University of Wisconsin Press.

Clarke, F.G. (1989), *Australia: A Concise Political and Social History*. Oxford: Oxford University Press.

Collier, J.F., M.Z. Rosaldo and S.J. Yanagisako (1982), 'Is There a Family? New Anthropological Views'. In *Rethinking the Family: Some Feminist Questions*, eds B. Thorne and M. Yalom. New York: Longman.

Connell, R.W. (1987), *Gender & Power*. Cambridge: Polity Press.

——— (1995), *Masculinities*. St Leonards: Allen & Unwin.

Connell, R.W., D.J. Ashenden, S. Kessler and G.W. Dowsett (1982), *Making the Difference: Schools, Families and Social Division*. Sydney: George Allen & Unwin.

Connell, R.W. and T.H. Irving (1992), *Class Structure in Australian History: Poverty and Progress*, 2nd edn. Melbourne: Longman Cheshire.

Cooper, W.E. and J.R. Ross (1975), 'World Order'. In *Parasession on Functionalism*, eds R. Grossman, L.J. San and T.J. Vance. Chicago: Chicago Linguistic Society.

Creed, G.W. (2000), '"Family Values" and Domestic Economics'. *Annual Review of Anthropology*, **29**: 329–355.

Curthoys, A. (1999), 'Family Fortress'. *The Weekend Australian*, 13.11.1999, Ed: 1, Pg: F06, 2494 words.

Das, V. (1995), 'National Honor and Practical Kinship: Unwanted Women and Children'. In *Conceiving the New World Order: The Global Politics of Reproduction*, eds F. Ginsburg and R. Rapp. Berkeley: University of California Press.

de Beauvoir, S. (1972), *The Second Sex*, trans. H.M. Parshley. Harmondsworth: Penguin Books.

de Vaus, D. (1997a), 'Ageing'. In *Australian Family Profiles: Social and Demographic Patterns*, eds D. de Vaus and I. Wolcott. Melbourne: Australian Institute of Family Studies.

——— (1997b), 'Divorce'. In *Australian Family Profiles: Social and Demographic Patterns*, eds D. de Vaus and I. Wolcott. Melbourne: Australian Institute of Family Studies.

——— (1997c), 'Family Structure'. In *Australian Family Profiles: Social and Demographic Patterns*, eds D. de Vaus and I. Wolcott. Melbourne: Australian Institute of Family Studies.

—————— (1997d), 'Marriage'. In *Australian Family Profiles: Social and Demographic Patterns*, eds D. de Vaus and I. Wolcott. Melbourne: Australian Institute of Family Studies.

de Vaus, D., S. Wise and G. Soriano (1997), 'Fertility'. In *Australian Family Profiles: Social and Demographic Patterns*, eds D. de Vaus and I. Wolcott. Melbourne: Australian Institute of Family Studies.

de Vaus, D. and I. Wolcott (1997), *Australian Family Profiles: Social and Demographic Patterns*. Melbourne: Australian Institute of Family Studies.

Delaney, C. (1995), 'Father State, Motherland, and the Birth of Modern Turkey'. In *Naturalizing Power: Essays in Feminist Cultural Analysis*, eds S.J. Yanagisako and C. Delaney. New York: Routledge.

Dempsey, K. (1992), *A Man's Town: Inequality between Women and Men in Rural Australia*. Melbourne: Oxford University Press.

—————— (1997a), *Inequalities in Marriage: Australia and Beyond*. Melbourne: Oxford University Press.

—————— (1997b), 'Trying to Get Husbands to Do More Work at Home'. *Australian and New Zealand Journal of Sociology*, **33**(2): 216–225.

Di Leonardo, M. (1992), 'The Female World of Cards and Holidays: Women, Families, and the Work of Kinship'. In *Rethinking the Family: Some Feminist Questions*, rev. edn, eds B. Thorne and M. Yalom. Boston: Northeastern University Press.

Docherty, J.C. (1983), *Newcastle: The Making of an Australian City*. Sydney: Hale & Ironmonger.

Donaldson, M. (1991), *Time of Our Lives*: Allen & Unwin.

Edgar, D. (1997), *Men, Mateship, Marriage: Exploring Macho Myths and the Way Forward*. Sydney: Harper Collins Publishers.

Edwards, R. (1979), *Contested Terrain: The Transformation of the Workplace in the Twentieth Century*. New York: Basic Books.

Ehrenreich, B. and D. English (1979), *For Her Own Good: 150 Years of the Experts' Advice to Women*. London: Pluto Press.

England, P. and B.S. Kilbourne (1990), 'Markets, Marriages and Other Mates'. In *Beyond the Marketplace: Rethinking Economy and Society*, eds R. Friedland and A.F. Bobertson. New York: de Gruyter.

Ernst, T. (1990), 'Mates, Wives and Children: An Exploration of Concepts of Relatedness in Australian Culture'. *Social Analysis*, **17**: 110–118.

Errington, S. (1990), 'Recasting Sex, Gender, and Power: A Theoretical and Regional Overview'. In *Power and Difference: Gender in Island Southeast Asia*, eds J.M. Atkinson and S. Errington. Stanford: Stanford University Press.

Fergie, D. (1988), 'On the Face of It: The Cultural Construction of Gender in Contemporary Australian Society'. *Canberra Anthropology*, **11**(1): 20–48.

Finch, J. (1989), *Family Obligations and Social Change*. Cambridge: Polity Press.

Firth, R.W., J. Hubert and A. Forge (1969), *Families and Their Relatives: Kinship in a Middle-Class Sector of London: An Anthropological Study*. London: Routledge & Kegan Paul.

Foucault, M. (1974), *The Order of Things: An Archaeology of the Human Sciences*. London: Tavistock Publications.

———— (1980), *The History of Sexuality: An Introduction*, trans. R. Hurley. New York: Vintage Books.

Fox, J.J. (1988), 'Origin, Descent and Precedence in the Study of Austronesian Societies'. Public Lecture in connection with De Wisselleerstoel Indonesische Studien. Delivered on 17 March 1988, Leiden University.

Franklin, S. and S. McKinnon (2000), 'New Directions in Kinship Study: A Core Concept Revisited'. *Current Anthropology*, **41**(2): 275–279.

Freeman, J.D. (1961), 'On the Concept of the Kindred'. *Journal of the Royal Anthropological Institute*, **9**: 192–220.

Funder, K., D. Edgar, D. Whithear, H. Brownlee, H. Glezer, M. Harrison, R. Hartley, P. McDonald, G. Ochiltree and I. Wolcott (1996), 'Family Studies in Australia'. *Marriage and Family Review*, **22**(3-4): 287–332.

Funder, K., M. Harrison and R. Weston (1993), *Settling Down: Pathways of Parents after Divorce*. Australian Institute of Family Studies.

Fürst, E.L. (1997), 'Cooking and Femininity'. *Women's Studies International Forum*, **20**(3): 441–449.

Galbraith, J.K. (1969), *The Affluent Society*, 2nd rev. edn. Harmondsworth: Penguin Books.

Game, A. and R. Pringle (1983), 'The Making of the Australian Family'. In *The Family in the Modern World*, eds A. Burns, G. Bottomley and P. Jools. Sydney: George Allen & Unwin.

Gilding, M. (1991), *The Making and Breaking of the Australian Family*. St Leonards, NSW: Allen & Unwin.

Gittins, R. (1997), 'The Boss Cracks the Whip'. *Sydney Morning Herald*, 9 April, p. 17.

Goodman, E. (1983), 'The Family and the Law'. In *The Family in the Modern World*, eds A. Burns, G. Bottomley and P. Jools. Sydney: George Allen & Unwin.

Goody, J. (1962), 'On Nannas and Nannies'. *Man*, **62**: 179–182.

———— (1983), *The Development of the Family and Marriage in Europe*. Cambridge: Cambridge University Press.

———— (2000), *The European Family: An Historico-Anthropological Essay*. Oxford: Blackwell Publishers.

Gorsuch, A.E. (1996), '"A Woman Is Not a Man": The Culture of Gender and Generation in Soviet Russia, 1921–1928'. *Slavic Review*, **55**(3): 636–600.

Grimshaw, P. (1983), 'The Australian Family: An Historical Interpretation'. In *The Family in the Modern World*, eds A. Burns, G. Bottomley and P. Jools. Sydney: George Allen & Unwin.

Grimshaw, P., M. Lake, A. McGrath and M. Quartly (1994), *Creating a Nation, 1788–1990*. South Yarra: McPhee Gribble Publishers.

Grosz, E.A. (1994), *Volatile Bodies: Toward a Corporeal Feminism*. St Leonards, NSW: Allen & Unwin.

Hakim, C. (1996), 'Labour Mobility and Employment Stability: Rhetoric and Reality on the Sex Differential in Labour-Market Behaviour'. *European Sociological Review*, **12**(1): 1–31.

Hamilton, A. (1975), 'Snugglepot and Cuddlepie: Happy Families in Australian Society'. *Mankind*, **10**(2): 84–92.

Hartley, R. and D. de Vaus (1997), 'Young People'. In *Australian Family Profiles: Social and Demographic Patterns*, eds D. de Vaus and I. Wolcott. Melbourne: Australian Institute of Family Studies.

Heng, G. and J. Devan (1992), 'State Fatherhood: The Politics of Nationalism, Sexuality and Race in Singapore'. In *Nationalisms and Sexualities*, eds A. Parker, M. Russo, D. Sommer and P. Yaeger. New York: Routledge.

Hextall, B., M. Millett and P. McGeough (1997), 'BHP's Real Target: 8,000 Jobs'. *Sydney Morning Herald*, 30 April, 1, 9.

Hobsbawm, E. (1978), 'Man and Woman in Socialist Iconography'. *History Workshop*, **6**: 121–138.

Hopkins, K. (1980), 'Brother-Sister Marriage in Roman Egypt'. *Comparative Studies in Society and History*, **22**: 203–354.

Horin, A. (1995), 'Gay Couple in Landmark Health Win: Suburban Revolution Redefined the Family'. *Sydney Morning Herald*, 21 July, 3.

Johnson, M. (1987), *The Body in the Mind: The Bodily Basis of Meaning, Imagination, and Reason*. Chicago: The University of Chicago Press.

Kapferer, B. (1988), *Legends of People, Myths of the State*. Washington: Smithsonian Institute Press.

Keen, I. (1994), *Knowledge and Secrecy in an Aboriginal Religion*. Oxford: Oxford University Press.

Keesing, R.M. (1975), *Kin Groups and Social Structure*. New York: Holt Rinehart and Winston.

——— (1990), 'Kinship, Bonding, and Categorization'. *The Australian Journal of Anthropology*, **1**(2-3): 159–167.

Lasch, C. (1978), *The Culture of Narcissism: American Life in an Age of Diminishing Expectations*, 1st edn. New York: Norton.

Lakoff, G. (1987), *Women, Fire, and Dangerous Things: What Categories Reveal About the Mind*. Chicago: University of Chicago Press.

Lakoff, G. and M. Johnson (1980), *Metaphors We Live By*. Chicago: University of Chicago Press.

Lakoff, G. and Z. Kovecses (1987), 'The Cognitive Model of Anger Inherent in American English'. In *Cultural Models in Language and Thought*, eds D. Holland and N. Quinn. Cambridge: Cambridge University Press.

Lewin, T. (2001), 'The Nation: Mother's Milk; Breast-Feeding: How Old Is Too Old?'. *New York Times*, 18 February, late edition – final edition, sec. 4.

McDonald, P. (1995), *Families in Australia: A Socio-Demographic Perspective*. Melbourne: Australian Institute of Family Studies.

Mcfarlane, A.J. (1987), 'Love and Capitalism'. *Cambridge Anthropology*, **11**(2): 22–39.

McGregor, C. (1997), *Class in Australia*. Ringwood, Victoria: Penguin Books Australia.

Martin, J.I. (1967), 'Extended Kinship Ties: An Adelaide Study'. *The Australian and New Zealand Journal of Sociology*, **3**(1): 44–63.

Matthews, J.J. (1984), *Good and Mad Women: The Historical Construction of Femininity in Twentieth-Century Australia*. North Sydney: Allen & Unwin.

Mennell, S., A. Murcott and A.H. Van Otterloo (1992), *The Sociology of Food: Eating, Diet and Culture*. London: Sage.

Merleau-Ponty, M. (1962), *The Phenomenology of Perception*, trans. C. Smith. London: Routledge & Kegan Paul.

Metcalfe, A.W. (1988), *For Freedom and Dignity: Historical Agency and Class Structures in the Coalfields of NSW*. Sydney: Allen & Unwin.

Metcalfe, A.W. and J. Bern (1994), 'Stories of Crisis – Restructuring Australian Industry and Rewriting the Past'. *International Journal of Urban and Regional Research*, **18**(4): 658–672.

———— n.d. 'Politics and Knowledge: The Making of Economic Crisis in the Hunter Valley'. Unpublished manuscript.

Middleton, C. (1974), 'Sexual Inequality and Stratification Theory'. In *The Social Analysis of Class Structure*, ed. F. Parkin. London: Tavistock Publications.

Mills, B. (1997), 'A Bitter Pill, but Possible to Swallow'. *Australian Financial Review*, 30 April, p. 27.

Millward, C. (1993), 'Extended Family Networks'. In *Paper Presented at the 4th Australian Family Research Conference, Manly, Sydney, 17-19 February*.

Millward, C. and D. de Vaus (1997), 'The Extended Family'. In *Australian Family Profiles: Social and Demographic Patterns*, eds D. de Vaus and I. Wolcott. Melbourne: Australian Institute of Family Studies.

Millward, C., I. Wolcott, D. de Vaus and G. Soriano (1997), 'Family Care'. In *Australian Family Profiles: Social and Demographic Patterns*, eds D. de Vaus and I. Wolcott. Melbourne: Australian Institute of Family Studies.

Morgan, D.H.J. (1996), *Family Connections: An Introduction to Family Studies*. Cambridge: Polity Press.

Morgan, D.L. (1993), *Successful Focus Groups: Advancing the State of the Art*. Newbury Park, Calif.: Sage Publications.

Morphy, H. (1984), *Journey to the Crocodile's Nest: An Accompanying Monograph to the Film 'Ma*Darrpa Funeral at Gurka'wuy'*. Canberra: Australian Institute of Aboriginal Studies.

Norris, K. (1993),. *The Economics of Australian Labour Markets*, 3rd edn. Melbourne: Longman Cheshire.

O'Connor, P. (1990), 'The Adult Mother/Daughter Relationship: A Uniquely and Universally Close Relationship?'. *Sociological Review*, **38**(2): 293–323.

Oxley, H.G. (1974), *Mateship in Local Organization: A Study of Egalitarianism, Stratification, Leadership and Amenities Projects in a Semi-Industrial Community of Inland New South Wales*. St. Lucia, QLD: University of Queensland Press.

Parliament of the Commonwealth of Australia; House of Representatives; Standing Committee on Community Affairs (1995), *A Report on Aspects of Youth Homelessness*. Australian Government Publishing Service.

Pick, D. (1989), *Faces of Degeneration: A European Disorder, c.1848–c.1918*. Cambridge: Cambridge University Press.

Pyke, K.D. (1996), 'Class-Based Masculinities: The Interdependence of Gender, Class, and Interpersonal Power'. *Gender & Society*, **10**(5): 527–549.

Rapp, R. (1992), 'Family and Class in Contemporary America: Notes toward an Understanding of Ideology'. In *Rethinking the Family: Some Feminist Questions*, rev. edn, eds B. Thorne and M. Yalom. Boston: Northeastern University Press.

Reiger, K.M. (1985), *The Disenchantment of the Home: Modernizing the Australian Family (1880–1940)*. Melbourne: Oxford University Press.

——— (1991), 'Motherhood Ideology'. In *Issues Facing Australian Families: Human Services Respond*, eds R. Batten, W. Weeks and J. Wilson. South Melbourne: Longman Cheshire.

Richards, L. (1985), *Having Families: Marriage Parenthood and Social Pressure in Australia*, rev. edn. Ringwood, Victoria: Penguin Books.

——— (1990), *Nobody's Home: Dreams and Realities in a New Suburb*. Melbourne: Oxford University Press.

Rosch, E. (1978), 'Principles of Categorization'. In *Cognition and Categorization*, eds E. Rosch and B.B. Lloyd. Hillsdale, N.J.: Lawrence Erlbaum Associates, Publishers.

Rose, S.O. (1992), *Limited Livelihoods: Gender and Class in Nineteenth-Century England*. Berkeley: University of California Press.

Rosenberg, G.S. and D.F. Anspach (1973), *Working Class Kinship*. Lexington, Mass.: Lexington Books.

Rosser, C. and C.C. Harris (1965), *The Family and Social Change; a Study of Family and Kinship in a South Wales Town*. London: Routledge & Kegan Paul.

Sartre, J.P. (1976–91), *Critique of Dialectical Reason: Vol. 1. Theory of Practical Ensembles*, trans. A. Sheridan-Smith. London: New Left Books.

Sawyer, M.C. (1989), *The Challenge of Radical Political Economy: An Introduction to the Alternatives to Neo-Classical Economics*. Hemel Hempstead: Harvester Wheatsheaf.

Schneider, D.M. (1969), 'Kinship, Nationality and Religion in American Culture: Toward a Definition of Kinship'. In *Forms of Symbolic Action: Proceedings of the 1969 Annual Spring Meeting of the American Ethnological Society*, ed. R.F. Spencer. Seattle: University of Washington Press.

——— (1980), *American Kinship: A Cultural Account*, 2nd edn. Chicago: University of Chicago Press.

Schneider, D.M. and R.T. Smith (1973), *Class Differences and Sex Roles in American Kinship and Family Structure*. Englewood Cliffs, N.J.: Prentice-Hall.

Sexton, E. (1997), 'A Painful Transition Ahead'. *Sydney Morning Herald*, 30 April, 9.

Short, P.M. n.d. [1994], 'Sharing, Reciprocity and Dependency: Family Relations in the Informal Economy'. Unpublished paper, Department of Anthropology and Sociology, University of Queensland.

Snooks, G.D. (1994), *Portrait of the Family within the Total Economy: A Study in Longrun Dynamics, Australia 1788–1990*. Cambridge: Cambridge University Press.

Stardardt, N. (1995), 'Male Bonding and Class Struggle in Imperial Germany'. *Historical Journal*, **38**(1): 175–194.

Stivens, M. (1974), 'Kinship and Class: A Study in a Sydney Suburb'. Master's thesis: University of Sydney.

———— (1978), 'Women and Their Kin'. In *Women United, Women Divided: Cross-Cultural Perspectives on Female Solidarity*, eds P. Caplan and J.M. Bujra. London: Tavistock Publications.

———— (1981), 'Women, Kinship and Capitalist Development'. In *Of Marriage and the Market: Women's Subordination in International Perspective*, eds K. Young, C. Wolkowitz and R. McCullagh. London: CSE Books.

———— (1985), 'The Private Life of the Extended Family: Family, Kinship and Class in a Middle-Class Suburb of Sydney'. In *Australian Ways: Anthropological Studies of an Industrial Society*, ed. L. Manderson. Sydney: Allen & Unwin.

Strathern, M. (1981), *Kinship at the Core: An Anthropology of Elmdon, a Village in North-West Essex in the Nineteen-Sixties*. Cambridge and New York: Cambridge University Press.

Turner, V.W. (1969), *The Ritual Process: Structure and Anti-Structure*. London,: Routledge & Kegan Paul.

Uhlmann, A.J. (2000), 'Incorporating Masculine Domination: Theoretical and Ethnographic Elaborations'. *Social Analysis*, **44**(1): 142–161.

———— (2001), 'Aspects of Kinship, Family and Gender in a Deindustrialising Australian Town'. A thesis submitted for the Degree of Doctor of Philosophy of the Australian National University, Canberra, April 2001.

———— (2004), 'The Sociology of Subjectivity, and the Subjectivity of Sociologists: A Critique of the Sociology of Gender in the Australian Family'. *British Journal of Sociology*, **55**(1): 79–97.

———— (2005), 'The Dynamics of Stasis: Historical Inertia in the Evolution of the Australian Family'. *The Australian Journal of Anthropology*, 2005, **16**(1): 18–30.

Weeks, W. (1995), 'Women's Work, the Gendered Division of Labour and Community Services'. In *Issues Facing Australian Families: Human Services Respond*, 2nd edn, eds W. Weeks and J. Wilson. South Melbourne: Longman Cheshire.

Weiss, B. (1996), *The Making and Unmaking of the Haya Lived World: Consumption, Commoditization, and Everyday Practice*. Durham: Duke University Press.

Weston, K. (1995), 'Forever Is a Long Time: Romancing the Real in Gay Kinship Ideologies'. In *Naturalizing Power: Essays in Feminist Cultural Analysis*, eds S.J. Yanagisako and C. Delaney. New York: Routledge.

Whitwell, G. (1989), *Making the Market: The Rise of Consumer Society*. Melbourne: McPhee Gribble Publishers.

Williams, B. (1995), 'Classification Systems Revisited: Kinship, Caste, Race and Nationality as the Flow of Blood and the Spread of Rights'. In *Naturalizing Power: Essays in Feminist Cultural Analysis*, eds S.J. Yanagisako and C. Delaney. New York: Routledge.

Williams, C. (1981), *Open Cut: The Working Class in an Australian Mining Town*. Sydney: George Allen & Unwin.

Willis, P.E. (1977), *Learning to Labour: How Working Class Kids Get Working Class Jobs*. Hampshire: Gower.

Willmott, P. and M.D. Young (1967), *Family and Class in a London Suburb*. London: New English Library.

Wolcott, I. (1997), 'Work and Family'. In *Australian Family Profiles: Social and Demographic Patterns*, eds D. de Vaus and I. Wolcott. Melbourne: Australian Institute of Family Studies.

Wolcott, I., R. Weston and I. Winter (1997), 'Family Income and Housing'. In *Australian Family Profiles: Social and Demographic Patterns*, eds D. de Vaus and I. Wolcott. Melbourne: Australian Institute of Family Studies.

Yanagisako, S.J. (1977), 'Women-Centered Kin Networks in Urban Bilateral Kinship'. *American Ethnologist*, **4**(2): 207–226.

Yanagisako, S.J. and J.F. Collier (1987), 'Toward a Unified Analysis of Gender and Kinship'. In *Gender and Kinship: Essays toward a Unified Analysis*, eds J.F. Collier and S.J. Yanagisako. Stanford: Stanford University Press.

Yeatman, A. (1983), 'The Procreative Model: The Social Ontological Bases of the Gender-Kinship System'. *Social Analysis*, **14**: 3–30.

Young, I.M. (1990a), 'Breasted Experience: The Look and the Feeling'. In *Throwing Like a Girl and Other Essays in Feminist Philosophy and Social Theory*, ed. I.M. Young. Bloomington: Indiana University Press.

——— (1990b), 'Pregnant Embodiment: Subjectivity and Alienation'. In *Throwing Like a Girl and Other Essays in Feminist Philosophy and Social Theory*, ed. I.M. Young. Bloomington: Indiana University Press.

——— (1990c), 'Throwing Like a Girl: A Phenomenology of Feminine Body Comportment, Motility, and Spatiality'. In *Throwing Like a Girl and Other Essays in Feminist Philosophy and Social Theory*, ed. I.M. Young. Bloomington: Indiana University Press.

Young, M.D. and P. Willmott (1962), *Family and Kinship in East London*, rev. edn. Harmondsworth, Middlesex: Penguin Books.

Zaretsky, E. (1982), 'The Place of the Family in the Origins of the Welfare State'. In *Rethinking the Family: Some Feminist Questions*, eds B. Thorne and M. Yalom. New York: Longman.

——— (1986), *Capitalism, the Family, and Personal Life*, rev. exp. edn. New York: Perennial Library.

Index

Aboriginal population 8, 94–5
abortion 30, 32, 174
adult-infant dichotomy 113, 119,
    122, 128–32, 136–40, 170
adultery 68
adulthood 108–9
affinal relations 97
age distinctions 107–9, 137
ageing population 28
ageing process 145–6
Allan, Graham 62–5
Anglo-Celtic kinship practice 8
anthropology 106, 143
apartments, living in 55
aunts 99–100, 107, 123
Australian Bureau of Statistics
    (ABS) 2, 27, 32, 34, 37–8,
    71–2, 84
Australian Institute of Family
    Studies (AIFS) 2, 37, 71–2, 84

baby boom 30
barbecues 158
Baxter, Janeen 81
bedrooms 55–6
BHP (company) 1–2, 4, 153
birth rates 31
Blackley, Leanne 144
bodily techniques 135
body, the, orientation to 124–9
Bourdieu, Pierre 3, 5, 45–9, 67, 102,
    111–13, 119–25, 156, 169–71, 176
bourgeois families 13–14, 23
Bourgois, P.I. 175
breastfeeding 16, 56, 95, 115,
    125–8

bureaucratic view of kinship
    98–105

Canberra 33
capitalism 11–15, 18, 37, 40–41,
    158–68
    and kinship practice 159–67
career women 81–2
casual work 166
Chayanov, Aleksandr Vasilevich
    160
child abuse 139
child labour 14
childbearing and childbirth 15,
    31–3, 43, 107, 162
childcare 17, 38, 148, 152, 164
childlessness, voluntary 176
child-rearing 16, 32–3, 43
children, reasons for having 172–5
children's rooms 55–6
Christmas presents 60
class conflict 17
    and gender style 153–8
class divisions 77, 81–2, 143–4, 153
    see also dominant and dominated
    classes
cliques 63, 65
cognitive-dissonance theory 173–4
cognitive prototypes, theory of 122
cognitive sciences 3, 170–71
cohabiting 59
Commonwealth Arbitration Court 18
communication styles 132–3
commuting 57
conjunct ordering 121–3
Connell, R.W. 146, 154